William Isaac Thomas
1863–1947

SOCIAL BEHAVIOR AND PERSONALITY

Contributions of W. I. Thomas to Theory and Social Research

Edited by

EDMUND H. VOLKART

NEW YORK
SOCIAL SCIENCE RESEARCH COUNCIL
1951

Printed in the United States of America

The Social Science Research Council was organized in 1923 and formally incorporated in 1924. Its members are chosen from seven associated professional societies in the social sciences and from related disciplines. It is the purpose of the Council to plan and promote research in the social fields.

ASSOCIATED ORGANIZATIONS

American Anthropological Association

American Economic Association

American Historical Association

American Political Science Association

American Psychological Association

American Sociological Society

American Statistical Association

COMMITTEE ON W. I. THOMAS' CONTRIBUTIONS TO SOCIAL SCIENCE

Donald Young, *Chairman*	Russell Sage Foundation
Herbert Blumer	University of Chicago
Thorsten Sellin	University of Pennsylvania
Dorothy Swaine Thomas	University of Pennsylvania
Staff: Edmund H. Volkart	Yale University

FOREWORD

Objective, detached, and friendly curiosity about people characterized both the professional and the personal life of W. I. Thomas. He always wanted to know more about how they lived, why they behaved as they did, and how such knowledge could best be acquired and ordered for communication to others. His interest was in people of all kinds; he studied preliterate and industrialized societies, peasants and the more advantaged classes, immigrants and the native born, minority as well as dominant groups, the young as well as the more mature. All races, nations, communities, and individuals could gain his absorbed interest if there was promise of some advance in understanding of human motivation and conduct.

The one person in whom it was difficult to interest W. I. Thomas was himself. Personal anecdotes could be drawn out of him on suitable occasions, but they commonly turned out to be more revealing about others. Attempts to obtain biographical statements of an introspective and self-analytical nature were always turned aside, less for reasons of modesty than of simple lack of interest. His correspondence might have been an alternative source for such information, but he did not save it. The fact that the man who established the personal document and the life history as basic sources in social science has left no such materials about himself explains the absence from this volume of any analysis of his personality and career. The extracts from his publications here presented afford a better understanding of the man than any biographical chapter which could be constructed from the memories of his friends and the fragmentary documents available. Consequently, the only biographical material included in this volume is the brief statement on pages 323 and 324.

The fact that all of Thomas' books were out of print during the later years of his life and that his articles were generally unavailable was of no serious concern to him. He was not even concerned that some of his most thoughtful writings remained in typescript or mimeographed form. Sociologists, social psychologists and others working in the field of social behavior, however, were troubled by the lack of ready access to his writings. Dorothy Swaine Thomas was among those so troubled. She consequently offered all the rights in his publications and manuscripts which had passed to her on his death to the Social Science Research Council without restriction of any kind but with the understanding that the need for future publication would be carefully considered. The offer was accepted with enthusiasm, and the Committee listed on page iv was appointed in 1949 to examine the possibilities and carry through any consequent proposal which might be approved by the Council.

This Committee reached agreement that a volume reviewing and integrating W. I. Thomas' major contributions to sociological and social-psychological theory and method, and making available a selection of his out-of-print and unpublished materials, should be prepared. Edmund H. Volkart drafted a prospectus for such a volume which was adopted by the Committee with minor modifications. He then accepted the Committee's invitation to prepare the selections specified in the prospectus for publication. This involved not only a considerable amount of difficult editorial work but also the writing of explanatory notes, analytical prefatory statements, and an integrating introductory chapter showing the development of W. I. Thomas' theory and method and placing his contributions in the pattern of the behavior disciplines. It is my belief that if W. I. Thomas were alive he would want to acknowledge Edmund Volkart not only as an editor but also as a collaborator.

DONALD YOUNG

PREFACE

This book is the joint product of many persons whose assistance is deeply appreciated and gratefully acknowledged.

The editor is indebted to the individual members of the Committee—to Donald Young, Herbert Blumer, Thorston Sellin, and Dorothy S. Thomas—who gave generously of their time and counsel. Thanks are also due to his colleagues at Yale University, especially to Maurice R. Davie and John Sirjamaki for reading, in a critical spirit, certain portions of the book; to A. Paul Hare, of the University of Chicago, for compiling the bibliography and for calling attention to material which otherwise would have been missed; to Janet Geraci, Jean Hickey, and Joan Brown for competent preparation of the original typescript.

A very special and grateful acknowledgment is accorded Mary Ellen Volkart who helped at every stage of preparation, and Eleanor C. Isbell whose judgment and discrimination contributed to the volume in many ways.

The selections contained herein are the responsibility of the editor. Editorial changes have been made only when it was possible to reduce repetition without distorting a line of thought. The general Introduction and the prefatory notes for each selection have been written in a more positive vein. The former is intended to be a systematic analysis of Thomas' basic theory, while the latter attempt to supply specific historical and theoretical orientations. Such footnotes as have been added indicate contrasts and developments in Thomas' thinking, as well as some pertinent recent material.

In the last analysis, this book belongs to W. I. Thomas. Such merits as it may possess are indisputably his by virtue of the import of his ideas and the lucidity with which he expressed them. It is fitting, therefore, to recall some prefatory remarks Thomas made when he edited *Source Book for Social Origins:* The following material "will be found very interesting, if read slowly. . . . On every score it deserves a wider recognition, and I should be happy if I could assist it to come into its own."

E. H. V.

CONTENTS

INTRODUCTION: SOCIAL BEHAVIOR AND THE DEFINED SITUATION

THE importance of W. I. Thomas in the development of American social science has been widely recognized by sociologists and social psychologists alike. It is generally conceded that his research and theory exercised considerable influence, and some of his works have long been regarded as classics among publications dealing with human society and behavior.

There has been some tendency, however, for particular concepts and theories to overshadow his more enduring contributions to the behavior sciences. For example, to some he is the father of the "situational" approach; others recall him as the senior author of *The Polish Peasant in Europe and America* and suppose that his most mature thought is to be found there; still others identify him by such concepts as the "four wishes," "social disorganization," or "definition of the situation," without knowing how, or whether, they are related to his fundamental scheme of thought.

The difficulty seems to be that few are familiar with the total range of Thomas' work, and as a consequence fragmentary conceptions abound. Many social scientists today assume that Thomas has little to offer in the way of systematic theory relevant to their work. In a limited sense they are correct in this view. Thomas did not write a final synthesis presenting his ideas in a systematic manner. Moreover, he had no formal doctrine which by implication would explain all kinds of behavior or social organization.

There is a difference, however, between an interpretive system of human social life and a system for studying that life so that it can be understood. Thomas' system is of the latter variety, but it is not so clearly apparent in his writings as one might wish. It must be reconstructed from his mature work. If this is done and his later ideas are viewed in conjunction with his earlier ones, there emerges the image of a person who was groping toward, and in some ways found, a fundamental position regarding the study of human behavior.

The essential features of this position may be summarized as follows:

1. The goal of social science is to obtain verifiable generalizations about human behavior.
2. Human behavior occurs only under certain conditions, which in the abstract may be represented by the concept of "situation."
3. The human situation often includes some factors common to both the observer and the actor, such as the physical environment, relevant social norms, and the behavior of others. The implication of this is that social science requires first-hand empirical description of the observable or "objective" aspects of the situation.
4. The human situation also includes some factors that exist only for the actors, i.e., how they perceive the situation, what it means to them, what their "definition" of the situation is. This implies that the subjective aspects of human life must be grasped by the investigator as much as the objective aspects. Moreover, the subjective must be understood in its real first-hand character, as opposed to imputed ideas of those factors (as represented by concepts of "needs," "wishes," "attitudes," etc.).
5. The methods of social science, therefore, must provide for the systematic analysis of both the objective and the subjective (experiential) aspects of human life.
6. Such a methodology requires the joint efforts of all the social sciences, including special techniques of obtaining data, such as the life history.
7. The social goal of this approach is to make available the kind of knowledge necessary and useful for the rational control of behavior.

In brief, Thomas' system is concerned with what must be studied, and how, if the vision of a realistic and ultimately useful social science is to be realized.

This introductory essay contains an elaboration of Thomas' system as it is outlined above. Its task is that of distilling many of his ideas into a single brief statement, thus attempting to supply a long-needed systematic interpretation of his fundamental thought. Here, the developments and contrasts in Thomas' thinking (which are made plain elsewhere in this volume) are subordinated to the task of clarifying his basic ideas and the unity which pervades them. It also seems desirable that some of the implications of these ideas should be considered but with no attempt at completeness. The reader should be left to draw his own conclusions.

One caution is necessary. Thomas was a profound and versatile thinker whose ideas are too rich to permit of but a single interpretation. Indeed, it would be presumptuous to claim that a relatively brief essay could adequately reflect the various facets of his thought. No such claim is made here. Rather, the following analysis should be construed as only one effort to make more explicit the central problems with which Thomas grappled. Other interpretations are not only possible, they are desirable.

The beginning of Thomas' system is to be found in his conception of the nature of social phenomena which is the province of social science investigation. This is important because his views in this respect came to differ considerably from those held by most so-called "pioneers" of social science. For them the possibility of such a science seemed to depend upon the extent to which social phenomena could be conceived in natural science terms. Thus Herbert Spencer interpreted the sequences of social institutions as obeying a universal "law" of evolution, and others took similar, though more extreme, positions by regarding society as an "organism" or by envisaging a "social physics." Their idea was to borrow concepts from the more successful physical sciences, impose them more or less directly upon social life, and thus make it appear that the study of social phenomena was really "scientific."

Thomas did not accept this kind of interpretation. To him such attempts were mechanistic, analogical, and spuriously scientific. Thus in 1909 he objected to "particularistic" interpretations of social data, as represented by Giddings' "consciousness of kind" and Durkheim's "constraint"; and later in the Methodological Note of *The Polish Peasant* he explicitly pointed out the inadequacy of mechanistic "cause and effect" concepts in the study of social life.

In his view these doctrines failed to present a realistic conception of human behavior and human experience. He thought they neglected precisely those things which make human social life unique: individual organisms living in groups, perceiving their environment, and attempting to come to terms with, or adjust to, the situations in which they find themselves.

Departing from these conceptions, Thomas took the view that the task of social science is to understand and interpret the phenomena of human adjustment as they are revealed in behavior:

> The central problem in the general life process is one of adjustment, and the forms of adjustive effort are "behavior."[1]

But adjustive behavior is manifest on both the individual and group levels of existence. Consequently, the social sciences

> are fundamentally concerned with relationships between individuals and individuals, individuals and groups, and groups and other groups.[2]

Behavior, however, is so complex in its elements and so changeable in its expression, that it rules out any such science as the early social theorists had envisioned:

> The chemist deals with elements which are relatively simple, while the behaviorist deals with actions which are in turn based on incommensurable physiological conditions . . . Moreover, the material of the chemist is static, does not change from time to time, while the material of the behaviorist (the human organism) is itself evolving. The individual is changing, under influences which cannot be measured. His response in situations changes with periods of physical, mental and emotional maturation and as a result of experiences in an endless variety of preceding situations. The student of behavior can therefore not hope to establish even the limited number of laws possible in the case of the exact scientist.[3]

The task of the social scientist is infinitely complex, defying overly simple comparisons with physical phenomena and their respective sciences. As Thomas remarked in 1938, he did not "believe in these comparisons between physics and sociology."[4]

[1] *Primitive Behavior* (New York: McGraw-Hill Book Company, 1937), p. 1.

[2] *Ibid.*

[3] W. I. Thomas and Dorothy S. Thomas, *The Child in America* (New York: Alfred A. Knopf, 1932), pp. 553-554.

[4] Unpublished "Proceedings" of a meeting of the Committee on Appraisal of Research, Social Science Research Council, December 10, 1938, p. 150.

The major difficulty with such comparisons is that they assume that social phenomena have uniform objective existence, and that social facts have identical meaning to all individuals and groups observing them. The suggestion is that human behavior somehow is equatable with the behavior of atoms and molecules, and thus the task of understanding that behavior is simplified.

Of course this is not true. Men do not live scientifically for the benefit of social scientists:

> It is also highly important for us to realize that we do not as a matter of fact lead our lives, make our decisions, and reach our goals in everyday life either statistically or scientifically. We live by inference. I am, let us say, your guest. You do not know, you cannot determine scientifically, that I will not steal your money or your spoons. But inferentially I will not, and inferentially you have me as guest.[5]

The import of this is that men, in their adjustive efforts, are never absolutely sure of the conditions to which they are adjusting. At any given moment it is impossible to determine all the conditions and factors which may exist. The real state of affairs may be known not at all or only partially. At any rate, it need not correspond to that which is subjectively experienced by the organism. Human behavior, however, occurs in terms of what is thought to exist. Men act "as if" the conditions really are as they imagine them to be.

To Thomas this is the crucial fact of human social life: adjustment is not an entirely mechanistic process in which cause and effect can be isolated simply by knowing the objective conditions and then observing the objective behavior. Intervening is the factor of subjective experience, which Thomas first conceptualized as "attitudes" and then as the "four wishes."

Later he discarded these particular concepts but retained the underlying principle that the study of social life demands concepts which will meet two criteria: they must mirror social reality in both its objective and subjective aspects, and at the same time they must hold out a promise of discovering scientific (i.e. verifiable) regularities of adjustive behavior. If human behavior is to be adequately

[5] "The Relation of Research to the Social Process," in W. F. G. Swann and others, *Essays on Research in the Social Sciences* (Washington: The Brookings Institution, 1931), pp. 189–190.

understood, its subjective components must be properly evaluated in relation to the objective components.

In *The Polish Peasant* the concepts of "values" and "attitudes" sufficed for this purpose, for at that time Thomas thought that the "laws" of social change might be discoverable through observation of the interaction of attitudes with social values. But in his later work, when he abandoned the search for social laws, Thomas emphasized the concepts of "situation" and "definition of the situation." These lie at the very heart of his social theory and represent his attempt to create a social science which would be true to its own phenomena rather than artificially derived from the physical sciences.

As an analytical tool the concept of "situation" serves several functions. Methodologically it provides for the observation of behavior under conditions which can in some measure be specified; descriptively it represents the way in which social life is experienced by men in society. For the present, interest centers on the latter function.

In Thomas' view the on-going social process as it is experienced in real life is best represented as a series of situations which evoke appropriate responses:

> The situation in which the person finds himself is taken as containing the configuration of the factors conditioning the behavior reaction. Of course, it is not the spatial material situation which is meant, but the situation of social relationships. It involves all the institutions and mores.[6]

Any behavior, by group or individual, cannot be understood apart from the situation in which it occurs and to which it is a potential adjustment. "Every concrete activity is the solution of a situation." [7]

But the situation, in this descriptive sense, is not to be thought of as having an entirely objective existence:

> The total situation will always contain more and less subjective factors, and the behavior reaction can be studied only in connection with the whole context, i.e., the situation as it exists in verifiable, objective terms, and as it has seemed to exist in terms of the interested persons.[8]

[6] *Ibid.*, p. 176.

[7] W. I. Thomas and F. Znaniecki, *The Polish Peasant in Europe and America* (2nd ed.; New York: Alfred A. Knopf, 1927), Vol. I, p. 68.

[8] *The Child in America*, p. 572.

Each individual or group comes into the situation with a different train of experience, a different outlook or perspective; and this in turn becomes a factor in the total situation, leading to different "definitions" of the situation and subsequently to different behavior.

The concept of "definition of the situation," therefore, is a necessary adjunct to that of the "situation" itself. In real life neither exists apart from the other, and thus they cannot be separately considered. In fact, the "definition of the situation" is the crucial link that connects experience and adjustive behavior to the situation:

> An adjustive effort of any kind is preceded by a decision to act or not act along a given line, and the decision is itself preceded by a *definition of the situation,* that is to say, an *interpretation,* or *point of view,* and eventually a policy and a behavior pattern. In this way quick judgments and decisions are made at every point in everyday life.[9]

As will be indicated later, the character of the definition in any given situation will depend upon the conjuncture of a variety of biological, physiological, psychological, social, and cultural factors.

The advantage of situational concepts over others that attempt to analyze social life lies in their genuineness. They are not imputations or inferences on the part of the social scientist, in the same way that "needs," "wishes," or "attitudes" are. They embody the main character of human experience as it appears to our common sense and in daily living. Rather than being imposed upon life, they spring from it and thus are uniquely appropriate tools for the realistic study of behavior and its accompanying human experience. This is revealed in the way Thomas used them to illumine the behavioral phenomena involved in the relationship of the individual to the group and in the process of social change.

One of the most important features of human existence is the fact that each individual is born into a group which possesses a going way of life, or a culture. In Thomas' terms a culture is composed of, or contains, "definitions of situations" which have been arrived at through the consensus of adults over a period of time. As a product of social life, these definitions are embodied in codes, rules, precepts, policies, traditions, and standardized social relationships. They are external to individuals, exercise some control over them, and have

[9] *Primitive Behavior,* p. 8.

an existence of their own which makes them amenable to study in and of themselves. In this respect Thomas' approach to culture is similar to that of Durkheim, Sumner, and others.

He differed from them, however, in at least one respect. Whereas Durkheim conceived of "social facts" as being caused by prior social facts, and Sumner conceived of the mores as representing "automatic" adjustments to life conditions, Thomas credited individuals with some power to form these common definitions. He spoke of "special definers of situations,"[10] men who by virtue of prestige, authority, or skill are in a position to influence the content of culture. These include persons who have the ability to make themselves believed: prophets, lawgivers, judges, and even scientists. Today they would be called "opinion makers," but the point is that Thomas was not a complete cultural determinist. By acknowledging the influence of individuals on culture he avoided the mechanistic implications of such doctrines as Sumner's "automatic adjustment," yet retained the possibility of scientific understanding.

On the other hand, Thomas was keenly aware of the influence of the group on the individual. Individual life is experienced as a series of situations, more or less unique to each society, and to which the group has attached its own definitions. Moreover, these take an active part in the social process:

> This defining of the situation is begun by the parents in the form of ordering and forbidding and information, is continued in the community by means of gossip, with its praise and blame, and is formally represented by the school, the law, the church.[11]

In the process of socialization the group endeavors to have the individual internalize its own definitions, to make them a part of his habitual self. Of course, only the individual can ever define his own situations and behave in them accordingly, but the effort of the group is to have him define situations in its own terms so the behavior will conform to social norms. Essentially the process is one of impressing upon the individual the existence of the group and its col-

[10] *Ibid.*

[11] "The Persistence of Primary-group Norms in Present-day Society and Their Influence in Our Educational System," in Herbert S. Jennings and others, *Suggestions of Modern Science Concerning Education* (New York: The Macmillan Company, 1917), p. 168.

lective judgment in such a way that these become factors in every situation.

In most cases the group succeeds. The individual does define most situations, most of the time, in a way which coincides with group norms. Without this large area of agreement between the collective judgment of the group and the individual definition, ordered social life, which is itself a social adjustment, would be impossible. In this connection it should be noted that even the most extreme radical in any society is radical in only a relatively few situations; in the rest he is a conformer.

Here is to be found Thomas' major contribution to what is now called "culture-personality" research. Using his "definition of the situation" concept, on both the group and individual levels, he was concerned with the extent to which cultural and personal definitions agree in actual life, and the reasons for agreement or divergence. From Thomas' standpoint the individual is never completely determined by his culture because of the great variety of forces involved in human behavior.

In cultural terms it is patent that the number of possible situations is infinite. Even in simple societies no single person knows all the situations the group provides nor does he know all the group definitions. Thus there are always some situations and norms of which the individual remains unaware. Further, in many situations the cultural definitions themselves are vague enough to permit diverse responses within certain limits. Respect for elders, as an instance, is a cultural definition; but what constitutes respect, and how it is expressed in behavior, varies widely not only from one society to another but also within a single society. Finally, some cultures permit a wider range of individualism than others, simply as a matter of policy or tradition. Culture cannot, therefore, be regarded as a set of rigid rules which can and must find expression in individual behavior.

To these factors there must also be added those of individual variability. Each person enters his situations with a somewhat different perspective than that of his fellows. People differ at birth, have different kinds and sequences of experience, and at any given moment are under the stress of different physiological conditions (fatigue, gaiety, excitement, etc.) which influence their perceptions. And the individual himself is constantly changing, if only in the sense of aging and having new experiences which become factors in later situations. In brief, there are personal determinants of behavior as well as group determinants, and the latter are seldom mechanically applied in human action.

This view of the individual also implies two further observations regarding the individual personality. One is that human personality cannot be merely "the subjective aspect of culture," as Thomas has been quoted as saying.[12] There are more determinants of personality than culture alone, as Thomas himself noted:

> . . . the particular behavior patterns and the total personality are overwhelmingly conditioned by the types of situations and trains of experience encountered by the individual in the course of his life.[13]

The other implication is that personality cannot be considered simply as a bundle of traits awaiting application to situations. Rather it is unique and dynamic, revealing itself only in adjustive efforts in various situations and being determined by a complex of internal and external factors. Such a conception casts some doubt on the utility and significance of tests which attempt to ascertain personality at a single point of time and in terms of static "entities."

Returning to the role of culture in individual behavior, it is now apparent that group definitions are only one element in the situations which confront the individual, and their efficacy depends upon other factors than training alone:

> The reaction of different individuals in the same culture to identical cultural influences will depend partly on their different trains of experience and partly on their biochemical constitutions and unlearned psychological endowments.[14]

Therefore it is quite impossible to imagine a society in which there would be complete agreement of personal and cultural definitions in all kinds of different situations. Adjustive efforts in each case proceed from different definitions having diverse antecedents:

[12] Ellsworth Faris is cited to this effect in Floyd N. House, *The Range of Social Theory* (New York: Henry Holt and Company, 1929), p. 169.

[13] "The Behavior Pattern and the Situation," *Publications of the American Sociological Society: Papers and Proceedings, Twenty-second Annual Meeting . . . 1927*, Vol. 22, p. 1.

[14] *Primitive Behavior*, p. 1.

The same situation or experience in the case of one person may lead this person to another type of adjustment; in another it may lead to crime; in another, to insanity, the result depending on whether previous experiences have formed this or that constellation of attitudes.[15]

These considerations lead to the conclusion that social behavior in a single culture is highly variable, within limits, and herein are found the roots of social change. No society is ever so perfectly organized that personal and cultural definitions agree at every point of social life. Variation from norms is inevitable. But from the standpoint of the traditional code such variations represent "social disorganization," or the *"decrease of the influence of existing social rules of behavior upon individual members of the group.* This decrease may present innumerable degrees, ranging from a single break of some particular rule by one individual up to a general decay of all the institutions of the group." [16] Thus some degree of social disorganization, or change, exists in all societies at all times.

The reasons for the decline in influence of social norms are to be found in a number of factors, including the number and kind of sanctions which uphold them, the extent to which they are capable of realizing individual interests, and so on. Thomas was particularly interested in those influences which produce "conflicting definitions of situations":

As long as the definitions of situations remain constant and common we may anticipate orderly behavior reactions. When rival definitions arise . . . we may anticipate social disorganization and personal demoralization. . . . the mass of delinquency, crime, and emotional instability is the result of conflicting definitions.[17]

Under conditions of primary group solidarity and isolation, the possibility of new and conflicting definitions is kept to a minimum, and the individual is incorporated into a rather tightly organized set of social norms. Both situations and the agreement of cultural and individual definitions of them remain relatively stable.

In the modern world, however, this is no longer true. The products of science, particularly those affecting communication and social mobility, have broken down the stability of the primary group and

[15] "The Behavior Pattern and the Situation," *op. cit.*, p. 11.
[16] *The Polish Peasant*, 1927, Vol. II, p. 1128.
[17] "The Behavior Pattern and the Situation," *op. cit.*, p. 13.

its norms. Now, the individual is confronted by a variety of situations, some of which are novel and others are simply ill-defined or subject to little consensus. The number of possible situations and the number of possible definitions have expanded almost to infinity:

> Every new invention, every chance acquaintanceship, every new environment, has the possibility of redefining the situation and of introducing change, disorganization or different type of organization into the life of the individual or even of the whole world.[18]

While this applies primarily to the situations of the modern world, it is, of course, true of all societies. Situations are not to be thought of as static sets of conditions. As they are experienced by individuals and groups they are fluid and dynamic, permitting the entrance of new stimuli which may affect their definition and the resulting behavior. And whether the behavior is organizing or disorganizing depends upon the point of view: that which is disorganizing from the standpoint of traditional norms may have the germs of a new type of organization, a new definition of the situation which in turn may be accepted and become a part of the culture.

In this connection Thomas' use of the "crisis" concept assumes importance. In a sense, he fused the notion of "crisis" with that of "situation" and "definition of the situation." So long as social life runs smoothly, so long as habits are adjustive, "situations" can scarcely be said to exist. There is nothing to define when people behave as anticipated. But when influences appear to disrupt habits, when new stimuli demand attention, when the habitual situation is altered, or when an individual or group is unprepared for an experiance, then the phenomenon assumes the aspect of "crisis."

A crisis is a threat, a challenge, a strain on the attention, a call to new action. Yet it need not always be acute or extreme:

> Of course a crisis may be so serious as to kill the organism or destroy the group, or it may result in failure or deterioration. But crisis, as I am employing the term, is not to be regarded as habitually violent. It is simply a disturbance of habit, and it may be no more than an incident, a stimulation, a suggestion.[19]

Nor is a crisis to be thought of as having a uniform objective existence, leading to automatic responses on the part of those who face it.

[18] *The Unadjusted Girl* (Boston: Little, Brown, and Company, 1925), p. 71.

[19] *Source Book for Social Origins* (4th ed.; Boston: Richard G. Badger, 1909), p. 18.

What may appear to be a crisis to an external observer may pass unnoticed by the participants; and contrariwise that which appears innocuous to some may have great significance for others. Thus, "the same crisis will not produce the same effect uniformly." [20]

Thomas regarded crises as among the most significant of human experiences, affecting the definitions of individuals and groups, their behavior, and finally influencing the content of culture and personality, as well as the rate and direction of social change. In society, a threat to security, a great depression, a war, may bring new definitions of situations which persist long after the events that evoked them. In history, crises have been related to the emergence of great men:

> The relation of the "great man" to crisis is indeed one of the more important points in the problem of progress. Such men as Moses, Mohammed, Confucius, Christ, have stamped the whole character of a civilization.[21]

In individuals, the entire personality may be affected by a single critical experience: the reading of a book, the accidental observation of an event, an incident with another person or group. How much of race prejudice, for example, might be traceable to a single unpleasant experience with a member of another race?

The significance of "crisis" lies in the fact that it may produce a fundamental outlook, a principle of life organization, which is incorporated into the culture on the one hand and the personality on the other. The reaction to crisis often develops a far-reaching definition, a base line from which a great variety of other situations are viewed. Thus in personal and social development crisis is a catalyst, disturbing old habits, evoking new responses, and becoming a major factor in charting new developments.

Thomas' principle of "crisis" is, of course, strikingly similar to Toynbee's thesis of "challenge and response" in historical civilizations and to the psychoanalysts' emphasis on the significance of traumatic experiences in personality disorders. The convergence of these three lines of thought suggests the value of more intensive study of men in critical situations. Recent studies of war experience and of "deprivation" are, in fact, steps in that direction.

[20] *Ibid.*

[21] *Ibid.*, p. 19.

From the foregoing it is apparent that Thomas' aim was to analyze social life as it appears in the experience of people who live it. The concepts of situation, definition of the situation, and crisis reflect that purpose. They also reflect his interest in the variability of social life, the extent to which individuals and groups have different experiences and consequently manifest different cultures and different personalities.

Throughout the development and use of these concepts his emphasis is on the necessity of understanding subjective experience in order to understand behavior. That is, we must know the beliefs, inferences, and perceptions which endow social situations with meanings not necessarily apparent to the observer. We must know when crises exist, and why they are crises. The relation between the objective situation and behavior is never a simple one of mechanical cause and effect, but one that is mediated by factors affecting the "definition" of the situation. The totality of these factors constitutes subjective experience, which functions as a selector and interpreter of all the elements present, and is the basis of adjustive behavior.

Here it must be stressed that the experience of a subject in a social situation may not coincide with the experience of the observing scientist. Indeed, the subject may perceive a number of elements in a situation which cannot be demonstrated to exist scientifically; but if they exist subjectively, behavior will depend upon this version of the situation. As Thomas put it: "If men define situations as real, they are real in their consequences." [22] The races of men may not exist except as anthropological constructs, but the idea of race influences responses in many situations. The social world is one in which subjective impressions can be projected onto life and thereby become real to the projectors.

Despite this emphasis on two kinds of reality, Thomas did not regard social phenomena as being other than "natural." They can be studied and understood, but they have a nature and means of operation of their own. The methods of social science, therefore, become especially important.

As Thomas saw it, the crucial methodological problem of social science is to study the objective aspects of social life in a way that

[22] *The Child in America*, p. 572.

is verifiable and at the same time to catch the subjective interpretations of the participants. If social science concentrates only on the objective features, it becomes superficial and artificial; if it focuses on the subjective alone, it becomes unverifiable in any real sense. With these criteria in mind Thomas suggested the "situational method," supplemented by the use of personal documents. Through them he hoped to grasp both the subjective and the objective in social life.

As a methodological tool the "situation" is a device for the observation and description of behavior as it occurs under different conditions. Dealing with the objective aspects of behavior, it approximates the method employed in the experimental sciences:

> The situational method is the one in use by the experimental physiologist and psychologist who prepare situations, introduce the subject into the situation, observe the behavior reactions, change the situation, and observe the changes in the reactions.[23]

Applying this conception to the study of social life:

> A study of the concrete situations which the individual encounters, into which he is forced, or which he creates will disclose the character of his adaptive strivings and the processes of adjustment. The study of the situation, the behavior in the situation, the changes brought about in the situation, and the resulting change in behavior represent the nearest approach the social scientist is able to make to the use of experiment in social research.[24]

Thus, while he eschewed artificial comparisons between natural and social science, Thomas nevertheless was aware of their affinity so far as fundamental methodology was concerned.

Of course, social science cannot begin with experiments in any rigorous sense of the term. It must begin with observations under ordinary conditions and then progress to those kinds of situations where variables can be more easily controlled:

> That is, reactions are first studied in the more "natural" situations and the factors involved in, and concomitant with, these situations are brought out in the behavior study. Then more controlled situations can be evolved which will allow for and rule out as many of the concomitant interfering factors as possible.[25]

[23] "The Behavior Pattern and the Situation," *op. cit.*, p. 2.

[24] "The Relation of Research to the Social Process," *op. cit.*, p. 177.

[25] *The Child in America*, p. 570.

Thomas believed that the case study must precede the more elaborate research involving statistical manipulation.

Nonetheless, in his view the situational method has "certain experimental, objective, and comparative possibilities" [26] not to be found in other approaches. In particular he contrasted it with the "social forces" approach, of which his "four wishes" were a variant.

At one time, 1923, Thomas regarded the "wishes" as an alternative approach to behavior study, as is indicated in the following passage:

> . . . even if our knowledge of the nervous system of man were complete we could not read out of it all the concrete varieties of human experience. The variety of expressions of behavior is as great as the variety of situations arising in the external world, while the nervous system represents only a general mechanism for action. We can however approach the problem of behavior through the study of the forces which impel to action, namely, the wishes, and we shall see that these correspond in general with the nervous mechanism.[27]

This suggests that while Thomas basically regarded behavior as situationally determined, he thought it might still be useful to view behavior from the standpoint of certain convenient classifications of human tendencies. Presumably the wishes were related to the nervous system and therefore more or less common to all men.

The "wish for security," for example, was based on the "instinct" of fear, in Thomas' scheme, and the "wish for response" on the "instinct" of love. The "wish for new experience" was emotionally related to the "instinct" of anger and the "near-instinct" of curiosity. Only the "wish for recognition" seemed to have no direct basis in the organism, but later he remarked that he thought this wish was a form of the "wish for response" and therefore based on love.[28]

Now if we disregard Thomas' use of such phrases as "forces which impel to action" or "the motor element, the starting point of activity" [29] to describe the wishes, it appears that they represent typical manifestations of the instincts as these latter are conditioned by social experience. In this scheme activity represents attempts to satisfy the demands of the organism, and Thomas hoped to classify and order

[26] "The Behavior Pattern and the Situation," *op. cit.*, p. 1.

[27] *The Unadjusted Girl*, pp. 3–4.

[28] Unpublished minutes of the Social Science Research Council Hanover Conference, August 23 – September 2, 1926, Vol. II, p. 331.

[29] *The Unadjusted Girl*, pp. 4, 40.

human experience in terms of the more or less typical categories which the wishes provided.

The difficulty came, however, when others began to regard the wishes as "causes" of behavior or used them to "explain" different activities. Of course, a great deal of human behavior could be related to them but Thomas realized that little was clarified thereby. For example, both sexual fidelity and promiscuity could be ascribed equally well to the "wish for response." Similarly the "wish for new experience" accounted alike for the behavior of the vagabond, the scientist, and the explorer. But why would the same wish lead to such different kinds of behavior?

Thus the wishes came to present a scientific dilemma. Assuming their basis in the nervous system did not permit the prediction of behavior, for this was clearly related to social situations. On the other hand, if the forms of behavior were known, it was impossible to infer with any degree of accuracy which wish or wishes had been operating. Thomas realized these difficulties, even while proposing the wishes as a possible approach:

> From the foregoing description it will be seen that wishes of the same general class—those which tend to arise from the same emotional background—may be totally different in moral quality. . . .
>
> Moreover, when a concrete wish of any general class arises it may be accompanied and qualified by any or all of the other classes of wishes.[30]

For strictly scientific purposes, therefore, the wishes were quite inadequate, although they may have possessed some utility as "constructs" or "intervening variables" in categorizing human experience.

Their major handicap was that they could not be demonstrated to exist, nor could their relation to concrete behavior be verified. They could only be plausibly illustrated in particular cases, and in the long run Thomas found their use more obscuring than enlightening:

> In the personality and psychiatric fields, for example, the difficulty has been that most of the studies have been made from the point of view of the inner life outward, i.e., rather than studying behavior in a variety of situations as a means of inferring drives, instincts, emotions, etc., the instincts, emotions, etc., have been assumed to have a reality of their own and behavior has been studied in terms of them. . . . and obscurity has been the general result.[31]

[30] *Ibid.*, p. 38.
[31] *The Child in America*, p. 570.

With these objections in mind Thomas turned to the situational approach.

Its methodological advantages in social science are several. In the first place it coincides with the aim of science in general, which is "to determine that under certain conditions certain results will follow in certain proportions." [32] Thus the problem of causation can be abandoned:

It is, in fact, desirable to abandon everywhere the idea of "causation" and approach problems in terms of "what antecedents have what consequences?" In the field of personality and culture the formulation of an adequate approach is: "Individuals differentiated in what ways and placed in what situations react in what patterns of behavior, and what behavioral changes follow what changes in situation?" [33]

Since the emphasis here is on the observation of behavior under different conditions, it is not necessary to think in simple terms of cause and effect.

A second advantage of the situational approach is that it provides an opportunity to bring out the variables involved in behavior. That is, by studying behavioral expressions comparatively in different situations, the various types of behavior determinants (biological, physiological, psychological, and cultural) and their relationships can be revealed. Thus, while the situational method does not study "original nature" directly, it does so indirectly since it

ignores or minimizes instincts and original nature and studies behavior reactions and habit formation in a great variety of situations comparatively. It assumes that whatever can be learned about original nature will be revealed in its reactions to these various situations.[34]

In this way the relative incidence and weight of the variables affecting behavior can be obtained empirically rather than through imputations. As Thomas noted, the situational procedure "by no means obscures the other factors; on the contrary, it reveals them." [35]

[32] *Ibid.*, p. 565.

[33] Unpublished "Report to the Social Science Research Council on the Organization of a Program in the Field of Personality and Culture" (1933, typescript), pp. 7–8. The complete report appears on pp. 290–318 infra (cf. p. 296).

[34] *The Child in America*, p. 561.

[35] "The Behavior Pattern and the Situation," *op. cit.*, p. 2.

A further advantage of the situational approach lies in its emphasis on the necessity of using control groups in social research. It may be found, for example, that a large percentage of delinquents are steady attendants at motion pictures, and the conclusion drawn that there is a causal relationship. But the precise relationship between motion pictures and delinquency would remain vague unless the proportion of regular attendants in the nondelinquent population were also known. If such a comparison is made and the relationship is a significant one, then the problem is opened up for further study: the kinds of pictures seen by both groups, the kinds of associates with whom the pictures are attended, and so on. In any case:

> In order to determine the relation of a given experience to delinquency it would be necessary to compare the frequency of the same experience in the delinquent group and in a group representing the general non-delinquent population.[36]

Here is a clear recognition that science depends upon inferences rigorously derived from controlled comparisons.

Yet Thomas also realized that in social science this procedure represents approximations more than it does exactness. Social situations are multidimensional, and it is difficult to specify all their elements:

> The impossibility of carrying on a strict experimentation in the social sciences is due also to our present inability to measure (or even adequately to recognize) the complexities of any given social situation or environment, and this renders impossible any equalizing of factors in two situations.[37]

This objection is all the more forceful because of the possible divergence between the situation as it "objectively" exists, and as it is "subjectively" experienced by the participants. It is this realization of two kinds of reality which makes it impossible "adequately to recognize" the complexities of any given situation.

Nevertheless, by stressing the need for observations under limited, if not exact, conditions Thomas was pointing social science in the right direction. He envisioned a series of studies which in successive steps would reduce the complexities of situations, make them more manageable, and thus help determine the significant factors in

[36] *The Child in America,* p. 573.

[37] "The Relation of Research to the Social Process," *op. cit.,* p. 183.

behavior. But these studies must be concerned with behavior as it happens and as it can be recorded systematically. The use of traditional historical data is therefore limited:

> We must first understand the past from the present. We must view the present as behavior. We must establish by scientific procedure the laws of behavior, and then the past will have its meaning and make its contribution.[38]

The situational approach reverses the somewhat common conception that the present must be understood in terms of the past. It also provides theoretical grounds for distinguishing history from social science, should such a distinction seem desirable.

Viewed in its general outline, the situational approach thus clarified social science methodology. Certainly its advantages are impressive; yet Thomas felt that the situational approach alone did not fulfill all the requirements of a genuine social science. Strictly speaking it dealt only with those objective features which the observing scientist could record and classify. There still remained the problem of grasping subjective experience, how the situation appeared to the persons being observed. It was in this connection that he introduced the use of "behavior documents" as source material into social science procedure—not merely as a convenience but as an absolute necessity:

> I am not suggesting that behavior can be adequately observed and recorded by the observational method or by statistical procedure. It appears, in fact, that the behavior document (case study, life record, psychoanalytic confession) representing a continuity of experience in life situations is the most illuminating procedure available. In a good record of this kind we are able to view the behavior reactions in the various situations, the emergence of personality traits, the determination of concrete acts, and the formation of life policies and their evolution.[39]

These documents, which he sometimes called "personal documents," vary widely in form, purpose, and utility. They include letters, diaries, autobiographies, and the more formal accounts of life experience gathered by social workers, social scientists, and psychiatrists for their own purposes. They all have in common the

[38] "The Persistence of Primary-group Norms," *op. cit.*, p. 196.
[39] "The Relation of Research to the Social Process," *op. cit.*, p. 188.

presentation of continuous experience as recorded by an observer (case record) or as reported by the individual himself (life history).

In Thomas' estimate the most important type is the life history in an undesigned form, that which is written without knowing that it may be used. Here there is less likelihood of falsity and a greater probability of more detailed information about the critical situations that have been experienced by the individual. Hence it has a greater potential value to social science than other kinds of documentary material. "Designed" records, on the other hand, such as published autobiographies, permit the subject deliberately or even unconsciously to conceal anything embarrassing or distasteful. Perhaps the poorest of all for scientific (as distinguished from therapeutic) purposes is the "designed" record which has been influenced by interested parties. Thomas was particularly critical of psychoanalysts in this regard, because of their tendency to indoctrinate patients with their own theories.

The use of personal documents in social science is to provide data on human experience from the standpoint of the subject. They are not useful in testing theories. By studying such documents we discover the *meanings* which various social situations have for the individual, his definitions of them, and the general "character of his adaptive strivings." [40]

Personal documents also have deficiencies. One objection that has been raised against them is that they are probably unreliable and invalid for research purposes. The argument is that individual introspections and memories cannot be observed or verified with any degree of certainty, that they are subject to personal biases, selections, and compensations, and that there is no way of determining their truth or falsity.

Thomas freely admitted these faults, but he also indicated the strength of personal documents:

> There are undoubtedly insuperable difficulties in the way of perfecting the life record on the side of objectivity and reliability. It is introspective, the memory is notoriously treacherous, observation is defective, phantasy, fabrication and bias play large roles. . . . But . . . it must be recognized that even the most

[40] "The Behavior Pattern and the Situation," *op. cit.*, p. 2.

highly subjective record has a value for behavior analysis and interpretation. A document, for example, prepared by one compensating for a feeling of inferiority or elaborating a delusion of persecution is as far as possible from objective reality, but the subject's view of the situation, how he regards it, may be the most important element for interpretation.[41]

The point is that we must have some means of uncovering subjective "definitions of situations," and personal documents aid in this task. They have a singular significance for the understanding of human experience and personality development. They cannot be ignored simply because they lack some of the hallmarks of empirical science:

. . . in everyday life in forming decisions and regulating social interaction, we are forced to utilize the testimony of others, their representations of reality, just as the courts are forced to use sworn testimony. In spite of the fact that the representations are not completely reliable, they are indispensable. A social psychology without records of experience would be like a court without testimony.[42]

Again, it has been suggested that personal documents be standardized in content. Presumably the idea is that if all records deal with the same categories of experience, the comparable data contained therein can be subjected to quantitative analysis. This view appears to be an elaboration of one of Thomas' ideas:

But this form of data [life histories] is capable of improvement and systematization, and will have valuable applications when considerable numbers of life histories adequately elaborated are employed in a comparative way in order to determine the varieties of the schematization of life in varieties of situations.[43]

But this does not mean standardization of content primarily for the purpose of statistical treatment. It simply means that comparative life histories will suggest the range of reactions which individuals can have to the same, or nearly the same, cultural influences. Such comparisons may also provide hypotheses about behavior which can later be tested more precisely through the use of statistical techniques.

Here is to be found Thomas' answer to the problem of the respective roles of case study and statistics in social science. They are

[41] "The Relation of Research to the Social Process," *op. cit.*, pp. 188–189.

[42] "Comment by W. I. Thomas," in Herbert Blumer, *An Appraisal of Thomas and Znaniecki's The Polish Peasant in Europe and America* (Social Science Research Council Bulletin 44, 1939), p. 84.

[43] "The Relation of Research to the Social Process," *op. cit.*, p. 188.

not mutually exclusive so much as they are complementary. The personal document is not designed to prove anything; rather, its unique value lies in the recounting of human experience in individual terms, at the same time revealing how different groups tend to define situations. Thus it can suggest critical variables and relationships which can then be reformulated so as to take advantage of the precision which statistics offers.

In particular Thomas thought that the personal document has hypothesis-forming importance, and provides data upon the following aspects of behavior:

(a) The systems of ideas and purposes of individuals as related to the general cultural patterns of society, and the relative compulsiveness of the various specific cultural stimuli.

(b) The trains of experience through which the individual's conception of his role in society is developed. . . .

(c) How organizations and institutions as they are (family, school, occupation, etc.) promote and interfere with individual adjustment.

(d) Whether the personality is essentially structured in infancy, and later maladjustments in the adolescent period (schizophrenia, crime) date back to that period, or whether childhood maladjustments are to a degree self limiting.

(e) What are the determining crises at adolescence and other periods of maturation and experience.

(f) The incentives involved in personality development and what necessities of human nature (organic and social urges) must always and everywhere be satisfied as conditions of an adjusted personality.

(g) The desire for intimacy, forms of intimacy, and the size of groups within which intimacies are possible, with special reference to the psychoses.

(h) The different reactions of different individuals to the same critical experience. For example, one may become insane, another commit suicide, another commit a crime, another continue unchanged, another adjust on a higher level of efficiency.

(i) To how many and what codes does the individual respond and what conflicts arise from this source. . . .

(j) Differences between verbal and actual behavior.[44]

The role of statistics, on the other hand, is to establish the relative weight of the suggested variables and their interrelationships. The human situation is complex; the variables are difficult to isolate and

[44] "Report . . . on the Organization of a Program in the Field of Personality and Culture," *op. cit.*, pp. 10–11 (infra, pp. 298–299).

measure. But in so far as they can be put into quantitative form, their significance must be tested statistically:

> Where the total situation is so complicated, the interrelations so numerous and measurement so necessary, the method will evidently be very intimately related to statistical procedure. Although it is impossible to set up real experimental control . . . , if groups of individuals roughly similar in a large number of attributes can be studied in varying situations the specific type of behavior resulting may be compared, statistically, for the different situations and inferences drawn as to the relative effects of the situations on the behavior.[45]

Even here, however, Thomas is cautious. In describing a comparative statistical study of delinquents with nondelinquents, he notes:

> But it must be obvious that very important aspects of the environment are probably not touched by these measurements, and likewise important aspects of personality make-up are not included. A study of this sort may be quite objective, give verifiable results and lead to guarded and careful inferences as to factors important in the etiology of crime, but it will very probably give a quite inadequate basis for the understanding of crime. In any interpretative study, by selecting out only those factors which are at the moment capable of quantitative expression, there is a necessary overweighting of those factors as against factors not readily expressed quantitatively.[46]

Similarly, he warns of the "premature quantification of the data," and the "absurd" application of statistical techniques to inexact data or data of a limited kind.[47]

With awareness of these pitfalls, however, statistics is an important part of social science equipment, providing in Thomas' scheme the principal techniques of verification, while case studies and life histories provide the concepts, categories, units, and variables which can be related in hypotheses to be verified. As he summarized the

[45] *The Child in America,* p. 565.

[46] *Ibid.,* p. 567.

[47] *Ibid.* Thomas' view on statistics was considerably influenced by Dorothy S. Thomas, co-author of *The Child in America.* Certainly Thomas had not emphasized the statistical approach prior to this time. Indeed, in his doctoral dissertation, he rejected an argument by Karl Pearson on the ground that it was "mainly statistical." See "On a Difference in the Metabolism of the Sexes," 1897, reprinted in *Sex and Society* (Chicago: University of Chicago Press, 1907) as "Organic Differences in the Sexes," p. 17, n. 1. In 1931, in "The Relation of Research to the Social Process," Thomas specifically cites Dorothy S. Thomas as "responsible for the items relating to statistical procedure in this paper" (*op. cit.,* p. 194, n. 6).

relationship of the two kinds of procedures, there is a constant interplay between them:

> What is needed is a continuous and detailed preparation and study of life histories along with the available statistical studies, to be used as a basis for the inferences drawn. And these inferences in turn must be continually subjected to further statistical analysis as it becomes possible to transmute more factors into quantitative form. The case study method and the "natural history" method must not only precede the more scientifically acceptable method in order to produce realistic hypotheses and indicate what units should be defined and isolated; they must also be used as a general background of reference to the more limited statistical findings, which lead, as we have indicated, to inferences which must be constantly checked for validity against the large mass of material not yet analyzable.[48]

Thus each type of research, the statistical and the case study, makes its own contribution to the scientific process. A genuine social science must employ both types complementally, rather than either one separately as advocates of one or the other often claim.

Thomas' methodology, then, provides for the study of behavior in both its objective and subjective aspects, each aspect having techniques appropriate to it. It also emphasizes the close link between theory and data, particular data suggesting hypotheses which in turn are tested against a new set of data assembled for the purpose. This close interdependence of fact and theory is now widely recognized, but not so when Thomas wrote. Then there was a tendency to be either descriptive (fact-gathering) or theoretical (speculative) with little effort to relate the results of the two processes except in the sense of illustration. Development of the situational approach, in this respect, was therefore a considerable contribution to the growth of empirical research and a more rigorous conception of social science methodology.

Such an approach, moreover, excludes none of the disciplines which deal with man. Being concerned with all aspects of human behavior, individual and group, subjective and objective, it provides a focus wherein all the social fields may join and make their particular contributions. After all, there is but one social science and the present disciplines merely represent a division of labor in the interests of convenience and intensiveness of study.

[48] "The Relation of Research to the Social Process," *op. cit.*, p. 190.

Indeed, Thomas suggested the major topics with which such a general social science must deal, indicating in a broad way how each of the disciplines fits into the total structure:

From this standpoint the problems of individual and group adjustment involve study of the following factors:

1. The culture situations to which the individual is to make adjustments (studies of cultures).

2. The devices and instrumentalities for adjusting the individual to the cultural situations (social organization and education).

3. The capacity and opportunity of the individual to be adjusted (constitutional factors, incentives, social position).

4. The failures of adaptation, meaning: for the individual, dependency, vagrancy, crime, alcoholism, drug addiction, psychoneurosis, etc.; and for the group, decline, subordination, extermination.

5. Changes in cultural situations (*e.g.*, internal mobility of populations, urbanization, migration, invasion, colonization, the dissemination of cultural traits, race prejudice, technological advance, shifting of occupation, changes in attitudes and values, etc.) requiring continuous readjustment of individuals and reorganization of culture and learning, and involving questions of the participation of individuals and groups in promoting and directing cultural change.[49]

Practically all of current social research comes within the purview of this framework and if the research is not to remain fragmentary and isolated it may well be conceived in this general context.

Yet Thomas' scheme is not a confining one, demanding a rigid adherence to problems defined a priori. He did not believe that science progresses in that manner. Rather it advances by "pursuing random inquiries "[50] proposed by imaginative, curious, and creatively intelligent men. Science is not practiced in a vacuum; it depends upon previous research, and the presence of problems growing out of it.

Apart from the advantages to social science which such a scheme possesses, there is also the matter of social import. Thomas' program has considerable social significance because it includes the study of practical problems which confront modern society in great abundance. These problems have a certain priority, not because they represent "abnormalities" and hence throw light on "normality"

49 *Primitive Behavior,* pp. 1–2.

50 "Report . . . on the Organization of a Program in the Field of Personality and Culture," *op. cit.*, p. 34 (infra, p. 318).

as Durkheim suggested, but because they are urgent. Indeed, Thomas saw no need for separating the normal from the abnormal:

> Defining the general problem as one of adjustive striving, the question arises whether concentration in the programs of study should be on the successful or the unsuccessful efforts of adjustment. It is, however, desirable that no formal separation should be made of the so-called "normal" and "abnormal" aspects of personality and behavior. The two phases should be taken as aspects of a process and as representing different degrees of adjustment. On the other hand, the unadjustments are the critical and practical aspects of the problem and it will be methodologically important and necessary to give particular attention to the maladjustments represented by delinquency, crime, . . . vagabondage, etc. . . . And while investigations of these maladjustive aspects of behavior should be made with reference to the cultural context in which they occur, . . . it will be desirable in some cases to take the maladjustment as the point of departure of the investigation.[51]

From Thomas' standpoint, which emphasizes subjective definitions of situations, all behavior is adjustive in some sense. Theoretically there is no maladjustment, except in the sense that society so defines this or that kind of act. The point is that in social science the behavior of individuals and groups must always be distinguished from the judgments which other individuals or groups pass upon it. Such judgments, and their determinants, are entirely separate problems.

Nevertheless, at any given time social norms do exist, and deviations from the norms are occurring. From the standpoint of the group these represent behavior problems, and from that of the social scientist such problems may be the initial point for study. Further, the situational method holds promise of solving these problems since it does not regard behavior as the inevitable product of innate, unchangeable biological forces.

On the contrary, the situational approach rejects such a particularistic view and finds that such factors as the biological are only elements in the total situation, which "represents the configuration of the factors conditioning the behavior." [52] By isolating the variables, measuring them as best we can, the situational approach holds out some hope of rational control of behavior:

[51] *Ibid.*, pp. 2–3 (infra, pp. 291–292).

[52] "The Behavior Pattern and the Situation," *op. cit.*, p. 1.

We regard this approach as the only one capable of giving a rational basis for the control of behavior which may be a substitute for the common sense, preceptual, ordering-and-forbidding type of control which has been traditional and which, to the degree that it had efficiency in the past, has now broken down.[53]

This does not mean that values and their creation lie within the province of the social scientist, but it does mean that if goals are once decided upon as desirable, the social scientist may then be in a position to help attain them:

It is recognized that the object of research in both the material and the social worlds is control, or it might be said to be the supplying of materials and situations for the satisfaction of human desires—the providing of what men want.[54]

In this way the social scientist repays the society which supports his work. In return he asks only that he be free to follow his investigations wherever they may lead, even if traditional norms or interpretations of behavior are thereby found to be inadequate. Social science can do no more than offer the fruits of its labor to those who carry the responsibility for public policy.

In sum, Thomas' conception of social science is peculiarly his own. It rests upon the fundamentals of all science as these may be applicable to the unique phenomena of human adjustment. Tentative and exploratory in nature, it does not supply answers so much as it suggests the questions that must be asked, the research that must be done, if a practical and realistic social science is to be attained.

Perhaps his most significant contribution in this direction is the elaboration of the "situation" as the real unit of human experience and thus the fundamental datum of the behavior sciences. This concept emphasizes and re-emphasizes the fact that human behavior occurs only under *certain conditions,* and that the principles of explanation must be sought through the analysis of situations. Rather than beginning with postulated factors—such as cultural, biological, or psychological determinants—and working toward the situation, the social scientist must work inductively from the situation, isolating and clarifying variables as he progresses.

[53] *The Child in America,* p. 561.

[54] "The Relation of Research to the Social Process," *op. cit.,* p. 175.

The influence of this conception along with its corollary, the "definition of the situation," is readily apparent in large areas of contemporary social science. Whether this influence is direct or indirect is of no great moment. The important thing is that similar views, even though differently elaborated, are now current.

Students of social stratification, for example, have adopted the position that classes must be determined in accordance with the way the people of a community define the class situation, rather than in accordance with arbitrary, objective criteria. Social behavior can then be studied in terms of the class categories which result from the consensus of individual definitions of social class. In this way reliable material is obtained from the subjective standpoint and then analyzed in an objective fashion. Similarly, much of contemporary work in attitude change, social norms, and the so-called "field" theories of behavior parallels Thomas' conceptions.

Yet for all the value which the situational concept seems to possess, some questions remain. It may be said that Thomas, despite the various definitions and illustrations he gave to the notion, seems curiously vague about it. At times the situation seems synonymous with a social institution, neighborhood, or group, but at others it means an event, an individual experience, or even a complete illusion. Moreover, in its social sense the situation seems to have no limits, or at least they are hard to define. Any single situation is so inextricably merged with others that it often appears to be a very dubious kind of abstraction with which to work.

Further, the concepts of both situation and crisis seem practically unidentifiable, except perhaps in retrospect or upon the testimony of interested parties. For research purposes, therefore, it is difficult to specify in advance what will be either a situation or a crisis to any particular individual or group. As a result, the scientific utility of these concepts may well be challenged.

To all this Thomas would probably reply that the concepts are incapable of precise definition because human experience is not of a kind which permits such precision. From the standpoint of persons in society, a situation or crisis may emerge without perceptible change in the environment simply because the environment is, so to speak, partly a projection of an inner condition. Presumably the only way in which such precision could be attained would be if all people had the same chains of experience and thus perceived all situations exactly alike—a state of affairs that can scarcely be imagined.

In the meantime what we have to deal with is the existence of subjective experience with objective consequences, that is, behavior "as if" things were as they are imagined to be. To Thomas this is the unique quality which separates human phenomena from all others. Moreover, he would insist that human social life must be considered in its own terms, whether vague or precise, perceptible to other observers or imperceptible, logical or illogical. Here is the very "stuff" of human existence. The concepts of situation and crisis are simply the best available means of realistically grasping this human experience in some measure, and so better understanding it.

In a broader sense Thomas' basic position on this point amounts to the formulation of a principle which is now more or less widely recognized, namely, that the nature of a science and the limits of its precision and powers of prediction are fixed by the nature of the phenomena being studied. The various physical sciences are by no means equal in their ability to measure and predict, yet the label "science" is not withheld from some of them for that reason. Each discipline must do what it can within the limits of its material. So it must be with social science: it must preserve those methods common to all science, and at the same time forge special tools to deal realistically and effectively with its own range of phenomena.

A further implication of Thomas' position is that it leads to the recognition of a new relativism in social science. This is not a restatement of the principle of cultural relativity, or associated notions, but an awareness of *points of view* in both social description and generalization.

On the descriptive level it suggests that "facts" do not have a uniform existence apart from the persons who observe and interpret them. Rather the "real" facts are the ways in which different people come into and define situations. Thomas cited a particular example:

> Thus, the behavior records of the child clinics are contributing important data by including the child's account of the difficult situation, the often conflicting definitions of this situation given by parents, teachers, etc., and the recording of such facts as can be verified about the situation by disinterested investigators.[55]

[55] *The Child in America,* p. 572.

The same situation, in other words, may have different meanings to the participants, and complete description involves the assembly and analysis of all the points of view. Meanings are as important to the social scientist as any set of objectively observed data.

In this connection the concept of "role" becomes especially significant. In any situation there may be an "ideal" role for a person, as defined by tradition; there may be the "real" role, as well; in addition the individual's definition of his role may vary as the situation changes, and different individuals may define the same role differently. In descriptive studies, therefore, it is not enough to say that a person has a certain kind of role: the standpoint which defines the role must also be specified.

The same implication applies at the level of scientific interpretation. There have been, for example, several different uses of the word "symbol" in social science, as when a psychoanalyst views some compulsive behavior, or when an anthropologist reports a marriage custom. In these cases it is seldom made clear whether the alleged "symbolism" is to be found in the ideas of the people being described, or whether it is an interpretive device in the mind of the social scientist himself. If it is the first, then statements about "symbolism" are merely descriptive; if the second, it is bona fide interpretation. Without explicit recognition of points of view, however, these matters remain unclear.

In retrospect, Thomas looms as more than a historical figure of importance. Directly and indirectly he has influenced the course of social science development, and his basic conceptions can be discerned in much of contemporary theory and research. If today it is difficult to appreciate his originality and authority, it is because so much of his work has been accepted into the body of social science. The study of adjustive behavior in situations, the use of control groups in research, the close interplay of fact and theory, the importance of life history material revealing subjective experience, the mutual interdependence of the social sciences, the recognition that all science is ultimately practical—all this has become common knowledge except to the most provincial.

Thomas' abiding concern was with the timeless problems of science as these are manifest in the realm of social behavior: the nature of the phenomena being studied, their conceptualization, and the methods appropriate to their analysis. To the extent that he clarified these problems and pointed the way to their solution, he has become a part of the culture of social science itself. He helped to define the scientific situation.

Part I

SOCIAL SCIENCE AND SOCIAL BEHAVIOR

1 THE NEED FOR A SOCIAL SCIENCE

Part I contains seven selections which trace the development of Thomas' conceptions of social science. In all of them he is concerned with the problems of conceptualization, method, technique, and practical application which are involved in the scientific study of human behavior. In addition to outlining Thomas' position, these selections contain some of the most influential writing in American social science. They reveal forcefully, and in detail, the questions which are of inescapable importance in the study of human life.

The first selection is from "The Persistence of Primary-group Norms in Present-day Society and Their Influence in Our Educational System," 1917, a brilliant essay on the social dilemmas of the modern world. This paper also introduced the concepts of the "four wishes," "definition of the situation," and the three personality types into American social science. But in this selection Thomas' major theme is the necessity of creating a social science in order to promote rational social control in a rapidly changing world. The primary group has broken down and its norms have lost their efficacy in regulating behavior. Traditional means of control are inadequate; natural science has proven itself beneficial even when disturbing the old norms; hence, argues Thomas, a science of the social world may prove equally practical. Only a method is required. These ideas were more fully developed in *The Polish Peasant,* 1918–20, but their clear statement here provides a suitable introduction to the selections that follow.

The Persistence of Primary-group Norms[1]

All that I have said up to this point impresses me . . . with the urgency of a more exact and systematic study of human behavior on a scale and with a method comparable with those already provided for the physical and biological sciences. We have a failure of the "common-sense" method, not only in education and the relation of races and nationalities, but in connection with crime, prostitution, slums, insanity, abnormality, labor problems and all kinds of unhappiness. It is only by following the example of the physical sciences

[1] In Herbert S. Jennings and others, *Suggestions of Modern Science Concerning Education* (New York: The Macmillan Company, 1917), pp. 159–197. The present selections may be found on pp. 188–191, 195–197. Other selections from this essay appear on pp. 111–115 and 226–231 infra.

and accumulating the largest possible amount of secure and varied information and establishing general and particular laws which we can draw on to meet any crisis as it arises that we shall be able to secure a control in the social world comparable to that obtained in the natural world, and to determine eventually the kind of world we want to live in. I take it that the only reason we have not followed the path of the natural sciences long ago is the partially unrealized fear of disturbing our behavior norms. For evidently there were laws and consequently practices in the physical world that would never have been discovered by the "common-sense" method, and obviously the same is true of the social world.

What the detailed procedure in such a science would be I am unable even to indicate. You have had examples of it in the preceding papers of this series,[2] and I have referred to one of the main problems in the earlier part of this paper—the laws of the conversion of one attitude or prepossession into another.[3] But the exact procedure could not be predicted in this field any more than it could have been predicted in the fields of physics and chemistry. The solution of problems gives rise to new problems.[4]

And in another respect a social science must be upon the basis of the physical sciences—it must go on endlessly and without reference to immediate practical applicability. The men who were instrumental in the constitution of the physical sciences pursued their problems as ends in themselves, without any reference to practical applicability. Their work was, to begin with, illegitimate anyway, hedonistic and disorderly, and the society which opposed it had no

2 The following papers appear on preceding pages in the same volume: Herbert S. Jennings, "The Biology of Children in Relation to Education"; John B. Watson, "Practical and Theoretical Problems in Instinct and Habit"; and Adolf Meyer, "Mental and Moral Health in a Constructive School Program."

3 Cf. current research on attitude change. A convenient summary of this research, from a particular point of view, may be found in David Krech and Richard S. Crutchfield, *Theory and Problems of Social Psychology* (New York: McGraw-Hill Book Company, 1948), especially chaps. v–vii. See also Carl I. Hovland, Arthur A. Lumsdaine, and Fred D. Sheffield, *Experiments on Mass Communication,* Studies in Social Psychology in World War II, Vol. 3 (Princeton: Princeton University Press, 1949), which reports some concrete investigations of attitude change, with particular emphasis on methodological problems.

4 Cf. "The Role of Methodology in the Development of Science," pp. 83–85 infra.

expectation of practical applicability, but anticipated only harmful disturbance of norms. But it happened that these men adopted the course which in the end yielded the largest number of results of practical applicability precisely because they had unlimited liberty in the setting and solution of problems, and thereby established the greatest variety of laws.

The sciences do reach a point where they are consciously turned in the direction of practical applicability, that is, they anticipate that by following certain directions certain practical results will appear (and the life of Pasteur is perhaps the best example of this); [5] but the history of the sciences shows that only a *method* quite free from dependence on practice can become practically useful in its applications. We do not know what the future of science will be before it is constituted and what may be the applications of its discoveries before they are applied. . . .

. . . The point is that we have not got a method in the social world. The primary-group norms are breaking down, mainly owing to the facilitated communication gained through discoveries in the natural sciences and their practical application. The very disharmony of the social world is largely due to the disproportionate rate of advance in the mechanical world.[6] We live in an entirely new world, unique, without parallel in history. History has not helped us. It cannot help us because we do not understand it; we do not even understand an election. We must first understand the past from the present. We must view the present as behavior. We must establish by scientific procedure the laws of behavior, and then the past will have its meaning and make its contribution.[7] If we learn the laws

[5] Cf. pp. 113–114 infra where, in another connection, Pasteur's scientific quest is described.

[6] Cf. the "culture-lag" hypothesis, in William F. Ogburn, *Social Change with Respect to Culture and Original Nature* (New York: B. W. Huebsch, 1922; Viking Press, 1928). Ten years earlier Thomas had written: "The human mind is a very precious possession, but it is also a very dangerous one. Its exercise implies the breaking up of old habits, both those growing out of animal instinct and those established through 'folk-thought,' and *the interval between the disturbance and the reaccommodation is necessarily one of anarchy* and laissez faire." ("The Significance of the Orient for the Occident," *American Journal of Sociology,* May 1908, pp. 735–736; italics ours.)

[7] Cf. this statement by Thomas in 1896: "A knowledge of the present must be combined with the knowledge of the past for an adequate understanding of any part of

of human behavior as we have learned the laws of mathematics, physics, and chemistry, if we establish what are the fundamental human attitudes, how they can be converted into other and more socially desirable attitudes, how the world of values is created and modified by the operation of these attitudes, then we can establish any attitudes and values whatever.

And we are not to speak of "ultimate" or "supreme" values. The ultimate value is the value you desire at the given moment. But if your "ultimate" values mean the abolition of war, of crime, of drink, of abnormality, of slums, of this or that kind of unhappiness, then you can secure these values, and you can secure whatever seem to you "ultimate" values afterwards, but they cannot be secured without a science of behavior, . . . [any] more than an "ultimate" mechanics or an "ultimate" medicine could or can be secured without the preceding sciences of mathematics, physics, and chemistry.

And, finally, if we recognize that social control is to be reached through the study of behavior, and that its technique is to consist in the creation of attitudes appropriate to desired values, then I suggest that the most essential attitude at the present moment is a public attitude of hospitality toward all forms of research in the social world, such as it has gained toward all forms of research in the physical world. . . .

---

the past." ("The Scope and Method of Folk-Psychology," *American Journal of Sociology*, January 1896, p. 441.)

2 METHODOLOGICAL NOTE

The Methodological Note which prefaced *The Polish Peasant,* 1918–20, may be regarded as a continuation and elaboration of the ideas set forth in the previous selection. Here again the inadequacies of "common-sense" sociology and the traditional "ordering-and-forbidding" technique of social control are emphasized, and a plea is made for the development of a social science which might have the values of prediction and control. The purpose of the Note was to outline the essentials of such a social science.

The first essential is that it discard the simple form of causation found in physical science. Reacting to Durkheim's dicta that "social facts" are caused by prior social facts, and that individual psychology is irrelevant to a social science, Thomas stresses the necessity of including subjective factors. Social science cannot remain wholly "objective." On the contrary it is fundamentally concerned with the interaction between objective "values" and subjective "attitudes." Social causation is complex and includes both a "value" aspect and an "attitude" aspect. The other important essential is that a science be developed which will have application to concrete social situations. This does not mean that social science is concerned only with immediate practical problems; it does emphasize the importance of discovering general laws of social change which will have applicability to such problems. Thus the Note attempted to supply the method which Thomas had previously found to be nonexistent.

Yet despite the elaborate phrasing to be found in the Note the scheme proposed remains relatively simple, not to say ambiguous. In this connection the reader is referred to Blumer's *An Appraisal of . . . The Polish Peasant,*[1] which contains not only a distinguished critique but also the rejoinders of Thomas and Znaniecki, and a spirited discussion by representatives of several disciplines.

Criticism notwithstanding, the Methodological Note remains a significant attempt to provide a theoretical frame of reference within which concrete research could be conducted. It called for comparative cultural studies, as well as intensive studies of a single culture and its subjective aspects. Valuable in theory, rich in insights, it is a social science classic. The following selections from the Note are intended to convey the general standpoint, including some portions which later were rejected by Thomas and criticized by other social scientists.

[1] Social Science Research Council Bulletin 44 (1939).

The Polish Peasant—
Methodological Note [2]

The marvelous results attained by a rational technique in the sphere of material reality invite us to apply some analogous procedure to social reality. Our success in controlling nature gives us confidence that we shall eventually be able to control the social world in the same measure. Our actual inefficiency in this line is due, not to any fundamental limitation of our reason, but simply to the historical fact that the objective attitude toward social reality is a recent acquisition.

. . . But the tendency to rational control is growing in this field also and constitutes at present an insistent demand on the social sciences.

This demand for a rational control results from the increasing rapidity of social evolution. The old forms of control were based upon the assumption of an essential stability of the whole social framework and were effective only in so far as this stability was real. In a stable social organization there is time enough to develop in a purely empirical way, through innumerable experiments and failures, approximately sufficient means of control with regard to the ordinary and frequent social phenomena, while the errors made in treating the uncommon and rare phenomena seldom affect social life in such a manner as to imperil the existence of the group; if they do, then the catastrophe is accepted as incomprehensible and inevitable. . . .

But when . . . social evolution becomes more rapid and the crises [3] more frequent and varied, . . . every one must be met in a more or less adequate way, for they are too various and frequent not to imperil social life unless controlled in time. The substitution of a conscious technique for a half-conscious routine has become, therefore, a social necessity . . .

The oldest but most persistent form of social technique is that of "ordering-and-forbidding"—that is, meeting a crisis by an arbi-

[2] The selection is from the second edition (New York: Alfred A. Knopf, 1927), Vol. I, pp. 1–69.

[3] For Thomas' earlier formulation of the "crisis" concept, see "The Psychology of Culture Change," pp. 218–220 infra.

trary act of will decreeing the disappearance of the undesirable or the appearance of the desirable phenomena, and using arbitrary physical action to enforce the decree. . . .

. . . In social life an expressed act of will may be sometimes a real cause, when the person or body from which it emanates has a particular authority in the eyes of those to whom the order or prohibition applies. But this does not change the nature of the technique as such. The prestige of rulers, ecclesiastics, and legislators was a condition making an act of will an efficient cause under the old régimes, but it loses its value in the modern partly or completely republican organizations.

A more effective technique, based upon "common sense" and represented by "practical" sociology, has naturally originated in those lines of social action in which there was . . . no place for legislative measures . . . Here, indeed, the act of will having been recognized as inefficient in directing the causal process, real causes are sought for every phenomenon, and an endeavor is made to control the effects by acting upon the causes, and, though it is often partly successful, many fallacies are implicitly involved in this technique; it has still many characters of a planless empiricism, trying to get at the real cause by a rather haphazard selection of various possibilities, directed only by a rough and popular reflection, and its deficiencies have to be shown and removed if a new and more efficient method of action is to be introduced.

The first of these fallacies has often been exposed. It is the latent or manifest supposition that we know social reality because we live in it, and that we can assume things and relations as certain on the basis of our empirical acquaintance with them. The attitude is here about the same as in the ancient assumption that we know the physical world because we live and act in it, and that therefore we have the right of generalizing without a special and thorough investigation, on the mere basis of "common sense." The history of physical science gives us many good examples of the results to which common sense can lead, such as the geocentric system of astronomy and the mediaeval ideas about motion. And it is easy to show that not even the widest individual acquaintance with social reality, not even the most evident success of individual adaptation to this reality, can offer any serious guaranty of the validity of the common-sense generalizations.

Indeed, the individual's sphere of practical acquaintance with social reality . . . is always limited and constitutes only a small part of the whole complexity of social facts. It usually extends over only one society, often over only one class of this society; this we may call the exterior limitation. In addition there is an interior limitation, still more important, due to the fact that among all the experiences which the individual meets within the sphere of his social life a large, perhaps the larger, part is left unheeded, never becoming a basis of common-sense generalizations. This selection of experiences is the result of individual temperament on the one hand and of individual interest on the other. In any case, . . . the selection is subjective—that is, valid only for this particular individual in this particular social position—and thereby it is quite different from, and incommensurable with, the selection which a scientist would make in face of the same body of data from an objective, impersonal viewpoint.[4]

Nor is the practical success of the individual within his sphere of activity a guaranty of his knowledge of the relations between the social phenomena which he is able to control. Of course there must be some objective validity in his schemes of social facts—otherwise he could not live in society—but the truth of these schemes is always only a rough approximation and is mixed with an enormous amount of error. When we assume that a successful adaptation of the individual to his environment is a proof that he knows this environment thoroughly, we forget that there are degrees of success, that the standard of success is to a large extent subjective . . . Two elements are found in varying proportions in every adaptation; one is the actual control exercised over the environment; the other is the claims which this control serves to satisfy. The adaptation may be perfect, either because of particularly successful and wide control or because of particularly limited claims.[5] Whenever the control within the given range of claims proves insufficient, the individual or the group

[4] Cf. Herbert Spencer, *The Study of Sociology* (New York: D. Appleton and Company, 1873), *passim* for similar views.

[5] For a similar discussion of adaptation, see pp. 173–174 infra.

can either develop a better control or limit the claims. And, in fact, in every activity the second method . . . plays a very important role. Thus the individual's knowledge of his environment can be considered as real only in the particular matters in which he does actually control it; his schemes can be true only in so far as they are perfectly, absolutely successful. And if we remember how much of practical success is due to mere chance and luck, even this limited number of truths becomes doubtful. Finally, the truths that stand the test of individual practice are always schemes of the concrete and singular, as are the situations in which the individual finds himself.

In this way the acquaintance with social data and the knowledge of social relations which we acquire in practice are always more or less subjective, limited both in number and in generality. Thence comes the well-known fact that the really valuable part of practical wisdom acquired by the individual during his life is incommunicable—cannot be stated in general terms; everyone must acquire it afresh by a kind of apprenticeship to life—that is, by learning to select experiences according to the demands of his own personality and to construct for his own use particular schemes of the concrete situations which he encounters. Thus, all the generalizations constituting the common-sense social theory and based on individual experience are both insignificant and subject to innumerable exceptions. A sociology that accepts them necessarily condemns itself to remain in the same methodological stage, and a practice based upon them must be as insecure and as full of failures as is the activity of every individual.

Whenever, now, this "practical" sociology makes an effort to get above the level of popular generalizations by the study of social reality instead of relying upon individual experience, it still preserves the same method as the individual in his personal reflection; investigation always goes on with an immediate reference to practical aims, and the standards of the desirable and undesirable are the ground upon which theoretic problems are approached. This is the second fallacy of the practical sociology, and the results of work from this standpoint are quite disproportionate to the enormous efforts that have recently been put forth in the collection and elaboration of materials preparatory to social reforms. The example of physical science and material technique should have shown long ago that only a scientific investigation, which is quite free from any dependence on practice, can become practically useful in its applications. Of course this does not mean that the scientist should not select for investigation problems whose solution has actual practical importance; the sociologist may study crime or war as the chemist studies dyestuffs. But from the method of the study itself all practical considerations must be excluded if we want the results to be valid. . . .

The third fallacy of the common-sense sociology is the implicit assumption that any group of social facts can be treated theoretically and practically in an arbitrary isolation from the rest of the life of the given society.[6] . . . If we start to study these facts . . . without heeding their connection with the rest of the social world, we must necessarily come to quite arbitrary generalizations. If we start to act upon these facts in a uniform way simply because their abstract essence seems to be the same, we must necessarily produce quite different results, varying with the relations of every particular case to the rest of the social world. This does not mean that it is not possible to isolate such groups of facts for theoretic investigation or practical activity, but simply that the isolation must come, not a priori, but a posteriori, in the same way as the distinction between the normal and the abnormal. The facts must first be taken in connection with the whole to which they belong, and the question of a later isolation is a methodological problem . . .

There are two other fallacies involved to a certain extent in social practice, although practical sociology has already repudiated them. The reason for their persistence in practice is that, even if the erroneousness of the old assumptions has been recognized, no new working ideas have been put in their place. These assumptions are: (1) that men react in the same way to the same influences regardless of their individual or social past, and that therefore it is possible

[6] In 1909 Thomas wrote: "No object can be completely understood when separated from the whole culture of which it is a part, and no culture can be understood when its fragments are dislocated." (*Source Book for Social Origins,* p. 857.) The extent to which Thomas followed this rule may be debatable, but here is one of the first theoretical objections to the comparative method used so freely by cultural evolutionists. His position has since been made a central tenet of "functional analysis."

to provoke identical behavior in various individuals by identical means; (2) that men develop spontaneously, without external influence, tendencies which enable them to profit in a full and uniform way from given conditions, and that therefore it is sufficient to create favorable or remove unfavorable conditions in order to give birth to or suppress given tendencies. . . .

And these fallacies of the common-sense sociology are not always due to a lack of theoretic ability or of a serious scientific attitude on the part of the men who do the work. They are the unavoidable consequence of the necessity of meeting actual situations at once. Social life goes on without interruption and has to be controlled at every moment. The business man or politician, the educator or charity-worker, finds himself continually confronted by new social problems which he must solve, however imperfect and provisional he knows his solutions to be, for the stream of evolution does not wait for him. He must have immediate results, and it is a merit on his part if he . . . endeavors to understand the social reality as well as he can before acting. Certainly social life is improved by even such a control as common-sense sociology is able to give . . . But in social activity, even more than in material activity, the common-sense method is the most wasteful method, and to replace it gradually by a more efficient one will be a good investment.

While, then, there is no doubt that actual situations must be handled immediately, we see that they cannot be solved adequately as long as theoretical reflection has their immediate solution in view. But there is evidently one issue from this dilemma, and it is the same as in material technique and physical science. We must be able to foresee future situations and prepare for them, and we must have in stock a large body of secure and objective knowledge capable of being applied to any situation, whether foreseen or unexpected. This means that we must have an empirical and exact social science ready for eventual application. And such a science can be constituted only if we treat it as an end in itself . . . The example of physical science and its applications show that the only practically economical way of creating an efficient technique is to create a science independent of any technical limitations and then to take every one of its results and try where and in what way they can be practically applied. The contrary attitude, the refusal to recognize any science that does not work to solve practical problems, in addition to leading to that inefficiency of both science and practice which we have analyzed above, shows a curious narrowness of mental horizon. We do not know what the future science will be before it is constituted and what may be the applications of its discoveries before they are applied; we do not know what will be the future of society and what social problems may arise demanding solution. The only practically justifiable attitude toward science is absolute liberty and disinterested help.[7] . . .

But if no practical aims should be introduced beforehand into scientific investigation, social practice has, nevertheless, the right to demand from social theory that at least some of its results shall be applicable at once, and that the number and importance of such results shall continually increase. As one of the pragmatists has expressed it, practical life can and must give credit to science, but sooner or later science must pay her debts, and the longer the delay the greater the interest required. This demand of ultimate practical applicability is as important for science itself as for practice; it is a test, not only of the practical, but of the theoretical, value of the science. A science whose results can be applied proves thereby that it is really based upon experience, that it is able to grasp a great variety of problems, that its method is really exact—that it is valid. The test of applicability is a salutary responsibility which science must assume in her own interest.

If we attempt now to determine what should be the object-matter and the method of a social theory that would be able to satisfy the demands of modern social practice, it is evident that its main object should be the actual civilized society in its full development and with all its complexity of situations, for it is the control of the actual civilized society that is sought in most endeavors of rational practice. But here, as in every other science, a determined body of material assumes its full significance only if we can use comparison freely, in order to distinguish the essential from the accidental, the simple

[7] When this was written the problem of freedom was no doubt more critical in the social than in the natural sciences. In recent years, however, the problem has been raised anew with reference to natural science—a condition that obviously invites analysis in terms of Thomas' "crisis" concept.

from the complex, the primary from the derived. And fortunately social life gives us favorable conditions for comparative studies, particularly at the present stage of evolution, in the coexistence of a certain number of civilized societies sufficiently alike in their fundamental cultural problems to make comparison possible, and differing sufficiently in their traditions, customs, and general national spirit to make comparison fruitful.[8] . . .

Another point to be emphasized with regard to the question of the object-matter of social theory is the necessity of taking into account the whole life of a given society instead of arbitrarily selecting and isolating beforehand certain particular groups of facts. We have seen already that the contrary procedure constitutes one of the fallacies of the common-sense sociology. . . . Still more harmful for the development of science is this fallacy when used in the comparative sociology which studies an institution, an idea, a myth, a legal or moral norm, a form of art, etc., by simply comparing its content in various societies without studying it in the whole meaning which it has in a particular society and then comparing this with the whole meaning which it has in the various societies.[9] We are all more or less guilty of this fault, but it pleases us to attribute it mainly to Herbert Spencer.[10]

[8] An interesting parallel to this view may be found in one of Thomas' earliest writings: "The substitution of action based on knowledge for action based on feeling is made possible . . . in society by the development of higher centers of control . . . The fact that such a substitution is one of the professed aims . . . of sociology gives peculiar interest to the examination of the forms of control which have dominated different types of society, and the determination of the conditions and forces leading from one form of control to another." ("The Scope and Method of Folk-Psychology," *American Journal of Sociology,* January 1896, p. 443.)

[9] It was not until 1936 that Linton codified the distinctions between the "form," "meaning," "use," and "function" of any cultural datum. However, here is a clear realization of the difference between the "meaning" of a cultural datum and its "form" (content). Similarly, in emphasizing the difference between the viewpoint of the member of a social group and that of the scientific observer, Thomas was a clear forerunner of the modern functionalists. Merton, at least, has recognized this. See Ralph Linton, *The Study of Man* (New York: D. Appleton-Century Company, 1936), pp. 402 ff., and Robert K. Merton, *Social Theory and Social Structure* (Glencoe: The Free Press, 1949), pp. 62–63 and p. 371, n. 69.

[10] Thomas had been critical of Spencer before. In particular he did not agree that "primitive man" was less inhibited than modern man; that ancestor worship was the original form of religion; or that the medicine man was the prototype from which all other professional and artistic occupations were derived. See *Source Book for Social*

In order to avoid arbitrary limitations and subjective interpretations there are only two possible courses open. We can study monographically whole concrete societies with the total complexity of problems and situations which constitute their cultural life; or we can work on special social problems, following the problem in a certain limited number of concrete social groups and studying it in every group with regard to the particular form which it assumes under the influence of the conditions prevailing in this society, taking into account the complex meaning which a concrete cultural phenomenon has in a determined cultural environment. In studying the society we go from the whole social context to the problem, and in studying the problem we go from the problem to the whole social context. And in both types of work the only safe method is to start with the assumption that we know absolutely nothing about the group or the problem we are to investigate except such purely formal criteria as enable us to distinguish materials belonging to our sphere of interest from those which do not belong there. But this attitude of indiscriminate receptivity toward any concrete data should mark only the first stage of investigation—that of limiting the field. As soon as we become acquainted with the materials we begin to select them with the help of criteria which involve certain methodological generalizations and scientific hypotheses. . . . We have to limit ourselves to certain theoretically important data, but we must know how to distinguish the data which are important. And every further step of the investigation will bring with it new methodological problems—analysis of the complete concrete data into elements, systematization of these elements, definition of social facts, establishing of social laws. All these stages of scientific procedure must be exactly and carefully defined if social theory is to become a science conscious of its own methods and able to apply them with precision . . . And it is always the question of an ultimate practical applicability which, according

---

Origins, pp. 24, 316, 734–735; also "The Relation of the Medicine-Man to the Origin of the Professional Occupations," *ibid.,* pp. 281–302. These criticisms did not prevent Thomas from saying that Spencer's *Principles of Sociology* remained "the most systematic and considerable attempt to interpret society as an evolution. And both the originality and the inadequacy of his views have greatly stimulated scientific inquiry." (*Ibid.,* p. viii.)

to our previous discussion, will constitute the criterion—the only secure and intrinsic criterion—of a science.

Now there are two fundamental practical problems which have constituted the center of attention of reflective social practice in all times. These are (1) the problem of the dependence of the individual upon social organization and culture, and (2) the problem of the dependence of social organization and culture upon the individual.[11] Practically, the first problem is expressed in the question, How shall we produce with the help of the existing social organization and culture the desirable mental and moral characteristics in the individuals constituting the social group? And the second problem means in practice, How shall we produce, with the help of the existing mental and moral characteristics of the individual members of the group, the desirable type of social organization and culture?

If social theory is . . . to solve these problems . . . it is evident that it must include both kinds of data involved in them—namely, the objective cultural elements of social life and the subjective characteristics of the members of the social group—and that the two kinds of data must be taken as correlated. For these data we shall use now and in the future the terms "social values" (or simply "values") and "attitudes." [12]

By a social value we understand any datum having an empirical content accessible to the members of some social group and a meaning with regard to which it is or may be an object of activity. Thus, a foodstuff, an instrument, a coin, a piece of poetry, a university, a myth, a scientific theory, are social values. Each of them has a con-

[11] These problems are not so very different from those stated in Thomas' earlier writings. For example, in "The Scope and Method of Folk-Psychology," *American Journal of Sociology,* January 1896, p. 435, he identified the main task of the "science of man" as "the determination of the developmental relation of individual to race consciousness, and the relation of both to accompanying institutions and usages." Similarly, in "The Province of Social Psychology," *ibid.,* January 1905, pp. 445–446, he states that social psychology is "the examination of the interaction of individual consciousness and society, and the effect of the interaction on individual consciousness on the one hand, and on society on the other." Allowing for differences in terminology, the basic conception appears quite similar throughout these various formulations.

[12] It has been suggested that the division of social phenomena into "attitudes" and "values" may be derived from Tarde. See Floyd N. House, *The Range of Social Theory* (New York: Henry Holt and Company, 1929), pp. 214–215, especially p. 215, n. 7.

tent that is sensual in the case of the foodstuff, the instrument, the coin; partly sensual, partly imaginary in the piece of poetry, whose content is constituted, not only by the written or spoken words, but also by the images which they evoke, and in the case of the university, whose content is the whole complex of men, buildings, material accessories, and images representing its activity; or, finally, only imaginary in the case of a mythical personality or a scientific theory. The meaning of these values becomes explicit when we take them in connection with human actions. The meaning of the foodstuff is its reference to its eventual consumption; that of an instrument, its reference to the work for which it is designed; . . . The social value is thus opposed to the natural thing, which has a content but, as a part of nature, has no meaning for human activity, is treated as "valueless"; when the natural thing assumes a meaning, it becomes thereby a social value. And naturally a social value may have many meanings, for it may refer to many different kinds of activity.

By attitude we understand a process of individual consciousness which determines real or possible activity of the individual in the social world. Thus, hunger that compels the consumption of the foodstuff; the workman's decision to use the tool; the tendency of the spendthrift to spend the coin; the poet's feelings and ideas expressed in the poem and the reader's sympathy and admiration; the needs which the institution tries to satisfy and the response it provokes; the fear and devotion manifested in the cult of the divinity; the interest in creating, understanding, or applying a scientific theory and the ways of thinking implied in it—all these are attitudes. The attitude is thus the individual counterpart of the social value; activity, in whatever form, is the bond between them. By its reference to activity and thereby to individual consciousness the value is distinguished from the natural thing. By its reference to activity and thereby to the social world the attitude is distinguished from the psychical state. . . .

But when we say that the data of social theory are attitudes and values, this is not yet a sufficient determination of the object of this science, for the field thus defined would embrace the whole of human culture and include the object-matter of philology and economics, theory of art, theory of science, etc. A more exact definition is therefore necessary in order to distinguish social theory from these sciences . . .

This limitation of the field of social theory arises quite naturally from the necessity of choosing between attitudes or values as fundamental data—that is, as data whose characters will serve as a basis for scientific generalization. . . . Scientific generalization must always base itself upon such characters of its data as can be considered essential to its purposes, and the essential characters of human actions are completely different when we treat them from the standpoint of attitudes and when we are interested in them as values. There is therefore no possibility of giving to attitudes and values the same importance in a methodical scientific investigation; either attitudes must be subordinated to values or the contrary. . . .

. . . The distinction of social from individual psychology and the methodological unity of social psychology as a separate science have not been sufficiently discussed, but we shall attempt to show that social psychology is precisely the science of attitudes and that, while its methods are essentially different from the methods of individual psychology, its field is as wide as conscious life.

Indeed, every manifestation of conscious life, however simple or complex, general or particular, can be treated as an attitude, because every one involves a tendency to action, whether this action is a process of mechanical activity producing physical changes in the material world, or an attempt to influence the attitudes of others by speech and gesture, or a mental activity which does not at the given moment find a social expression, or even a mere process of sensual apperception. . . .

But of course not all the attitudes found in the conscious life of a social group have the same importance for the purposes of social psychology at a given moment . . . On the one hand, the task of every science in describing and generalizing the data is to reduce as far as possible the limitless complexity of experience to a limited number of concepts, and therefore those elements of reality are the most important which are most generally found in that part of experience which constitutes the object-matter of a science. And thus for social psychology the importance of an attitude is proportionate to the number and variety of actions in which this attitude is manifested. The more generally an attitude is shared by the members of the given social group and the greater the part which it plays in the life of every member, the stronger the interest which it provokes in the social psychologist, while attitudes which are either peculiar to a few members of the group or which manifest themselves only on rare occasions have as such a relatively secondary significance, but may become significant through some connection with more general and fundamental attitudes.* . . .

Thus, the field of social psychology practically comprises first of all the attitudes which are more or less generally found among the members of a social group, have a real importance in the life-organization of the individuals who have developed them, and manifest themselves in social activities of these individuals. . . .

But when we study the life of a concrete social group we find a certain very important side of this life which social psychology cannot adequately take into account, . . . and which during the last fifty years has constituted the central sphere of interest of the various researches called *sociology* . . . more or less explicit and formal *rules* of behavior by which the group tends to maintain, to regulate, and to make more general and more frequent the corresponding type of actions among its members. . . . The rules of behavior, and the actions viewed as conforming or not conforming with these rules, constitute with regard to their objective significance a certain number of more or less connected and harmonious systems which can be generally called *social institutions,* and the totality of institutions found in a concrete social group constitutes the *social organization* of this group. And when studying the social organization as such we must subordinate attitudes to values . . .

Sociology, as theory of social organization, is thus a special science of culture . . . and is in so far opposed to social psychology as the general science of the subjective side of culture. But at the same

* In connection, indeed, with the problems of both the creation and the destruction of social values, the most exceptional and divergent attitudes may prove the most important ones, because they may introduce a crisis and an element of disorder. And to the social theorist and technician the disorderly individual is of peculiar interest as a destroyer of values, as in the case of the anti-social individual, and as a creator of values, as in the case of the man of genius.

[Editor's note: This footnote and all others designated with asterisks in this volume are direct quotations of footnotes appearing in the works of W. I. Thomas which are here reproduced.]

time it has this in common with social psychology: that the values which it studies draw all their reality, all their power to influence human life, from the social attitudes which are expressed or supposedly expressed in them; if the individual in his behavior is so largely determined by the rules prevailing in his social group, it is certainly due neither to the rationality of these rules nor to the physical consequences which their following or breaking may have, but to his consciousness that these rules represent attitudes of his group and to his realization of the *social* consequences which will ensue for him if he follows or breaks the rules. And therefore both social psychology and sociology can be embraced under the general term of social theory, as they are both concerned with the relation between the individual and the concrete social group, though their standpoints on this common ground are quite opposite, and though their fields are not equally wide, social psychology comprising the attitudes of the individual toward *all* cultural values of the given social group, while sociology can study only one type of these values—social rules—in their relation to individual attitudes.

We have seen that social psychology has a central field of interest including the most general and fundamental cultural attitudes found within concrete societies. In the same manner there is a certain domain which constitutes the methodological center of sociological interest. It includes those rules of behavior which concern more especially the active relations between individual members of the group and between each member and the group as a whole. It is these rules, indeed, manifested as mores, laws, and group-ideals and systematized in such institutions as the family, the tribe, the community, the free association, the state,[13] etc., which constitute the central part of social organization and provide through this organization the essential conditions of the existence of a group as a distinct cultural entity and not a mere agglomeration of individuals; and hence all other rules which a given group may develop and treat as obligatory have a secondary sociological importance as compared with these. But this does not mean that sociology should not extend

[13] Cf. the universal "type-institutions" suggested by Bronislaw Malinowski in *A Scientific Theory of Culture and Other Essays* (Chapel Hill: University of North Carolina Press, 1944), pp. 54–66.

its field of investigation beyond this methodological center of interest. . . . Of course it can be determined only a posteriori how far the field of sociology should be extended beyond the investigation of fundamental social institutions, and the situation varies from group to group and from period to period. . . .

. . . The great and most usual illusion of the scientist is that he simply takes the facts as they are, without any methodological prepossessions, and gets his explanation entirely a posteriori from pure experience. A fact by itself is already an abstraction [14] . . . The question is only whether we perform this abstraction methodically or not, whether we know what and why we accept and reject, or simply take uncritically the old abstractions of "common sense." If we want to reach scientific explanations, we must keep in mind that our facts must be determined in such a way as to permit of their subordination to general laws. . . . And only if social theory succeeds in determining causal laws can it become a basis of social technique, for technique demands the possibility of foreseeing and calculating the effects of given causes, and this demand is realizable only if we know that certain causes will always and everywhere produce certain effects.

Now, the chief error of both social practice and social theory has been that they determined, consciously or unconsciously, social facts in a way which excluded in advance the possibility of their subordination to any laws. The implicit or explicit assumption was that a social fact is composed of two elements, a cause which is either a social phenomenon or an individual act, and an effect which is either an individual act or a social phenomenon. Following uncritically the example of the physical sciences, which always tend to find the one determined phenomenon which is the necessary and sufficient condition of another phenomenon, social theory and social practice have forgotten to take into account one essential difference between physical and social reality, which is that, while the effect of a physical phenomenon depends exclusively on the objective nature of this phenomenon and can be calculated on the ground of the latter's empirical content, the effect of a social phenomenon depends in addition on the subjective standpoint taken by the individual or the group toward this phenomenon and can be calculated only if we

[14] Cf. "There is no such thing as description completely devoid of theory" (*ibid.*, p. 7).

know, not only the objective content of the assumed cause, but also the meaning which it has at the given moment for the given conscious beings. This simple consideration should have shown to the social theorist or technician that a social cause cannot be simple, like a physical cause, but is compound, and must include both an objective and a subjective element, a value *and* an attitude. . . .

The fundamental methodological principle of both social psychology and sociology—the principle without which they can never reach scientific explanation—is therefore the following one:

The cause of a social or individual phenomenon is never another social or individual phenomenon alone, but always a combination of a social and an individual phenomenon.

Or, in more exact terms:

The cause of a value or of an attitude is never an attitude or a value alone, but always a combination of an attitude and a value.[15] . . .

The ideal of social theory, as of every other nomothetic science, is to interpret as many facts as possible by as few laws as possible, that is, not only to explain causally the life of particular societies at particular periods, but to subordinate these particular laws to general laws applicable to all societies at all times—taking into account the historical evolution of mankind which continually brings new data and new facts and thus forces us to search for new laws in addition to those already discovered. But the fact that social theory as such cannot test its results by the laboratory method, but must rely entirely on the logical perfection of its abstract analysis and synthesis, makes the problem of control of the validity of its generalizations particularly important. The insufficient realization of the character of this control has been the chief reason why so many sociological works bear a character of compositions, intermediary between philosophy and science and fulfilling the demands of neither. . . .

The ultimate test of social theory, as we have emphasized through-

[15] In 1938, at a special conference on Blumer's appraisal of *The Polish Peasant,* Thomas remarked in his rejoinder: "I approve our separation of attitudes and values, or psychological sets and tendencies to act, on the one hand, and the external stimuli to action on the other, and of our general description of the interaction of these factors, but I think we went too far in our confident assumption that we shall be able to lay bare the complete and invariable nature of this interaction and thus determine the *laws* of 'social becoming.' " ("Comment by W. I. Thomas," in Blumer, *op. cit.,* p. 83.)

out the present note, will be its application in practice, and thus its generalizations will be also subject in the last resort to the check of a possible failure. However, practical application is not experimentation. The results of the physical sciences are also ultimately tested by their application in industry, but this does not alter the fact that the test is made on the basis of laboratory experiments. The difference between experiment and application is twofold: (1) The problems themselves usually differ in complexity. The experiment by which we test a scientific law is artificially simplified in view of the special theoretic problem, whereas in applying scientific results to attain a practical purpose we have a much more complex situation to deal with, necessitating the use of several scientific laws and the calculation of their interference. . . . (2) In laboratory experiments the question of the immediate practical value of success or failure is essentially excluded for the sake of their theoretical value. . . . But in applying scientific results in practice we have essentially the practical value of success or failure in view. It is unthinkable that a chemist asked to direct the production of a new kind of soap in a factory should test his theory by direct application and risk the destruction of a hundred thousand dollars worth of material, instead of testing it previously on a small scale by laboratory experiments. Now in all so-called social experiments, on however small a scale, the question of practical value is involved, because the objects of these experiments are men; the social scientist cannot exclude the question of the bearing of his "experiments" on the future of those who are affected by them. He is therefore seldom or never justified in risking a failure for the sake of testing his theory. Of course he does and can take risks, not as a scientist, but as a practical man; that is, he is justified in taking the risk of bringing some harm if there are more chances of benefit than of harm to those on whom he operates. His risk is then the practical risk involved in every application of an idea, not the special theoretic risk involved in the mere testing of the idea. And, in order to diminish this practical risk, he must try to make his theory as certain and applicable as possible before trying to apply it in fact, and he can secure this result and hand over to the social practitioner generalizations at least approximately as applicable as those of physical science, only if he uses the check of contradiction by new experience. This means that besides using only such generalizations as can be contradicted by new experiences he must not wait till new experiences impose themselves on him by accident, but must search for them, must institute a systematic method of *observation*. And, while it is only natural that a scientist in order to form a hypothesis and to give it some amount of probability has to search first of all for such experiences as may corroborate it, his hypothesis cannot be considered fully tested until he has made subsequently a systematic search for such experiences as may contradict it, and proved those contradictions to be only seeming, explicable by the interference of definite factors.[16] . . .

We cannot enter here into detailed indications of what social technology should be, but we must take into account the chief point of its method—the general form which every concrete problem of social technique assumes. Whatever may be the aim of social practice—modification of individual attitudes or of social institutions— . . . we never find the elements which we want to use or to modify isolated and passively waiting for our activity, but always embodied in active practical *situations,* which have been formed independently of us and with which our activity has to comply.

The situation is the set of values and attitudes with which the individual or the group has to deal in a process of activity and with regard to which this activity is planned and its results appreciated. Every concrete activity is the solution of a situation. The situation involves three kinds of data: (1) The objective conditions under which the individual or society has to act, that is, the totality of values—economic, social, religious, intellectual, etc.—which at the given moment affect directly or indirectly the conscious status of the individual or the group. (2) The pre-existing attitudes of the individual or the group which at the given moment have an actual influence upon his behavior. (3) The definition of the situation, that is, the more or less clear conception of the conditions and consciousness of the attitudes. And the definition of the situation is a neces-

[16] This statement emphasizes one of the major contributions of the Methodological Note, at least to sociology: it discouraged aimless fact-gathering and led to more fruitful efforts relating fact and theory.

sary preliminary to any act of the will, for in given conditions and with a given set of attitudes an indefinite plurality of actions is possible, and one definite action can appear only if these conditions are selected, interpreted, and combined in a determined way and if a certain systematization of these attitudes is reached, so that one of them becomes predominant and subordinates the others. It happens, indeed, that a certain value imposes itself immediately and unreflectively and leads at once to action, or that an attitude as soon as it appears excludes the others and expresses itself unhesitatingly in an active process. In these cases, whose most radical examples are found in reflex and instinctive actions, the definition is already given to the individual by external conditions or by his own tendencies. But usually there is a process of reflection, after which either a ready social definition is applied or a new personal definition worked out.

3 THE BEHAVIOR PATTERN AND THE SITUATION

After publication of *The Polish Peasant,* Thomas wrote *Old World Traits Transplanted,*[1] 1921, and *The Unadjusted Girl,* 1923, both of which proved to be further contributions to theory and research. In December 1926 he was elected President of the American Sociological Society. His Presidential Address, at its annual meeting in 1927, was published as "The Behavior Pattern and the Situation," from which the following selection is taken.

The view presented in it is at some variance with his previous writings. It differs from *The Polish Peasant* in that the attitude-value scheme is subordinated to other conceptions. It differs from *The Unadjusted Girl* in that motives, in the form of the "four wishes," have also receded into the background. Taking their place is the "situation," not only as a determinant of behavior but also as a methodological tool. Indeed, most of the paper is a description of various research which exemplifies the situational approach.

Thus the following selection marks another stage in the development of Thomas' methodological position. It represents a transition between the "search for social laws" approach which marked his earlier thinking to the "situational-probabilities" approach more fully developed in *The Child in America,* 1928. "The Behavior Pattern and the Situation" emphasizes the advantages to be gained from the study of behavior reactions in different situations, a comparative approach which provides the social scientist with an approximation of an experimental method.

Presidential Address
American Sociological Society, 1927[2]

The lines of social research have largely converged on the question of behavior reactions and the processes involved in their formation and modification. It appears that the particular behavior patterns and the total personality are overwhelmingly conditioned by the types of situations and trains of experience encountered by the indi-

[1] This volume, while published over the names of Park and Miller, was primarily the work of Thomas. Evidence for this statement may be found on p. 259 infra, in a recent letter of Mr. Allen T. Burns, who was General Director of the Americanization Studies, of which the volume in question was a part.

[2] *Publications of the American Sociological Society,* Vol. 22, pp. 1–13.

vidual in the course of his life. The question of heredity remains a factor, but this is also being studied in terms of behavior; it is, in fact, defined as the phylogenetic memory of experience—memory organically incorporated.

In approaching problems of behavior it is possible to emphasize—to have in the focus of attention for working purposes—either the attitude, the value, or the situation. The attitude is the tendency to act, representing the drive, the affective states, the wishes. The value represents the object or goal desired, and the situation represents the configuration of the factors conditioning the behavior reaction. It is also possible to work from the standpoint of adaptation—that is, how are attitudes and values modified according to the demands of given situations.

Any one of these standpoints will involve all the others, since they together constitute a process. But I wish to speak at present of the situational procedure as having certain experimental, objective, and comparative possibilities and as deserving of further attention and elaboration. As I have said, the emphasis of this standpoint by no means obscures the other factors; on the contrary, it reveals them. The situations which the individual encounters, into which he is forced, or which he creates, disclose the character of his adaptive strivings, positive or negative, progressive or regressive, his claims, attainments, renunciations, and compromises. For the human personality also the most important content of situations is the attitudes and values of other persons with which his own come into conflict and cooperation, and I have thus in mind the study of types of situation which reveal the role of attitudes and values in the process of behavior adaptation.

The situational method is the one in use by the experimental physiologist and psychologist who prepare situations, introduce the subject into the situation, observe the behavior reactions, change the situation, and observe the changes in the reactions. Child[3] rendered one point in the situation more stimulating than others by applying an electric needle or other stimulus and made heads grow where tails would otherwise have grown. The situational

[3] Charles M. Child, *Physiological Foundations of Behavior* (New York: Henry Holt and Company, 1924).

character of the animal experimentation of the psychologists is well known. The rat, for example, in order to open a door, must not only stand on a platform placed in a certain position, but at the same time pull a string. . . .

The study of behavior with reference to situations which was begun by Verworn, Pfeffer, Loeb, Jennings,[4] and other physiologists and was concerned with the so-called "tropisms," or the reaction of the small organism to light, electricity, heat, gravity, hard substances, etc., was continued, or paralleled, by the experiments of Thorndike, Yerkes, Pavlov, Watson, Köhler,[5] and others with rats, dogs, monkeys, and babies as subjects, but until quite recently no systematic work from this standpoint has involved the reactions of the individual to other persons or groups of persons. That is to say, the work has not been sociological, but physiological or psychological.

Recently, however, there have developed certain directly sociological studies of behavior based on the situation. These are either experimental in the sense that the situations are planned and the behavior reactions observed, or advantage is taken of existing situations to study the reactions of individuals comparatively.

We may notice first the significant work of Bühler, Hetzer, and Tudor-Hart * upon the earliest social reactions of the child. Working

* Charlotte Bühler, Hildegard Hetzer, and Beatrix Tudor-Hart, *Sociologische und psychologische Studien über das erste Lebensjahr* (Quellen und Studien zur Jugendkunde), Jena, 1927.

[4] Max Verworn (1863–1921), German physiologist, *Allgemeine Physiologie* (5th ed.; Jena: G. Fischer, 1909); Jacques Loeb (1859–1924), German-American physician and physiologist, *The Mechanistic Conception of Life* (Chicago: University of Chicago Press, 1912), and *The Organism as a Whole—From a Physicochemical Viewpoint* (New York: G. P. Putnam's Sons, 1916); W. Pfeffer (1845–1920), German botanist, *Pflanzenphysiologie* (2nd ed.; Leipzig, 1897); and Herbert S. Jennings, American zoologist, *Contributions to the Study of the Behavior of Lower Organisms* (Carnegie Institution of Washington Publication No. 16, 1904), which popularized "trial and error" behavior, and *Behavior of the Lower Organisms* (New York: Columbia University Press, 1923).

[5] Edward L. Thorndike, *Animal Intelligence* (New York: The Macmillan Company, 1911), and *Educational Psychology* (New York: Lemcke and Buechner, 1903), among others; Robert M. Yerkes, *Almost Human* (New York: Century Co., 1925); I. P. Pavlov, *The Work of the Digestive Glands* (tr. W. H. Thompson; London: Charles Griffin & Company, 1902), and *Conditioned Reflexes* (tr. G. V. Anrep; London: Oxford University Press, 1927); John B. Watson, *Behavior* (New York: Henry Holt and Company, 1914), and *Behaviorism* (New York: W. W. Norton & Company, 1930); and Wolfgang Köhler, *The Mentality of Apes* (tr. Ella Winter; New York: Harcourt, Brace & Company, 1926).

in the Vienna clinics they divided 126 children into 9 groups of 14 each, the first group containing children 3 days old and under, and the last group containing those 4–5 months old, and experimenting with sound-stimuli they observed the rate at which the child learns to separate out and give attention to the human voice among other sounds. All the children noticed all the sounds (striking a porcelain plate with a spoon, rattling a piece of paper, and the human voice) sometimes, but the reaction of the newborn to noises in the first weeks is far more positive than the reaction to the voice, even to loud and noisy conversation: 92 per cent of frequency to the noises and 25 per cent to the voice. But in the third week the proportion is about the same, and in the fourth week the reaction is more frequent to the voice. The first positive reaction to the voice, other than listening, is a puckering of the lips, a sucking movement. The quality of the voice or the person speaking is at first of no significance. A child of three months when scolded angrily laughed gleefully. As yet angry tones had not been associated with punishment. A voice of any kind meant feeding.

Working with another group of 114 children, not newborn but borrowed from nursing mothers at a milk depot, placing them together in groups of two or more, and giving them toys, the most various reactions were disclosed in the unfamiliar situation. Some were embarrassed and inactive; others were openly delighted; some pounced upon the toys and paid no attention to the children; others explored the general environment; some robbed their companions of all the toys; others proffered, exchanged, or exhibited them; some were furious in the new situation, already, in the first year, positively negativistic. It is impossible to say to what degree these children had been conditioned by association with their mothers and how far the reactions were dispositional. But it is plain that by the end of the first year the most positive personality trends had been established. At this early age the experimenters think they distinguish three main personality types: the dominant, the amiable or humanitarian, and the exhibitionist, or producer.

Situational work of this type is now being carried on in several child-study institutes in the United States, and is foundational for the work in which we are more directly interested. Anderson and Goodenough, for example, and their associates, working in Minneapolis and observing the reactions of children among themselves in spontaneous play, found that a given child participating in play actively with all the other members of the group successively might be found leading or dominating in 95 per cent of the situations, whereas another child, under the same conditions, was found to be in the leading position only 5 per cent of the time. That is, within a constant period one child is getting twenty times as much practice in meeting social situations in a given way as a second child. We have here a type of organization of behavior where not only the lack of practice but the habit of subordination will have the most far-reaching consequences in the development of efficiency and personality. Observations will now be undertaken by the same observers on the effect of the alteration of the composition of groups with the object of giving the less dominant children opportunity to assume more important roles.*

Another item in the program of this institute is the study of habit formation in connection with games of skill. It has appeared that the children develop idiosyncrasies in their technique of throwing a ring at a peg. If an effort, however awkward, happens to be successful, the child tends to adopt and perseverate in this method, regardless of his later insuccesses.** Evidently the fixation of many undesirable social habits has this origin. Whimpering, crying, lying, vomiting, bed-wetting have had an initial success in dominating the mother, and may become a part of the child's behavior repertory. It is to be remembered also that the initiation of one mode of reaction to a situation tends to block the emergence of other types of reaction. Moreover, it appears from other sources that children are capable of developing dual and contrasting behavior reactions in different types of situations. Miss Caldwell,[6] in Boston, working mainly with Italian children, has astonishing records showing consistently defiant, destructive, negativistic behavior in the home and

* John E. Anderson, "The Genesis of Social Reactions in the Young Child," *The Unconscious; A Symposium,* pp. 69–90.
** *Ibid.*

[6] Grace M. Caldwell, Records of the Boston North End Habit Clinic (manuscript).

relatively orderly behavior in the nursery school. And this duality of behavior is carried on for years—bad in one situation, good in another.

Freeman and his associates[7] in Chicago are now publishing a situational study of the greatest importance based on the placing of about six hundred children in foster homes, in response, apparently, to the following challenge by Terman:[8] "A crucial experiment," Terman says, "would be to take a large number of very young children from the lower classes and after placing them in the most favorable environment obtainable compare their later mental development with that of the children born into the best homes." In this experiment comparisons were made between results on intelligence tests which had been given before adoption, in the case of one group, and the results after they had been in the foster home a number of years. Another comparison was made between children of the same family who had been placed in different homes, the home being rated on a scheme which took into consideration the material environment, evidence of culture, occupation of foster father, education and social activity of foster parents. Both of these comparisons had held heredity constant, letting the situation vary. A third comparison held environment constant, letting heredity vary, that is, concerning itself with a comparison of the intelligence of the own children of the foster parents and of the foster children. The results, stated in a word, show that when two unrelated children are reared in the same home, differences in their intelligences tend to decrease, and that residence in different homes tends to make siblings differ from one another in intelligence. This study is limited to the question of intelligence, but it is obvious that a fundamental study of behavior could be made by the same method.

Esther Richards,[9] of the Phipps Psychiatric Clinic in Baltimore, has been experimenting with psychopathic children by placing them in homes and on farms and moving them about until a place is

[7] Frank N. Freeman and others, "The Influence of Environment on the Intelligence, School Achievement, and Conduct of Foster Children," *Yearbook of the National Society for the Study of Education,* Vol. 27 (1928), pp. 103–217.

[8] Lewis M. Terman, *The Measurement of Intelligence* (Boston: Houghton Mifflin Company, 1916), p. 116.

[9] Esther L. Richards, "The Significance and Management of Hypochondriacal Trends in Children," *Mental Hygiene,* 7:43–69 (1923).

found in which they are adjusted. She discovered that there were whole families of hypochondriacs showing no symptoms of organic deficiency. To be "ailing, and never so well" had become a sort of fashion in families, owing, perhaps, to the hysterical manifestations of the mother. These attempts are rather uniformly successful as long as the parents remain away from the child. One boy had been manifesting perfect health and robust activity on a farm, but conceived a stomach ache on the appearance of his mother, which disappeared with her departure. And it is the prevailing psychiatric standpoint that the psychoneuroses—the hysterias, hypochondrias, schizophrenias, war neuroses, etc., are forms of adaptions to situations.

Dr. Harry Stack Sullivan[10] and his associates, working at the Sheppard and Enoch Pratt Hospital, Baltimore, are experimenting with a small group of persons now or recently actively disordered, from the situational standpoint, and among other results this study reveals the fact that these persons tend to make successful adjustments in groupwise association between themselves. . . .

The psychologists and social workers connected with the juvenile courts and child clinics, the visiting teachers, and other organizations are now preparing extensive records tending to take the behavior of the child in connection with all the contacts and experiences which may have influenced the particular delinquency or maladjustment. And finally the regional and ecological behavior surveys with which Park, Burgess, Thrasher, Shaw, Zorbaugh, and others are identified attempt to measure the totality of influence in a community, the configuration and disposition of social stimuli, as represented by institutions, localities, social groups, and individual personalities, as these contribute to the formation of behavior patterns.

The merit of all these exploratory approaches is that they tend to bring out causative factors previously neglected and to change the character of the problem. Thrasher's[11] study of 1,313 gangs in Chicago changes the character of the crime problem, and this study merely opens up a new situation. Other researches, not yet published, will show that, recruited from the gangs, criminal life is as definitely

[10] A report of this research has not been discovered. Perhaps Thomas received it verbally from Dr. Sullivan.

[11] Frederic M. Thrasher, *The Gang* (Chicago: University of Chicago Press, 1927).

organized in Chicago as the public school system or any other department of life, the criminals working behind an organization of "irreproachable" citizens. Shaw [12] has studied the cases of boys brought before the juvenile court in Chicago for stealing with reference to the number of boys participating, and finds that in 90 per cent of the cases two or more boys were involved. It is certain that many of the boys concerned were not caught, and that the percentage of groupwise stealing is therefore greater than 90 per cent. This again throws a new light on the nature of the problem of crime. Again, Burgess and Shaw have studied the incidence of delinquency for different neighborhoods and find that in the so-called "interstitial zones," lying along the railroad tracks and between the better neighborhoods, the boys are almost 100 per cent delinquent, while in other neighborhoods there is almost no delinquency. Burgess found one ward in a city of 12,000 population with about eight times as many cases of juvenile delinquency as in any of the other wards.*

These are examples of factors of delinquency which turn up or come to the front in the course of the exploration of situations. But with reference to the relationship of the factors, their distribution in the ratio of delinquency, or even the certitude that we are aware of all the factors, we are in one respect in the position of the person who gives false testimony in court. We overweight the standpoint acquired by our particular experience and our preconceived line of approach. . . .

The psychiatrist Kempf,[13] speaking of the diagnosis and classification of nervous diseases, has given the opinion that if twenty cases were given to twenty psychiatrists separately for diagnosis and their findings were sealed and given to a committee for a comparison of the results the whole system of diagnosis would blow up. And something of this kind would happen if students of delinquency, under the same conditions, attempted to name the causative factors in a crime wave or in the heavy incidence of delinquency in a given

* E. W. Burgess, "Juvenile Delinquency in a Small City," *Journal of Criminal Law and Criminology*, VI, 726–28.

[12] Clifford R. Shaw, "Correlation of Rate of Juvenile Delinquency with Certain Indices of Community Organization and Disorganization," *Publications of the American Sociological Society*, Vol. 22, pp. 174–179.

[13] Edward J. Kempf, *Psychopathology* (St. Louis: C. V. Mosby Company, 1920).

locality. The answers would certainly be weighted on the side of bad heredity, gang life, poverty, commercialized pleasure, decline of the church, post-encephalitic behavior disturbances, etc., according to the different standpoints represented.

Since the establishment of the first juvenile court in 1899 there has been a very careful elaboration of procedure with reference to the treatment of the young delinquent—systematic study of the case, oversight in the home or in a detention home, placing in good families, psychiatric social workers, visiting teachers, attempts to improve the attitudes of parents toward children, recreation facilities, children's villages and farm schools—and there is, I think, a general impression that there is a steady improvement, an evolution of method, and a gradual approach to a solution of the problem of delinquency. But there is no evidence that juvenile-court procedure or any procedure tends to reduce the large volume of juvenile delinquency. This is not surprising in view of the present rapid unstabilization of society connected with the urbanization of the population, the breakdown of kinship groups, the circulation of news, the commercialization of pleasure, etc. But it is more significant that the methods of the juvenile courts, when applied by their best representatives and in the most painstaking way, cannot be called successful in arresting the career of children who once appear in court, that so many first offenders become recidivists and eventually criminals. Healy and Bronner, who were the first court psychologists, and whose work commands the highest respect in the world, have recently reviewed this point on the basis of the records of their cases during the past twenty years in Chicago and Boston. They say:

> Tracing the lives of several hundred youthful repeated offenders studied long ago by us and treated by ordinary so-called correctional methods reveals much repetition of offense. This is represented by the astonishing figures of 61 per cent failure for males (15 per cent being professional criminals and 5 per cent having committed homicide), and 46 per cent failure for girls (19 per cent being prostitutes). Thus in over one-half the cases in this particular series juvenile delinquency has continued into careers of vice and crime. . . . This is an immense proportion to be coming from any series of consecutive cases studied merely because they were repeated offenders in a juvenile court. It represents a most disconcerting measure of failure.*

* Healy and Bronner, *Delinquents and Criminals: Their Making and Unmaking,* pp. 201–2.

They mention that no less than 209 of the 420 boys whom they knew when they appeared in the Chicago juvenile court had later appeared in adult courts, and of these 157 had received commitment to adult correctional institutions 272 times. The first court appearance is thus not to be regarded as the initiation of a reform, but in many youthful offenders it appears as a sort of confirmation or commencement ceremony initiating a criminal way of life. There are, indeed, many records of positive successes under juvenile court treatment, especially among the cases of Healy and Bronner, but the most successful workers confess that they do not know how they obtained their successes, whether through their own efforts or through spontaneous changes in the child.

Now there is reason to believe that we are deluded or not properly informed as to the efficiency of other behavior-forming situations and agencies on which we are confidently relying for the control of behavior and the development of normal personality. We assume that good families produce good children, but certain of the experimental nursery schools, selecting their children carefully in order to avoid material already spoiled, find nevertheless that they have drawn from the best families a large percentage of problem children. Our school curricula, based on reading ability and lesson-transfer, drive many children gifted along perceptual-motor lines into truancy and delinquency. It would be possible to show by cases that the home and the school are hardly less unsuccessful behavior-forming situations than the juvenile court.

Naturally the greatest amount of attention, up to the present, has been given to the study of abnormal behavior in the forms which come to public attention, become a nuisance; but behavior difficulties are widespread in the whole population, and it is certain that we can understand the abnormal only in connection with the normal, in relation to the whole social process to which they are both reactions. The same situation or experience in the case of one person may lead this person to another type of adjustment; in another it may lead to crime; in another, to insanity, the result depending on whether previous experiences have formed this or that constellation of attitudes.

The answer is, we must have more thoroughgoing explorations of situations.[14] In our planning we should include studies and surveys of behavior-forming situations, measurements of social influences which will enable us to observe the operation of these situations in the formation of delinquent, emotionally maladjusted, and stable personalities and determine the ratios. A plan of this kind . . . proposes to take selected localities or neighborhoods in given cities, including, for example, the interstitial zones where delinquency is highest and the good neighborhoods where delinquency is lowest, and study all the factors containing social influence.

A survey of this kind would involve a study of all the institutions—family, gang, social agencies, recreations, juvenile courts, the daily press, commercialized pleasure, etc.—by all the available techniques, including life-records of all the delinquent children and an equal number of non-delinquent children, for the purpose of tracing the effects of the behavior-forming situations on the particular personalities. . . .

[14] Twenty-three years later, another President of the American Sociological Society was making the same point by referring to the "situation" as one of the neglected problems in social psychology. See Leonard S. Cottrell, Jr., "Some Neglected Problems in Social Psychology," *American Sociological Review,* December 1950, pp. 705–712.

4 THE METHODOLOGY OF BEHAVIOR STUDY

The following selection was published as the last chapter of *The Child in America,* 1928, by W. I. and Dorothy S. Thomas. Other chapters describe various approaches to behavior problems of the young, and offer critical appraisals of the many different schemes of understanding, explaining, and controlling youthful behavior. The last chapter is a summing up of these procedures, with further suggestions for research. At the least it is a clear statement of the situational approach; at most it is a penetrating essay on the nature of science and its limitations and advantages in behavior study.

Several features of the selection are noteworthy. There is, for example, the discussion of the advantages of the "how" approach over the "why" approach to behavior. In this connection it must be remembered that the "motivational" or "social forces" school had been very active in the early years of the century, postulating certain "motives" or "interests" or "forces" as the "cause" of behavior. Thomas himself had conceived of the "four wishes" and used them as the principal tool for analysis in *The Unadjusted Girl,* 1923. Now his view is that research cannot begin with such postulates; rather we must infer motives from observations of how men behave in different situations. This marks an important modification in his thought.

There is also the discussion of the use and misuse of statistics in social research, developing the point that they are useful in the process of verification and in furnishing grounds for further hypotheses. Thomas' major objections to some of the statistical studies of that time were that they apply overly precise formulae to faulty data, and tend to assume that statistical correlations "tell the whole story."

Finally, it should be noted that the importance of subjective experience to a science of behavior is still emphasized. In this connection Thomas' discussion of the life history as a source of research material should prove especially useful to students of culture and personality.

The Child in America—Concluding Chapter [1]

The ultimate object of scientific study is prediction, for with prediction we can have control. This is best accomplished by the experi-

[1] The selection is taken from the third printing (New York: Alfred A. Knopf, 1932), pp. 553–573. By permission.

mental scientist. The chemist, for example, can predict and control, within limits, because he has learned by experience that certain materials in certain situations always behave in the same way. He can prepare his situations, introduce his materials and get uniform reactions. He is able to measure influence because his materials are stable and he can control all the influences reaching them, or if they change and enter combinations he is able to measure the changes and record the combinations and again predict. The scientist is able to determine a limited number of *laws*—that under given conditions given results will invariably follow. He is not, however, able to give a *complete* causal explanation of any phenomenon. . . . In order to do this it would be necessary to begin with the formation of the material world, determine every force and measure every influence in the universe in the order of their reciprocal action down to the present moment.

The complete determination of the causation of any act of human behavior would be a task not less impossible than this. The chemist deals with elements which are relatively simple, while the behaviorist deals with actions which are in turn based on incommensurable physiological conditions—an incredibly complicated integration of endocrines, enzymes, blood chemicals, chromosomes, various nervous systems, behaving as a whole. Moreover, the material of the chemist is static, does not change from time to time, while the material of the behaviorist (the human organism) is itself evolving. The individual is changing, under influences which cannot be measured. His response in situations changes with periods of physical, mental and emotional maturation and as result of experiences in an endless variety of preceding situations. The student of behavior can therefore not hope to establish even the limited number of laws possible in the case of the exact scientist. He may hope to be able to determine that in certain situations certain reactions will usually follow. He will be able to make *inferences* but probably unable to establish *laws*. This would imply, then, not a *complete* but an *adequate* causal explanation of behavior.[2]

[2] This position is an interesting contrast to the one taken in *The Polish Peasant*. Thomas and Znaniecki were more optimistic about the discovery of the laws of "social becoming" than Thomas is here, as indicated by use of the word "inferences." Later on,

It is desirable, therefore, to set up, if possible, a methodological procedure in behavior studies which will fix some limits to the behavior universe, as the scientist fixes some limits to the material universe, and at the same time give data for an adequate prediction and control. . . .

Among all the intricacies of the physiological system there are two major features of far-reaching consequences for behavior. One of them relates to the basic appetites and contains the so-called hunger and sex drives, representing the conditions of organic continuity—nutrition and reproduction.[3] The other relates to the presence in the organism of certain preformed tendencies to behave in specific action patterns, whereby the organism is more or less predestined by its internal structure to behave in given ways. These unlearned action tendencies are the so-called instincts. . . .

The traditional interpretations of behavior have worked from this approach and with these data. Focusing on "instincts," "consciousness," "original nature," they attempted to explain why the organism behaves in given ways in view of its internal nature and structure, and the attempt has led to a great deal of controversy and much confusion. . . .

We are not anxious to discourage behavior studies from the standpoint of the mechanisms of the organism. On the contrary, it is very useful to have the data provided by Carlson on hunger and Watson on the "instincts," etc.[4] In interpretation it is necessary to work with hypotheses, which are heuristic devices employed in the search for meaning—to be abandoned if the data do not provide a sufficient number of corroborations. The hypotheses should be as many as possible and for this purpose the data of the "inner environment," the unlearned and learned "attitudes," "norms," "values," "goals,"

---

as he became more accustomed to statistics, Thomas started to think in terms of "probabilities." See p. 89 infra.

[3] Cf. "Food and sex . . . were the great original stimuli to action and culture." ("The Scope and Method of Folk-Psychology," *American Journal of Sociology,* January 1896, p. 445.)

[4] See A. J. Carlson and H. Ginsburg, "The Tonus and Hunger Contractions of the Stomach of the New-Born," *American Journal of Physiology,* 38:29–32 (1915); and John B. Watson, *Psychology From the Standpoint of a Behaviorist* (2nd ed.; Philadelphia: J. B. Lippincott Company, 1924).

etc., are useful. . . . But if we take a social situation . . . where a child is placed at birth in his mother's arms, and trace the reactions of both for a period of time, we shall find that *measurable interpretations can be made in terms of the behavior expressions but not in terms of the behavior mechanisms.*[5] . . .

Taking up these problems, it will be possible to interpret the behavior of the child at this early age in terms of his "original nature"—the physiologically based hunger and the instinctive love response, leading to a fixation on the mother up to a certain point, but no further. As a result of the intimacy we may have a habit system in which response is overemphasized. It is expressed eventually in clinging to the mother, crying when separated, jealousy, emotional outbursts, etc. The child is then able to use these reactions as power devices to control the mother. Through the tantrum he can secure petting, candy, or anything he wants. . . .

In the meantime the hunger and its satisfaction has resulted in growth and the organism is integrating (musculature, nervous system, glands, etc.) for performances—for the pursuits, explorations, conflicts, skills, goals, careers of adult life in a society containing more enmity reactions than love reactions. As growth and integration progress the motor activities become more diversified, and we have play and curiosity and exploration. At this point there begins to be a hampering of the child's movements by the mother which . . . provokes resistance. Consequently some confusion arises in the attempt to trace causation. If "obstinacy," "negativism," "destructiveness," "tantrums" . . . are forms of naughtiness designed to hold the attention and provoke the response of the mother, they appear to be also "performance" expressions, a fight with the mother when she attempts to hamper the child's movements in her effort to conform him to a code. . . .

It will be seen that it has been possible up to this point to interpret the child's behavior somewhat successfully from either of the two standpoints, that of "original nature," or that of "situation," but if we should continue the attempt to interpret his behavior in terms of "original nature" we should have to fall back on the pseudo-

[5] Omitted here is a description of the work of Hetzer and Tudor-Hart, for which see pp. 61–62 supra.

instincts . . . and to assume differences in constitution,[6] in blood chemistry, in the operation of endocrine organs, in the preponderance of this or that "instinct" and we should run into endless speculations and have after all no program of treatment. These speculations formed the content of the older psychological, sociological and educational literature.[7]

The behavioristic or situational approach, on the other hand, ignores or minimizes instincts and original nature and studies behavior reactions and habit formation in a great variety of situations comparatively. It assumes that whatever can be learned about original nature will be revealed in its reactions to these various situations. We regard this approach as the only one capable of giving a rational basis for the control of behavior which may be a substitute for the common sense, preceptual, ordering-and-forbidding type of control which has been traditional and which, to the degree that it had efficiency in the past, has now broken down.[8] . . .

The aim of scientific research is to determine that under certain conditions certain results will follow in certain proportions. We have pointed out . . . that the student of human behavior is not able to set up a situation in which there is a sufficient degree of control to produce true experimental methods of the type of those in the chemical laboratory. He has not been able to hold other factors constant, while he measures the influence of the variation of some particular factor, and everywhere the complications of the data have led to difficulties in the way of objective analysis. The approaches that have been made from the morphological, physiological and psychometric points of view have attempted to isolate some specific part of the human being from the behavior complex and to relate this specific part to the total remaining part. The isolated factor may be quite simple, as, for example, some product of body metabolism such as the hydrogen ion concentration in the saliva, or quite complicated, as abstract intelligence or mechanical abilities. The

[6] Cf. Thomas' early view that "differences in temperament in individuals" are the result of "chemical constitution." ("The Scope and Method of Folk-Psychology," *op. cit.*, p. 442.)

[7] This is essentially the point made in 1911 by Edward C. Hayes in "The 'Social Forces' Error," *American Journal of Sociology*, 16:613–625.

[8] See pp. 40–41 supra for another discussion of this point.

measurement of a specific factor, if it be simple enough, can often be done with great accuracy. The investigation of its relationship to other behavior variables, however, becomes a very complicated matter.

Where the total situation is so complicated, the interrelations so numerous and measurement so necessary, the method will evidently be very intimately related to statistical procedure. Although it is impossible to set up real experimental control for the solution of a problem, if groups of individuals roughly similar in a large number of attributes can be studied in varying situations the specific type of behavior resulting may be compared, statistically, for the different situations and inferences drawn as to the relative effects of the situations on the behavior. A study of this sort may often give results that are very good approximations to the experimental type of situation. This is well illustrated in Freeman's study of foster children[9] . . .

A converse application of statistics in lieu of experimentation is seen in studies of the criminal. Here the problem is to find by how many measurable qualities the criminal is differentiated from those who do not commit crimes. Groups of criminals are matched with groups of non-criminals in certain respects and the significance of any differences found in other measurable respects is determined statistically (Goring).[10] Of course, in all such studies clear-cut, definite results are seldom obtained because of the complexity of what is being measured, and because of the large part that unmeasurable factors play in proportion to those that can be measured. For instance, in the study of the criminal the most adequate approach that has been made, from the point of view of the use of statistics as leading to a situation that approximates experimentation, is a study that compares a group of young delinquents in institutions with boys of the same age, social class, etc., who have not become delinquent. Both groups were given intelligence tests, tests for mechanical aptitudes, tests to determine psychoneurotic responses, and data were collected as to nationality, occupation of parents,

[9] See p. 64 supra for a summary of Freeman's study.

[10] Charles Goring, *The English Convict* (London: His Majesty's Stationery Office, 1913).

size of family, room space per person in the home (Slawson).[11] But it must be obvious that very important aspects of the environment are probably not touched by these measurements, and likewise important aspects of personality make-up are not included. A study of this sort may be quite objective, give verifiable results and lead to guarded and careful inferences as to factors important in the etiology of crime, but it will very probably give a quite inadequate basis for the understanding of crime. In any interpretative study, by selecting out only those factors which are at the moment capable of quantitative expression, there is a necessary overweighting of those factors as against factors not readily expressed quantitatively. With regard to the factors measured, provided they are in a comparable form, an estimate may be made of their *relative* importance as compared with each other. That is, relationships within the group of measured factors will be accurately defined, but factors which cannot be measured readily (or at all) will receive no attention.

In some of the approaches which we have studied this premature quantification of the data is quite obvious, as in the studies that depend on ratings of traits. A large number of persons will be judged on a trait, say, aggressiveness. This may be done by ranking them from the most aggressive to the least aggressive, assigning numerical values for degrees of aggressiveness, or describing, in behavior terms, "degrees" of aggression thought to be equal distances apart, having the judgments made in behavior terms and then assigning values. These methods are all full of pitfalls. The instrument of measurement, i.e., a human "judge," is erroneous and inconsistent. It is never certain how much of the judge and how much of the subject appears in the actual judgment or "measurement." Tabulations resulting from these judgments are difficult to interpret. Statistical manipulations of the data, the application of complicated methods which have definite meaning only when applied to data of a strictly defined and limited character, are absurd. . . .

Another difficulty often found in these investigations is that one part of the problem can be measured directly, in genuinely quantitative terms, but in the comparisons and correlations that must be

[11] John Slawson, *The Delinquent Boy* (Boston: Richard G. Badger, 1926).

made other parts of the problem will be of this pseudo-quantitative sort. For example, a perfectly objective study of individual differences in speed of handwriting may be made. The investigator, however, wishes to study not speed of handwriting, which seems to have little general importance, but general "speed of movement" and "speed of decision" which seem to be weighted with great social significance. Instead, however, of making studies which would show the various relationships of various sorts of speed in the same individuals (which would probably take years of work) this handwriting test will be called a test of "speed of movement," and an attempt will be made to validate it by correlating it with the judgments various people may make of the speed of movement and decision of the individuals taking the tests. This is a short-cut method, based on the assumption that judgments will be made on the basis of recalling observations of "speed of movement" in a large number of natural situations. Assuming that the problem was a good one, that there is a relation between speed of handwriting and speed of decision (which may be doubted) the investigator wants to prove too much in too little time and the results will have little scientific value.

Another variety of this procedure is brought about by an over-simplification of the problems of human behavior. This is frequently seen in persons who have approached the field from another field where high scientific standards prevail, say, from the field of biochemistry. The investigator may have worked out and applied an accurate method of determining certain biochemical states. He assumes (rightly) that personality, temperament, the emotions, etc., have a biochemical base and wishes to work out the relationship of his very accurately determined biochemical index to personality or temperament or "behavior." And in study after study we find him accepting subjective, grossly inconsistent "ratings" of the personality and behavior factors, correlating them with his very accurately defined index and giving interpretations that seem to assume an equally scientific basis for both of the correlatives. This procedure is probably partly due to the naïveté often found in research workers in their approach to the problems of fields other than their own, particularly the more intangible social and psychic fields, but it is partly due also to the lateness of development of objective studies in these fields so that the choice for the investigator from another field is this imperfect sort of correlation or none at all.

Among the approaches which we have reviewed, the psychometric has had the advantage over the others in that it has had two full decades of development during which interest and stimulation in the field have been intense. Not only has the very wide application of intelligence tests resulted in a standardization and development of norms of performance, but it has led to the accumulation of many valuable data on the concomitants of performance on these tests. These concomitants have been found to be occupational, geographical, "cultural" (in the sense of superior material environment), racial and educational (in the sense of the amount of schooling received). This wide application of the tests and the definite knowledge of so many of the concomitants of the results have pointed the way for the development of controls and for the study of probable causation. This has led to the possibility of determining the effect of certain of these concomitant factors on variations in others—notably studies such as Freeman's, where the effect of changed environment on the IQ variability was tested. It has also led to important studies of IQ in relation to delinquency, whereby control has been exercised by equalizing delinquent and non-delinquent groups for certain of these concomitant factors. It will be seen also that so long as the psychometrists clung to the idea that they were dealing with "original nature" in their test results, and that original nature was unmodifiable, that the responses were concomitants of differing original natures, and that being unmodifiable (or so only within narrow limits) original nature was producing the differing responses, very little good behavior material was evolved. When, however, they utilized this knowledge of concomitants to set up controlled experiments, put aside for a moment the question of the unmodifiability of original nature and changed individuals about from one situation to another and recorded the actual changes in their intellectual behavior, interesting light was thrown on "original nature" by the situational study. . . .

It is desirable therefore, that other behavior fields should analyze their materials in terms of the situation. In the personality and psychiatric fields, for example, the difficulty has been that most of the studies have been made from the point of view of the inner life outward, i.e., rather than studying behavior in a variety of situations as a means of inferring drives, instincts, emotions, etc., the instincts, emotions, etc., have been assumed to have a reality of their own and behavior has been studied in terms of them. There has been a tendency to pre-determine what "types" of reactions a set-up would bring out, and obscurity has been the general result. The really fruitful studies have been those that have been based on widespread observation and objective recording of behavior in varying situations, and it is this type of study that leads to the possibility of the development of controls. That is, reactions are first studied in the more "natural" situations and the factors involved in, and concomitant with, these situations are brought out in the behavior study. Then more controlled situations can be evolved which will allow for and rule out as many of the concomitant interfering factors as possible. Through studies of this sort we learn *how* people behave and from them we can then infer *why* people behave as they do. . . .

We are of the opinion that verification, through statistics,[12] is an important process in most of the fields of the study of human behavior. Relationships can be indicated, various processes can be evaluated, if the data are in a form where statistical methods may legitimately be applied, and if the interpretations keep within the limitation of the assumptions on which the methods were based. Probably the greatest distrust of statistics has come through the unwise manipulations of data that are often made, through the expression in terms of great precision of results obtained when complicated formulae are applied to very inexact data, and through the totally erroneous assumption on the part of many statisticians that the statistical results tell all that can be told about the subject.

What is needed is continual and detailed study of case-histories and life-histories of young delinquents along with the available statistical studies, to be used as a basis for the inferences drawn. And these inferences in turn must be continually subjected to further statistical analysis as it becomes possible to transmute more factors into quantitative form. Statistics becomes, then, the continuous process of verification. As it becomes possible to transmute more and more data to a quantitative form and apply statistical methods, our

[12] See p. 24, n. 47, supra.

inferences will become more probable and have a sounder basis. But the statistical results must always be interpreted in the configuration of the as-yet unmeasured factors and the hypotheses emerging from the study of cases must, whenever possible, be verified statistically.

The behavior document (case study, life-record, psychoanalytic confession) represents a continuity of experience in life situations. In a good record of this kind we are able to view the behavior reactions in the various situations, the emergence of personality traits, the determination of concrete acts and the formation of life policies, in their evolution. Perhaps the greatest importance of the behavior document is the opportunity it affords to observe the attitudes of other persons as behavior-forming influences, since the most important situations in the development of personality are the attitudes and values of other persons. . . .

It has been strongly objected, especially by the adherents of the school of "behaviorism," that this introspective method has no objectivity or validity. What they mean is that these records will not reveal the mechanisms of behavior, the process of consciousness, what is going on inside of us when we think and act, and with this we are in agreement. But the unique value of the document is its revelation of the situations which have conditioned the behavior, and concerning this there can be no doubt.[13]

There may be, and is, doubt as to the objectivity and veracity of the record, but even the highly subjective record has a value for behavior study. A document prepared by one compensating for a feeling of inferiority or elaborating a delusion of persecution is as far as possible from objective reality, but the subject's view of the situation, how he regards it, may be the most important element for interpretation. For his immediate behavior is closely related to his definition of the situation, which may be in terms of objective reality or in terms of a subjective appreciation—"as if" it were so. Very often it is the wide discrepancy between the situation as it seems to others and the situation as it seems to the individual that brings about the overt behavior difficulty. To take an extreme example, the warden

[13] Cf. Leo W. Simmons, "Concerning the Analysis of Life Histories" in his *Sun Chief* (New Haven: Yale University Press, 1942), pp. 385–397.

of Dannemora prison recently refused to honor the order of the court to send an inmate outside the prison walls for some specific purpose. He excused himself on the ground that the man was too dangerous. He had killed several persons who had the unfortunate habit of talking to themselves on the street. From the movement of their lips he imagined that they were calling him vile names, and he behaved as if this were true. If men define situations as real, they are real in their consequences.[14]

The total situation will always contain more and less subjective factors, and the behavior reaction can be studied only in connection with the whole context, i.e., the situation as it exists in verifiable, objective terms, and as it has seemed to exist in terms of the interested persons. Thus, the behavior records of the child clinics are contributing important data by including the child's account of the difficult situation, the often conflicting definitions of this situation given by parents, teachers, etc., and the recording of such facts as can be verified about the situation by disinterested investigators.

In the field of psychiatry the context becomes particularly significant, and it is desirable to have here a multiplication of records showing how situations are appreciated and motivate behavior, but the records should be made not without regard to the factual elements in the situation. To the degree that the psychiatric cases are approached from the standpoint of the total situation it will appear that the problems of behavior taken all together assume an aspect of totality. The unfortunate separation of the "abnormal" from the "normal" in behavior studies will disappear, and the abnormal, pathological and criminal behavior reactions will appear not as "disease" but as socially (and individually) undesirable behavior reactions in given situations, and from this standpoint they will lend themselves more readily to study from the behavioristic standpoint.

The situational approach, utilizing statistical methods and the life-record, is capable of throwing light on many problems whose

[14] This sentence, one of the most quoted in the literature, has recently been attributed to Znaniecki rather than Thomas. See Howard Becker, "Interpretive Sociology and Constructive Typology," in Georges Gurvitch and Wilbert E. Moore, eds. *Twentieth Century Sociology* (New York: The Philosophical Library, 1945), p. 80, n. 21. The evidence for this view appears quite scanty, inasmuch as the sentence does not appear in *The Polish Peasant,* despite Becker's reference to that effect.

etiology remains obscure. For example, in the literature of delinquency we find under the heading "causative factors" such items as the following: Early sex experience, 18% for boys and 25% for girls; bad companionship, 62% for both sexes; school dissatisfaction, 9% for boys and 2% for girls; mental defect, 14%; premature puberty, 3%; psychopathic personality, 14%; mental conflict, 6.5%; motion pictures, 1%, etc. Now it is evident that many young persons have had some of these experiences without becoming delinquent, and that many mentally defective persons and psychopathic personalities are living at large somewhat successfully without any record of delinquency; some of them are keeping small shops; others are producing literature and art. How can we call certain experiences "causative factors" in a delinquent group when we do not know the frequency of the same factors in a non-delinquent group? [15] In order to determine the relation of a given experience to delinquency it would be necessary to compare the frequency of the same experience in the delinquent group and in a group representing the general non-delinquent population. It is obviously absurd to claim that feeblemindedness or psychopathic disposition is the *cause* of crime so long as we have no idea of the prevalence of these traits in the general population. Similarly, the Oedipus complex (mother fixation) and Electra complex (father fixation) are weighted by the Freudians and made prominent sources of the psychoneuroses and of delinquency, whereas the clinical records show a multitude of cases where children with behavior disturbances are either indifferent to the parents or directly hate them. Again, with regard to economic factors as cause of crime we find, for example, in the records of the White-Williams Foundation of Philadelphia (an organization dealing primarily with non-delinquent children) the same unfavorable economic conditions, broken homes, etc., which are usually assigned as "causative factors" in the studies of delinquency, but in this case without delinquency. The simple expedient of using a control group would aid in clarifying this question of causative factors. . . .

[15] Thomas was groping for this significant methodological point as early as 1896. In his first paper, he pointed out the defects in Lombroso's approach to the study of criminals: measuring only criminals and failing to compare his findings with those from "normal individuals." See "The Scope and Method of Folk-Psychology," *op. cit.*, p. 438.

5 THE ROLE OF METHODOLOGY IN THE DEVELOPMENT OF SCIENCE

The following selection is from a letter written to Robert E. Park in 1928. In it Thomas considers the relation of methodology to scientific progress, describing the latter as a product of curiosity that moves from "point to point." Using examples from both natural and social science, Thomas shows that problems are the inspiration to research. The scientist is curious and asks leading questions. As answers emerge, other questions are suggested and other scientists pursue them. Thus science moves endlessly, from point to point, in response to the problems created by its own progress. In all this, formal methodology plays a subordinate role determined by the kinds of problems to be solved.

The implications of this statement for the persistent problem of how to study human behavior are clear. Methodology is not an end, it is a means to further comprehension and illumination of the variables involved in behavior. No one method can be postulated as all-encompassing. Rather, the methods in any given case will depend upon the kind of question asked about behavior and upon the character of the work that has gone before.

This view is so justly famous and so characteristic of Thomas that further comment is not required. It may be remarked, however, that Thomas' own development closely paralleled the course of scientific progress he so vividly describes here.

Letter to R. E. Park [1]

It is my experience that formal methodological studies are relatively unprofitable. They have tended to represent the standpoint developed in philosophy and the history of philosophy. It is my impression that progress in method is made from point to point by setting up objectives, employing certain techniques, then resetting the problems with the introduction of still other objectives and the modification of techniques. For example, Galvani or someone else gets a reaction from a frog's leg by the application of electricity. This may suggest to Pfeffer or Verworn the application of electricity to a basin containing infusoria. It is then determined that these

[1] Quoted in Herbert Blumer, *An Appraisal of . . . The Polish Peasant* (Social Science Research Council Bulletin 44, 1939), pp. 166–167.

organisms show positive and negative reactions, that these reactions are dependent upon the state of nutrition, etc., and the whole question of the tropisms is opened up. These and other investigators then introduce other stimuli—heat, light, acids, food, hard surfaces, etc.—and get still other reactions. There is then developed a mechanistic school of behavior and Loeb devotes himself, among other things, to the attempt to secure by certain manipulations reactions from inorganic material identical with those shown by living material. At this point Jennings, conditioned either by religion, philosophy or democracy—at any rate, suspicious of the mechanistic assumptions—sets up experiments to determine that these microörganisms show a certain amount of judgment and self-determination in their reactions to the stimuli. Child then raises the question as to the effects of various stimuli applied to particular portions of the body surface of the organism. He discovers that the stimulation is not transmitted in full force from the point of contact, and proceeds to structuralize the organism at will by the differential application of stimuli.

In all of this, there is no formal attention to method but the use of some imagination or mind from point to point. The operator raises the question, at appropriate points, "What if," and prepares a set-up to test this query.

Similarly, in our own line, some of us, in connection with some experience, raised a question, "What would happen if we were able to secure life records of a large number of persons which would show their behavior reactions in connection with their various experiences and social situations?" After some experimentation, yourself [Park], Shaw and others have been interested in the preparation of very systematic and elaborate life-histories. In this connection it is noted that the behavior of young persons is dependent upon their social status [2] and the regions in which they live. Studies are then made from the ecological standpoint. It is discovered that children brought into the juvenile court are predominantly from certain localities in the city. The rate of delinquency is related to gang life and gang life is related to localities. Thrasher then makes a study of the gang from

[2] For recent research bearing on this point see August B. Hollingshead, *Elmtown's Youth* (New York: John Wiley & Sons, 1949).

this standpoint. As comparative observations multiply, Shaw undertakes to determine how the cases of boys brought into the juvenile court for stealing are connected with their gang life and determines that 90 percent of these boys did their stealing in groups of two or more. In the search for the causes of delinquency, it then appears that the delinquent and nondelinquent are often very much alike in their behavior reactions. It is then recognized that it is impossible to study the delinquent population without at the same thing studying the nondelinquent, and at present we have introduced the plan of using nondelinquent groups as a control in connection with studies of the causation of delinquency.

In all this, also, we move from point to point without necessarily any formidable attempt to rationalize and generalize the process. It is only, in fact, so far as sociology is concerned, since we abandoned the search for standardized methods based largely on the work of dead men, that we have made the beginnings which I have indicated.[3]

[3] In this connection it should be pointed out that Thomas stimulated many of the fruitful, empirical studies in American sociology. There has been some tendency to ignore this fact. However, Park has written that Thomas' work established the tradition of research at Chicago, where many of these studies were made. In particular Park emphasized the importance of *Source Book for Social Origins,* 1909, in lifting American sociology from its concern with "social problems" to a concern with theoretical problems. The ideas it contained, he said, found "a consistent expression in most, if not all, of the subsequent published studies of the students and instructors in sociology at Chicago." See his brief "Notes on the Origin of the Society for Social Research," in the *Bulletin* of the Society for Social Research, August 1939. (The editor is indebted to A. Paul Hare for sending him a copy of this article.)

Similarly, Pauline Young has written: "There is perhaps no other single sociologist who has so profoundly influenced American field research students as has Dr. Thomas." (*Scientific Social Surveys and Research,* New York: Prentice-Hall, 1939, p. 78.)

6 RESEARCH AND THE SOCIAL PROCESS

In the period 1930–31 The Brookings Institution invited nine major figures in the social sciences to a general seminar for the purpose of discussing problems of method. Thomas was invited along with Beard, Ogburn, Schlesinger, and others, and presented the paper reproduced in the present section.

By this time his methodological position was perhaps clearer than ever before. Fundamentally, all the social sciences study human behavior; the best way to study it is through the comparison of behavior reactions in different situations, using both statistics and life documents; the purpose is more adequate control of behavior.

Thus the following selection derives from the preceding ones. Yet there are differences. His proposal for cooperative research under institutional auspices is a new development; and the suggestion that there are three "general forms" of behavior research is a more specific formulation of his ideas than appears elsewhere. Finally, the last paragraph (the gist of which had appeared before) indicates a return to the consideration of general cultural problems and their comparative study. This bore fruit in *Primitive Behavior*, 1937.

In the present connection, however, it is sufficient to note that the following selection is in many ways Thomas' most complete statement on social science and social behavior.

The Relation of Research to the Social Process [1]

It is recognized that the object of research in both the material and the social worlds is control, or it might be said to be the supplying of materials and situations for the satisfaction of human desires—the providing of what men want. There can be no question that there has been research since the world began. The bow and arrow, the spring trap, the invention of poisons, and so on, represent research by primitive man;[2] and even the life of animals is a constant experimentation and a learning process.

1 From W. F. G. Swann and others, *Essays on Research in the Social Sciences* (Washington: The Brookings Institution, 1931), pp. 175–194. By permission.

2 Cf. Thomas' statement in 1907: "Modern inventions are magnificent and seem quite to overshadow the simpler devices of primitive times; but when we consider the precedents, copies, resources, and accumulated knowledge with which the modern

What we have in mind at present is, of course, a more organized and continuous approach which we call scientific. From this standpoint the achievements in the physical and biological sciences have been positive and enormous. No one questions that medical research has modified the social process and secured greater control of one of the aspects of life, as when Koch discovered the tubercular bacillus; . . . or when Bruce in British Uganda, seeking the cause of sleeping sickness, caused specimens of all insects from all localities to be sent in by the chiefs and the missionaries, made a spot map of the incidence of sleeping sickness and spot maps of the incidence of all the insects, and through superimposition discovered that the map of sleeping sickness and the map representing the tsetse fly coincided.

The physical and biological sciences have the advantage of experimentation and instrumentation, and are impeded by less resistance to change than is the field of social interaction. In the social sciences the problem is not mainly the control of the material world but of the behavior of individuals as members of a society. The subject matter of all the social sciences is in fact fundamentally behavior. And here experimentation with the human materials is limited, and resistance to change is more stubborn on account of the sanctity of custom and the rivalry of personal interests. . . .

The student of behavior whether social psychologist, sociologist, criminologist, or psychiatrist, is at present approaching the problem of behavior from the situational standpoint. The situation in which the person finds himself is taken as containing the configuration of the factors conditioning the behavior reaction. Of course, it is not the spatial material situation which is meant, but the situation of social relationships. It involves all the institutions and mores—family, gang, church, school, the press, the movies, and the attitudes and values of other persons with which his own come in conflict or cooperation. The individual always possesses a repertory of attitudes (tendencies to act) and values (goals toward which the action is directed), depending in each case on biological constitution on the

---

investigator works, and, on the other hand, the resourcelessness of primitive man in materials, ideas, and in the inventive habit itself, I confess that the bow and arrow seems to me the most wonderful invention in the world." ("The Mind of Woman and the Lower Races," in *Sex and Society*, pp. 278–279.)

one hand and social conditioning on the other. A study of the concrete situations which the individual encounters, into which he is forced, or which he creates will disclose the character of his adaptive strivings and the processes of adjustment. The study of the situation, the behavior in the situation, the changes brought about in the situation, and the resulting change in behavior represent the nearest approach the social scientist is able to make to the use of experiment in social research. . . .

The mathematician, Poincaré, has thus described the basic procedure of analysis and of classification as approached by the natural sciences:

> The most interesting facts are those which can be used several times, those which have a chance of recurring. We have been fortunate enough to be born in a world where there are such facts. Suppose that instead of eighty chemical elements we had eighty million, and that they were not some common and others rare but uniformly distributed. Then each time we picked up a new pebble there would be a strong probability that it was composed of some unknown substance. Nothing that we knew about other pebbles would tell us anything about it. [On the basis of likeness, we are able to form rules.] As soon as the rule is well established, as soon as it is no longer in doubt, the facts that are in conformity with it lose their interest. We cease to look for resemblances and apply ourselves before all else to differences, and of these differences we select first those that are most accentuated, not only because they are the most striking but because they will be the most instructive.*

In the social sciences the situation is not essentially different from that in the natural sciences. The main difficulty at present is not that our behavior data are beyond the application of scientific method but that so few elements have yet been isolated, and that the experimental factors are producing a process of constant change in the materials we are studying. At any given moment, however, a set of rules (codes or standards) exists, and the deviations from these rules as represented by, let us say, the commission of crime are the material for our immediate study. The isolation of various behavior and experiential elements in this group, and their comparison with the recurrences of these elements in the non-deviating population is the further problem. The fact that our knowledge must of necessity be very meager until we have further fundamental research should

* Poincaré, Henri, *Science and Method,* pp. 17, 20.

not, of itself, be discouraging. It is, indeed, now admitted that even the physicist and chemist have a limited appreciation of their facts and that they are obliged to proceed (with considerable success) as though what they do not know does not exist.

In a good experiment in physics or chemistry, the influence of a given factor is measured by excluding all interfering factors. The change in the original material with the introduction of a specific factor can then be measured. Repetition of the experiment should give the same results, subject only to an experimental error. In the social field, if a factor has been discovered to be strongly associated with (for example) crime, in a given complex environment, its influence as a causative factor can be inferred only by excluding it in a situation in which all other factors are kept the same as in the original situation. But in experiments dealing with humans (or even animals and plants), interfering stimuli cannot be excluded, influence cannot be directly measured, and inferences as to causality become much less certain. Direct experimentation is here never clear-cut. So many other influences are brought to bear besides the one which it is intended to measure, that only by a widespread statistical comparison of various situations can any adequate inferences emerge. These inferences will never have the certainty of "laws"; they will always be in terms of probability.[3] The better the experiment, the less dependent are the inferences on statistical manipulation. The impossibility of carrying on a strict experimentation in the social sciences is due also to our present inability to measure (or even adequately to recognize) the complexities of any given social situation or environment, and this renders impossible any equalizing of factors in two situations.[4]

The inadequacy of research techniques in the social field may be illustrated by the attempts of criminologists to determine "crimi-

[3] Cf. "Now I should like to say . . . I don't believe in these comparisons between physics and sociology, that is, . . . you never have the same experimental control of a situation . . . we seek high degrees of probability." (From Thomas' remarks reported in unpublished "Proceedings" of the Committee on Appraisal of Research, Social Science Research Council, December 10, 1938, p. 150.) This completes Thomas' evolution from the confident search for "laws," through a more moderate view about "inferences," to the position expressed above. See p. 71, n. 2, supra.

[4] Cf. pp. 74–75 supra.

nal types." These studies have always assumed a marked differentiation of the criminal in some one respect from the rest of mankind. Thus, we have had theories of the criminal type as representing physical anomaly; all criminals possess these anomalies (exceptions are occasionally admitted) and mankind generally does not. Persons possessing these anomalies who have not committed crimes are "potential criminals," who will, presumably, commit the next series of crimes. We have had similar theories representing the criminal as the mentally abnormal type; for example, criminals are feebleminded, and the non-criminal feeble-minded are potential criminals. Exceptions are rarely allowed, but it has been conceded that "There remain a few children of normal and superior intelligence whose delinquency must be accounted for in some other way." * Finally, we have theories asserting the typical criminal to be emotionally disordered (psychopathic).

All these attempts to define the criminal type assume some sharp differentiation of a group of mankind in their inherited tendencies or early conditioning, and assume further that the correlation between this sharply differentiated characteristic and the commission of crime is practically perfect. But when empirical checks of these assumptions have been made, the correlations were destroyed. . . . This has been the fate of all theories which have attempted to define a criminal type. A factor, the incidence of which in the general population is assumed to be slight, has been found to be preponderant among a group of criminals. It is, therefore, assumed to define a type generally or specifically related to criminality (that is, either *the* criminal type, irrespective of crime, or a particular type, such as the murderer). As data are accumulated regarding the incidence of this trait generally, it is found to be present in various groups of the non-criminal population. In other words, it has not been found that any trait or characteristic is the exclusive attribute of the criminal; he does not exist as a pure type.

These theories have, however, often contained a significant element. A correlation will be found to exist between a given attribute and criminal behavior, e.g., criminal groups will be found to have somewhat disproportionate numbers of persons of low-grade intel-

* Williams, I. H., "Delinquent Boys of Superior Intelligence," *Journal of Delinquency*, Vol. I, p. 34.

ligence as compared with groups of the general population. The theory of type will not hold, but a factor of some etiological importance may emerge.

From concerning ourselves with a single factor, we pass to a consideration of a multiplicity of factors which may be involved, and the isolation of these factors from each other and the study of their inter-relationship become problems of fundamental importance. The method becomes that of multiple rather than single classification. Each variable must be considered in terms of other variables. The perspective must constantly be shifted from one factor of significance to other factors involved. In this way an estimate of the strength of a single factor may be secured, as well as the strength of several concomitant factors. The realistic approach to the criminal is in terms of concomitance of various factors (physical, mental, cultural) and their inter-relationship as compared with those of non-criminal groups. It is not a question of "all or none" of a given attribute being possessed by a criminal group and thus differentiating a type. It is rather a question of "how much" and "in what other relationships" this attribute exists in various groups of criminals as compared with various other groups.

I may suggest that research into behavior as related to the social process may take three general forms:

(1) Detailed accounts of the processes involved and the changes in behavior and attitudes occurring in radical situational changes for individuals and groups of individuals. These accounts would be in the nature of case histories and documentary analyses of the situations produced in the ordinary course of events by social change, by certain empirical therapeutic measures, etc. Immigration is one of the most satisfactory situations of the kind produced by or in society . . . The movement of populations from the country to the city, the slum areas in the city, the geographical culture areas, the varying culture configurations and behavior patterns of races and nationalities, are other examples. Empirical therapeutic measures are represented by foster-home placements, the experiments of Dr. Esther L. Richards * in moving psychopathic children from one family situation to another until adjustment was made, and those of Dr.

* "The Significance and Management of Hypochondriacal Trends in Children," *Mental Hygiene,* Vol. 7, pp. 48–49.

Harry Stack Sullivan in promoting the association of psychopaths in groups among themselves. Detailed life histories of individuals reveal changed behavior as associated with situational change. These studies and documents have value both as focussing upon the totality of the processes involved in these changes (or rather the resultants of these processes) giving, so to speak, a behavior perspective, and as indicating what factors should be isolated for more careful investigation.

(2) The study and evolution of environment. The inadequacy of the measurement of environmental influences has been apparent in all studies which have purported to show the effects of change of environment. Most of these studies can claim to have shown only that change in behavior was associated with a change in environment or situation. No adequate definition or measurement of the factors present in the new situations and absent in the old has been made. The sociologists, psychiatrists, and social workers have all attempted to indicate the factors associated with the change, but too often the determinations have been rationalizations. The attempts to quantify environment have been generally absurd. The Whittier scale is a composite of ratings of a home on the basis of necessities, neatness, size, "parental conditions" and parental supervision. The Minnesota scale consists of a detailed elaboration of material equipment with an amazing system of weighting, presumably on the basis of the degree of "culture" indicated by the possession of certain articles (alarm clock rated 1, mantel clock 2, grandfather's clock 3, etc.). Neither of these, nor any known attempts at composites, can be said to give any adequate picture of the environmental processes. Even those factors which can be readily investigated have received little attention, for example, the morphology of the family (that is, its composition with regard to age, sex, maturity, occupational and relationship range), income and expenditure, housing, and so on. Much record is needed simply to give a definition of environment in direct, quantitative terms.

(3) The development of a more accurate technique in observing and recording. The inadequacy of behavior recording is perhaps even more obvious. The recent development of observational techniques in the study of the social behavior of young children is throwing light upon the pitfalls in the way of reliable behavior records. The

definition of the unit of behavior to be observed has been found to be a problem demanding much careful experimentation, in order to produce adequate control of the observer. . . .

Behavior analysis and interpretation will also be furthered through the development of the longitudinal approach to the life history. It is important not only to examine many types of individuals with regard to their experiences at various past periods of life in different situations, but it is important also to follow through groups of individuals into the future, getting a continuous record of experiences as they occur.

It is also highly important for us to realize that we do not as a matter of fact lead our lives, make our decisions, and reach our goals in everyday life either statistically or scientifically. We live by inference. I am, let us say, your guest. You do not know, you cannot determine scientifically, that I will not steal your money or your spoons. But inferentially I will not, and inferentially you have me as guest.

What is needed is a continuous and detailed preparation and study of life histories along with the available statistical studies, to be used as a basis for the inferences drawn. And these inferences in turn must be continually subjected to further statistical analysis as it becomes possible to transmute more factors into quantitative form. The case study method and the "natural history" method must not only precede the more scientifically acceptable method in order to produce realistic hypotheses and indicate what units should be defined and isolated; [5] they must also be used as a general background of reference to the more limited statistical findings, which lead, as

[5] Robert C. Angell raised the same question in 1945, in a discussion of the use of statistics in sociological research: "Theoretical research, especially in the early stages, is much more a matter of finding the right categories than of measuring within them. The danger is that some will be content with inappropriate variables just because they can measure them. . . . [This] is a position which seems to be gaining ground in some quarters. To the writer at least, it represents a real threat to sound scientific work." He also quotes Stuart A. Rice to the same effect. (See "A Critical Review of the Development of the Personal Document Method in Sociology, 1920–1940," in Louis Gottschalk, Clyde Kluckhohn, and Robert Angell, *The Use of Personal Documents in History, Anthropology, and Sociology,* Social Science Research Council Bulletin 53, 1945, p. 224.) For a similar view see Parsons, "The Present Position and Prospects of Systematic Theory in Sociology," in Georges Gurvitch and Wilbert E. Moore, eds. *Twentieth Century Sociology,* p. 47.

we have indicated, to inferences which must be constantly checked for validity against the large mass of material not yet analyzable.

. . . [Turning] now to the examples of regional surveys, which disclosed a relation between behavior and specific urban areas, in order to understand the causal relationships it would be necessary to study the social influence of a given area of high delinquency on the juvenile population. And in order to do this it would be necessary (1) to make studies of the institutions and agencies exercising influence—home and family, school, church, boys' and girls' clubs, gangs, recreation centers, kind of work, commercialized pleasures, etc.; (2) to use a control group of non-delinquent boys and girls equal to the total number of delinquent boys and girls in the same region; (3) to equalize the factors in the two groups so as to make the data comparable and capable of quantification, comparing the individuals of the two groups, for example, with reference to intelligence, psychoneurotic responses, abnormal marital relation of parents (death, divorce, separation), nationality of parents, occupation of parents, educational background (including years in school and grade finished, kind of school attended, attendance in school, age at leaving school), occupational history, sex history, etc., and (4) to prepare detailed case histories and life histories of delinquents and non-delinquents as a means of judging the influence of the existing institutions and agencies.

Similar studies should then be made in various other selected regions of the same city and eventually in different cities. The urban regions and the different cities as wholes present very different cultural milieus. There is a different distribution and emphasis of influences. . . .

The systematic comparison of regions and cultures would eventually be important in forming hypotheses and policies. While it will be possible and, in some cases, necessary for these researches to go on separately, it is desirable that all the problems of crime causation and prevention be viewed and studied together and simultaneously in given situations, regions, and populations; that the same individuals be involved from all the standpoints, and that different local areas be studied by the same method and compared.

Eventually programs of the same kind should be carried out among selected racial and national groups, for example, the Italians, the Scandinavians, the Germans, the Russians, the Japanese, the Chinese, etc., with reference to determining the relation between behavior and social structure comparatively. Studies of this kind would be particularly rich in hypothesis-forming materials.

If there were time, I should like to make some concrete suggestions as to the method of approach in determining the social influence of certain concrete factors in the total situation as they are related to behavior, especially to deviate behavior. I have in mind such things as population factors, family organization and disorganization, economic factors, alcoholism and drug addiction, the newspaper and crime literature, and the motion picture.

I will mention, however, another item that seems to me of importance. It appears that the present academic and often rationalistic approach to problems relating to the social process is not of a type best adapted to understanding and controlling the social process, and that a more adequate type of approach has been developed by the great industrial organizations as, for example, the American Telephone and Telegraph Company and the General Electric Company. In these organizations problems are set by the central investigations, but "pure" research is often far behind the immediate needs of these problems. Therefore, chemists, physicists, and other specialists are assigned laboratory work in their own fields, with no immediate practical ends, but with the general purpose of speeding up the development of particular aspects of the field. If an institution were similarly organized for the study and control of behavior, it would naturally be limited in the immediate research set-up to those elements of behavior which have already been isolated by the separate disciplines. And it would be further limited by the imperfect methods of measurement existing in these separate disciplines. As a matter of immediate procedure, the best available techniques in the psychological, anthropometric, psychiatric, biochemical, economic, and social-behavior fields should be applied with equal care to the study of individuals and groups deviating in given ways from given norms. Preliminary explorations in which some single typological or other factor may seem worth investigating could be carried out on a more limited scale, for purposes of checking on possible factors that should be later incorporated in the larger studies.

It is obvious that the research program of an institution would be retarded by the slow development of techniques in each of the separate disciplines upon which it must draw. It would, therefore, be essential to turn the attention of investigators in this field to the investigation of elements which the institution considered important. The originating and coordinating agency would be the institution itself. Much of the wasted effort in typological studies in criminology has been due to the fact that an investigator who is familiar with his own technique applies it to a group of criminals, without any knowledge of criminal behavior or criminology. The investigators from the several fields should be essentially technicians who are able to apply their existing techniques in directions suggested by the staff of the institution and develop new techniques for application in these directions. For example, the institution might direct the attention of economists to problems of measuring labor stability and encourage specific development in psychology, physiology, sociology, and the other social sciences which would presumably prove of value to the eventual relation of elements in the field of criminal behavior.

It has been evident to you that in attempting to outline an approach to the examination of the social process I have had in mind the deviate behavior in anti-social lines. I have done this for the sake of concreteness. But there is a more comprehensive and normal type of behavior reaction going on every day before our eyes which has to do with the participation of the masses of the population, often whole populations, in common sentiments and actions.[6] It is represented by fashions of dress, mob action, war hysteria, the gang spirit, Mafia, omerta, Fascism, popularity of this or that cigarette or tooth paste, the quick fame and infamy of political personalities. It uses language —spoken, written, and gesture. It is emotional, imitative, largely irrational and unconscious, weighted with symbols, and sometimes outrageous. It is capable of manipulation and propagation by leading personalities and the public print. Its results are commonly and pub-

[6] Cf. Herbert Blumer, "Collective Behavior," in A. M. Lee, ed. *New Outline of the Principles of Sociology* (New York: Barnes and Noble, 1946), pp. 167–222.

licly accepted definitions of situations. Its historical residuum constitutes the distinctive character of races, nationalities, and communities.[7] In this region lies the psychology of the evolution of public opinion and of social norms. I am ready to believe that this is the social process which you would have chosen to have presented here at this time. But we are not prepared at present to do much more than rationalize about this larger social process. It would be necessary to break it up into special aspects, as I have attempted to indicate, and to make a long-time job of it. This would be possible if there were a redistribution of attention and money which would place behavior research on something like a parity with research in the biological and physical fields.

[7] Thirty-five years before this was written Thomas was concerned with the same problem, only then from the point of view of instincts and "temperament." See "The Scope and Method of Folk-Psychology," *American Journal of Sociology,* January 1896, pp. 442–443. The same problems are still receiving attention, as evidenced by the spate of studies of "national character."

7 THE COMPARATIVE STUDY OF CULTURES

Thomas' last publication was *Primitive Behavior,* 1937, a monument to cultural relativity, and a departure from the fields which had occupied his attention for the preceding 25 years. It was the *Source Book for Social Origins,* 1909, brought up to date, with new material and interpretations. The opening pages presented his basic approach and they are reprinted here as the concluding selection of Part I.

After placing the study of cultures in the broader context of social science, Thomas discusses three theories of some historical importance: the evolutionist, the racial, and the geographical-economic interpretations. These are rejected for various reasons, and in their place Thomas reaffirms "definition of the situation" as his analytical tool. From this point of view each society meets its problems (adapts) through defining situations, and these definitions constitute the objective conditions to which individuals must adapt. The definitions, however, vary in time and place, and the rest of the book describes the variability of definition with respect to the same or similar events.

When the selection is viewed in the context of Thomas' entire development as a theorist, it will be seen as a further extension of the situational approach. Just as the study of other species than our own eventually is useful to us, so is the study of other cultures than our own—particularly in emphasizing different group reactions to the same or similar situations.

Thus the following selection is not only Thomas' last theoretical writing; it is also an endeavor to apply the same method and concept to materials of broader significance.

Primitive Behavior—
Introductory Chapters [1]

The social sciences are fundamentally concerned with relationships between individuals and individuals, individuals and groups, and groups and other groups. Language, gossip, customs, codes, institutions, organizations, governments, professions, etc., are concerned with the mediation of these relationships.

[1] By permission from *Primitive Behavior,* copyright 1937, McGraw-Hill Book Company, Inc. The selection comprises all of Chapter I, "The Comparative Study of Cultures," pp. 1–7, and part of Chapter II, "Methodological Approach," pp. 8–9.

The central problem in the general life process is one of adjustment, and the forms of adjustive effort are "behavior." In a human as distinguished from an animal society the problem of the adjustments of individuals and groups is related to a cultural situation, that is, one in which a body of values has been accumulated and preserved (mainly through the instrumentality of language) in the form of institutions, mores, and codes, together with a reinforcing set of attitudes or tendencies to act in conformity with prescribed behavior patterns or norms. The attitudes and values, or, we may say, the attitudes toward values, which reflect the personality of the individual are the result of a process of conditioning by the influences of the cultural milieu, eventuating in a body of habits.

The reaction of different individuals in the same culture to identical cultural influences will depend partly on their different trains of experience and partly on their biochemical constitutions and unlearned psychological endowments. Local, regional, nationalistic and racial groups are in turn conditioned, in the formation of their behavior patterns and habits, by their several trains of experience and conceivably by their particular biochemical and psychological constitutions.

From this standpoint the problems of individual and group adjustment involve study of the following factors:

1. The culture situations to which the individual is to make adjustments (studies of cultures).

2. The devices and instrumentalities for adjusting the individual to the cultural situations (social organization and education).

3. The capacity and opportunity of the individual to be adjusted (constitutional factors, incentives, social position).

4. The failures of adaptation, meaning: for the individual, dependency, vagrancy, crime, alcoholism, drug addiction, psychoneurosis, etc.; and for the group, decline, subordination, extermination.

5. Changes in cultural situations (e.g., internal mobility of populations, urbanization, migration, invasion, colonization, the dissemination of cultural traits, race prejudice, technological advance, shifting of occupation, changes in attitudes and values, etc.) requiring continuous readjustment of individuals and reorganization of cul-

ture and learning, and involving questions of the participation of individuals and groups in promoting and directing cultural change.

In this connection it is a frequent experience that the problems of a given situation are soluble only by going outside that immediate situation. Thus the widest and seemingly most irrelevant excursion from human situations is the exploration of the cosmic universe, but the hypothesis-forming implications of this research for our own material universe have been pointed out by an eminent astronomer:

> The variable stars are our main measuring tools for getting out into the universe beyond and outside our own system. It is very difficult to find out anything about our own milky way because we ourselves are inside this system. We can study it only by studying the other systems, and the more we learn about them directly, the more we will learn about our own system, indirectly.*

The employment of the microscope instead of the telescope and spectroscope has enabled the biologists to push exploration to the other extreme, in the direction of the examination of the life and behavior of invisible and parasitic forms of existence, and this direction of research, which originally seemed also quite irrelevant to the problem of the human universe, has eventually reacted very positively on the control of human diseases. Thus, to take a single example, malaria is caused by a parasite which must develop its life cycle in two unrelated hosts, the earlier stages in the stomach of a mosquito and the later stages in the red blood corpuscles of humans. Humans bitten by infected mosquitoes contract malaria, and sound mosquitoes biting infected humans are infected, and a vicious circle is thus established. But if mosquitoes are unable to bite humans the parasites cannot be propagated and malaria disappears. Similarly, experiments with garden peas, guinea pigs and fruit flies have thrown a light on human heredity not directly obtainable from humans.

It is well known also that the theory of evolution as formulated by Darwin and his contemporaries had a profound influence upon the development of all the social sciences and more particularly on anthropology and sociology. Darwin also went outside the immediate situation and examined comparatively the modification of life on the morphological side during the whole of geological time, and

* Shapley, H., *New York Times,* Jan. 1, 1931.

fixed what Huxley later called "man's place in nature," which was, in fact, among the animals.

The years following the publication of Darwin's *Origin of Species* were, of course, an exciting period, and a formative one for anthropology. A new and vivid interest was aroused for those great groups of mankind called "savages," "primitives," "uncivilized," "lower races," "natural races," and recently by Faris "preliterates," [2] and for about seventy years these groups have been studied with increasing intensity and improved techniques, partly from the standpoint of the antiquity of man and the derivation of his varieties and partly from that of the evolution of human institutions.

At the present moment all the social sciences have become more or less concerned with the problem of human behavior, especially in its relation with the problems of education, the intercourse of nationalities, the contacts of races, delinquency, crime, insanity, etc., and more generally with reference to the progressive unstabilization of society, and there is a renewed and wider interest in the comparative examination of the specific cultural systems of racial and national groups and the behavior of individuals in the specific cultural situations, corresponding again with Professor Shapley's dictum that the more we learn about other systems directly the more we shall learn about our own system indirectly.

Historically the study of primitive societies has been prominently associated with the three following points of view:

1. That cultural evolution, as shown in social institutions, would be found to emerge and proceed in a regular order and invariable unilinear sequence, the same steps being taken in the same order by each and every division of mankind in so far as they were taken at all.

Tylor, who was prominent in the foundation of modern anthropology, emphasized the theory of the unilinear development of cultures and illustrated it by a comparison drawn from geology:

> The institutions of man are as distinctly stratified as the earth on which he lives. They succeed each other in series substantially uniform over the globe,

[2] More recently Melville J. Herskovits has argued for the term "nonliterates." See *Man and His Works* (New York: Alfred A. Knopf, 1948), p. 75.

independent of what seem the comparatively superficial differences of race and language, but shaped by similar human nature acting through successively changed conditions in savage, barbaric, and civilized life.*

The assumptions of this straight-line evolutionary theory have been well stated by Rivers, who at the same time rejects it in favor of a historical approach to be noticed later:

[Formerly] the aim of the anthropologist was to work out a scheme of human progress according to which language, social organization, religion, and material arts had developed through the action of certain principles or laws. It was assumed that the manifold peoples of the earth represented stages in this process of evolution, and it was supposed that by the comparative study of the culture of these different peoples it would be possible to formulate the laws by which the process of evolution had been directed and governed. It was assumed that the time order of different elements of culture had been everywhere the same; that if matrilineal institutions preceded patrilineal in Europe and Asia, this must also have been the case in Oceania and America; that if cremation is later than inhumation in India, it has also been later everywhere else. This assumption was fortified by attempts to show that there were reasons, usually psychological in nature, according to which there was something in the universal constitution of the human mind, or in some condition of the environment, or inherent in the constitution of human society, which made it necessary that patrilineal institutions should have grown out of matrilineal, and that inhumation should be earlier than cremation.**

From the standpoint of the cultural evolutionists, the lowest savages, represented by the Tasmanians and Australians, were taken as representing the first phase of cultural evolution, and the "folkways" of European peasants, their periodic festivals superstitions, etc., were regarded as "survivals" from the first phase. Inferences were also made as to the original state of man from certain reported practices of contemporary savages, suggesting that their cultures contained also survivals. If in some savage groups wives were loaned in a hospitable way this was assumed to be a survival of primitive promiscuity, and, similarly, if the tabus against incestuous cohabitation were broken periodically (as in certain ceremonies) this was interpreted as evidence of a prior stage of general "consanguineous marriage." It was noticed also that in certain tribes near relatives of a girl cohabited with her

* Tylor, E. B., "On a Method of Investigating the Development of Institutions . . . ," *Jour. Anth. Inst.*, 18:269.

** Rivers, W. H. R., *History and Ethnology*, 3–4 (The Macmillan Company. By permission).

immediately before marriage, excluding the groom temporarily, and this, termed by Lubbock the "expiation of marriage," was regarded as a sort of resentful gesture on the part of family members and a survival from a period when sexual communism prevailed. The mock resistance on the part of the bride and her relatives to her removal to the residence of the groom was interpreted as a survival of marriage by capture, etc.[3]

2. That the higher cultures are the result of superior inborn mental endowment in the racial divisions which they represent.

The Darwinian formulation of evolution, which on the physical side meant the gradual building up of the higher organic forms through the modification of the lower ones, was especially favorable to the view that the "lower" races were incompleted in their mental evolution. It had, in fact, required no Darwinian theory to convince the white man that the black and yellow races were mentally inferior and thus incapable of originating higher forms of culture. This was, for example, the argument in America in justification of slavery, and the earlier ethnological reports on the inability of savages to count more than three or five or to reason logically pointed also in this direction. Spencer and Galton were prominent in formulating this view but it is notable that Tylor did not base his evolutionary argument on alleged differences in mental endowment of the races of lower and higher cultures. He was influenced by the general concept of evolution derived from geology as well as biology and explicitly avoided the identification of his view with the question of mental differences, in the following terms:

[3] As early as 1909 Thomas was pointed in his criticism of Westermarck on this issue: " . . . I may add that the reader will find his (Westermarck's) great defect in his method of regarding certain practices as vestiges of assumed antecedent conditions of whose existence these so-called vestiges are the guarantee. . . . To note only a single instance, Westermarck has collected many pages of what he calls survivals from a period of marriage by capture. But there is good reason to think that marriage by capture was never a general practice. . . . And the alleged survivals of capture in historical times, of which Westermarck makes so much, are probably to be regarded merely as systematized expressions of the coyness of the female . . . It became 'good form' and a trait of modesty in a girl not to yield without a show of avoidance, and under these conditions ceremonial avoidance became elaborate. But it does not lead us back to a condition of actual capture." (*Source Book for Social Origins*, 1909, pp. 532–533.) For a somewhat similar view of the same point see *Sex and Society*, 1907, p. 189.

For the present purpose it appears both possible and desirable to eliminate considerations of hereditary varieties or races of man, and to treat mankind as homogeneous in nature, though placed in different grades of civilization.*

The most thoroughgoing transfer of the concept of organic evolution to a social problem was made by the criminologist Lombroso, who defined the criminal, at least the "born criminal," as one whose physical, mental and moral evolution has failed to take place regularly or completely, and who consequently remains in the stage of our "brutal prehistoric ancestors." Lombroso and his followers attempted to enumerate the physical marks or "stigmata" of the criminal (protuberant lower jaw, deformed cranium, scanty beard, etc.). The criminal type was thus regarded as an "atavism" or throwback to an incompleted stage of evolution. In this case the question of race development was not involved, but to the extent that the Lombrosian theory prevailed it was confirmatory of the view that the backward races represented an incompleted development.

This view has also naturally enough become associated with colonial policies, nationalistic aspirations, and race prejudice and at present has its most organized expression in the theory of Nordic or Anglo-Saxon superiority. Originating strangely enough with a Frenchman (Gobineau), this position is held by certain students of heredity, eugenics, race biology, and physical anthropology, in Germany, Scandinavia, and America, and is urged by a number of popular and chauvinistic writers.[4]

3. That different rates of progress and levels of culture among the racial populations are due to more and less favorable geographic positions and economic conditions.

As long ago as Hippocrates and Aristotle a relation was pointed out between raw materials, geographic position, and climate on the one hand and the character of given civilizations on the other. The concept was emphasized later by Bodin and Montesquieu in France, by the geographer Ritter in Germany, by the historian Buckle in

* Tylor, E. B., *Primitive Culture,* 1:7.

[4] Arthur de Gobineau, *The Inequality of Human Races* (tr. Adrian Collins; New York: G. P. Putnam's Sons, 1915); for other versions of racial theories, see Madison Grant, *The Passing of the Great Race* (New York: Charles Scribner's Sons, 1916), and Lothrop Stoddard, *The Rising Tide of Color Against White World-Supremacy* (New York: Charles Scribner's Sons, 1920).

England, and systematically developed by the anthropo-geographer Ratzel in Germany and by his disciple Semple in America. In America also Huntington has emphasized particularly the efficiency of culture as related to climate, and Wissler, among others, has been prominent in the delimitation of specific culture areas and culture complexes.[5]

From this general standpoint what is variously termed the "ecological area," the "geographical province," the "area of characterization" determines the physical type of plants, animals, and humans, the character of civilizations, and the fate of nations. It is claimed that the great civilizations have arisen under favorable conditions of climate and material resources, and their decline, as in Greece, is interpreted as due to climatic change, denudation of forests, introduction of malaria, or the expansion of the population beyond the available supply of certain material values. Simkhovitch, for example, has attempted to trace the decline of the Roman empire to an inadequate supply of hay.*

It is plain that the material culture of an area will, as Dixon has expressed it, reflect the "permissive" character of the environment.[6] Certain values may be absent and certain activities may be excluded. The Eskimo will not be able to cultivate corn or build houses and boats of wood, and the tropical African will not wear furs, build houses of snow, or construct blubber lamps. Moreover, great aggrega-

* Simkhovitch, V. G., "Hay and History," *Polit. Sci. Quart.*, 28:385–403; "Rome's Fall Reconsidered," *ibid.*, 31:201–243.

[5] See "Airs, Waters, and Places" in F. Adams, ed. *The Genuine Works of Hippocrates* (2 vols.; London, 1849); the *Politics* of Aristotle; J. Bodin, *The Six Books of a Commonweale* (tr. Richard Knolles; London: G. Bishop, 1606); Baron de Montesquieu, *The Spirit of Laws* (tr. Thomas Nugent, rev. by J. V. Prichard; London: G. Bell and Sons, 1902); Carl Ritter, *Die Erdkunde im Verhältniss zur Natur und zur Geschichte des Menschen* (2 vols.; Berlin: G. Reimer, 1817–18); Henry T. Buckle, *Introduction to the History of Civilization in England* (London: G. Routledge & Sons, 1904); Friedrich Ratzel, *Anthropogeographie* (2 vols.; Stuttgart: J. Engelhorn, 1891–99); Ellen C. Semple, *Influences of Geographic Environment* (New York: H. Holt and Company, 1911); Ellsworth Huntington, *Civilization and Climate* (3rd ed.; New Haven: Yale University Press, 1924); Clark Wissler, *Man and Culture* (New York: Thomas Y. Crowell Company, 1923). Most of these are discussed in Franklin Thomas, *The Environmental Basis of Society* (New York: The Century Co., 1925).

[6] An interesting comparison may be found in Thomas' 1909 statement: "Nature may affect the rate and particular form of progress and limit its degree, but human society takes the same general pattern everywhere." (*Source Book for Social Origins*, p. 130.)

tions of men are in general dependent upon fertile soil, agriculture, cattle, and mineral resources, and political history has a certain relation to the mass of population. But even so, we find that populations circumvent unfavorable conditions on the one hand or fail to utilize them on the other. The Egyptian civilization may be correlated with the fertility of the Nile Valley but the comparable civilizations of the Incas of Peru and the Mayas of Central America were developed on an unfavorable mountain plateau and in what is now a tropical jungle, while the Indians of the fertile regions of the United States developed nothing comparable. It has also been pointed out that different types of culture may emerge successively in an identical environment and that two groups living simultaneously side by side in the same general environment may show very different patterns of behavior and culture.*

No one of these standpoints will be emphasized in the following discussion. On the contrary, it will be assumed:

1. That diversities in behavior and culture are the result of different interpretations of experience, resulting in characteristic behavior reactions and habit systems, and that a uniform course of cultural and behavioral evolution is consequently out of the question.[7]

2. That theories of difference in degrees of mental endowment among races and populations and of inborn racial "psyches" have not been sustained; that such differences as may possibly exist have not played a noticeable role in the development of behavior and culture, and that the manifest group psyches are not inborn but developed through experience and habit systems.[8] . . .

* Dixon, R. B., *The Building of Cultures,* 28 ff.

[7] In his early writings Thomas accepted the evolutionist position without much challenge. See, for example, *Sex and Society,* 1907, *passim.* There are some scattered statements indicating doubt, but it was in 1909 that he stated categorically that we cannot "assume a straight and uniform line of development among all the races." (*Source Book for Social Origins,* p. 25.) In brief, Thomas seems to have considered the unilinear hypotheses and then to have rejected them long before some others did, e.g. Robert Briffault, *The Mothers* (3 vols.; New York: The Macmillan Company, 1927). More recently, evolutionary views have been clarified considerably by Leslie A. White. See *The Science of Culture* (New York: Farrar, Straus and Company, 1949).

[8] With reference to biological theories of the racial variety, Thomas pointed out as early as 1905 that it was necessary to distinguish between the mental ability of an

3. That emphasis should be placed on the culture area[9] rather than the natural environment. In their adjustive strivings territorially isolated groups develop, through their specific experiences, characteristic values and habits, some of them unique, and the circulation of these traits, their migration from area to area, and the borrowing back and forth, represents a sort of social inheritance, and is perhaps the main basis of social change and of advance to the cultural level termed "civilization." . . .

Employing the term "culture" to represent the material and social values of any group of people, whether savage or civilized (their institutions, customs, attitudes, behavior reactions) the structuralization of cultures, their diversification and the direction of their development, the total configuration of the patterns they contain, and the reaction of personalities to the cultural situation can best be approached in terms of *the definition of the situation.* An adjustive effort of any kind is preceded by a decision to act or not act along a given line, and the decision is itself preceded by a *definition of the situation,* that is to say, an *interpretation,* or *point of view,* and eventually a policy and a behavior pattern. In this way quick judgments and decisions are made at every point in everyday life. Thus when approached by a man or beast in a lonely spot we first define the situation, make a judgment, as to whether the object is dangerous or harmless, and then decide ("make up our mind") what we are going to do about it.

On the social level these definitions and the patterns they initiate are represented by moral and legal codes, political policies, organizations, institutions, etc.;[10] they originate in adjustive reactions, are

---

individual and the state of knowledge or culture of the group. Thus he stated that what have often been regarded as "biological differences separating social groups are not really so," but are "dependent on social environment." ("The Province of Social Psychology," *American Journal of Sociology,* January 1905, p. 452.) For a clearer denial of racial determinism see "The Mind of Woman and the Lower Races," 1907, reprinted in *Sex and Society,* pp. 260–262.

[9] Cf. Thomas' early view that "when cultures are displayed by regions and understood as wholes, it is . . . possible to compare the different regions and the different cultural elements in the different regions." (*Source Book for Social Origins,* 1909, p. 857.) This appears to be a clear forerunner of the "culture area" concept of the American anthropologists; as a research suggestion, it foreshadows current "area study" programs.

[10] Cf. "The Primary Group and the Definition of the Situation," pp. 226–231 infra.

developed through language, gossip, argument, and conflict; there appear special definers of situations—medicine men, prophets, lawgivers, judges, politicians, scientists; culture epochs and mass conversions (Christianity, Mohammedanism, the German Reformation, the French Revolution, popular government, fascism, communism, prohibition, etc.) are inaugurated by the propaganda of definitions of situations.

Examining this standpoint among primitive groups we find that they notice and magnify situations which we fail to notice, or disregard; that different tribes define the same situation and pattern the behavior in precisely opposite ways; that the same tribe may define the situation for one set of objects in one way and for another set in another; that a trivial situation may initiate a pattern which expands and ramifies and is stepped up to a position of emotional and social importance; that the same pattern may include a variety of meanings and applications;[11] that in different populations an identical pattern may have different meanings and applications; that a pattern may change to its opposite and back again, and even back and forth, with changing circumstances; that in some regions a pattern may be extraordinarily emphasized, in others quite incidental, and in still others entirely lacking; that different cultures may be more or less dominated by particular definitions and patterns; that reactions on the physiological (visceral-emotional) level may initiate patterns which are subsequently rationalized; that there is a tendency (which may be termed "perseverative") to step up patterns to unanticipated extremities.

[11] Cf. Robert K. Merton, *Social Theory and Social Structure* (Glencoe: The Free Press, 1949), p. 51.

Part II

SOCIAL BEHAVIOR AND PERSONAL DYNAMICS

8 THE FOUR WISHES

As the title of Part II indicates it is concerned primarily with Thomas' approaches to and conceptions of the individual, his personality, and the various forces which organize the personality and give it direction. In this connection it is important to note that Thomas gradually moved from a theory emphasizing internal dynamics to one emphasizing external dynamics (social influences). The first topic to be considered, then, is Thomas' conative theory centering around the concept of the "four wishes."

Generally, Thomas' wishes are taken to mean those of "new experience," "security," "response," and "recognition." In actuality, the wish for "mastery" appears in earlier formulations in place of the wish for "response." Moreover, what Thomas intended by the concept of "wish" seems unsettled. In this circumstance it seems desirable that the several versions of the wishes be presented so that they may be compared and some conclusions drawn.

The wishes made their first appearance in "The Persistence of Primary-group Norms," 1917, from which the following selection is taken. Here Thomas is trying to construct a scheme of "intervening variables" to link behavior with the demands and potentialities of the human organism. Fundamentally there are the "appetites" for food and sex. Then there are "original emotional reactions," derived from Watson, and conceptualized as "fear," "rage," and "joy" or "love." Thomas' wishes appear to be related to the organism, yet not quite a part of it; they are further products of appetites and original emotional reactions, yet still common to all men.

In reading the following selection it should be noted that although four wishes are mentioned, Thomas is mainly concerned with only two.

Original Formulation of the Wishes [1]

In his treatment of the infantile emotions Professor Watson suggested that we have greatly overstated the number of the original emotional reactions, and he is inclined to reduce them to three types —those connected with fear, those connected with rage and those connected with joy or love.

In a study of a particular immigrant group (the Poles) I have found that human behavior seems to represent four fundamental types of

[1] "The Persistence of Primary-group Norms," in Herbert S. Jennings and others, *Suggestions of Modern Science Concerning Education*, pp. 159–167.

interests or wishes—those connected with the desire for new experience, those connected with the desire for mastery, those connected with the desire for recognition, and those connected with the desire for safety or security,—recognizing of course that all forms of behavior can eventually be reduced to the two fundamental appetites, food-hunger and sex-hunger, the one necessary to preserve the life of the individual and the other necessary to preserve the life of the species.

It would perhaps be fanciful to assume that all interest could be reduced to terms of organic motion—physiological expansion in rage and joy, physiological contraction in fear,—as the physicists reduce all reality to velocity and changes in velocity,—but actually we find the development of emotional states and of intelligence directly connected with the power of movement in space. Broadly speaking, the vegetable and the animal differ in their organic economy in the fact that the vegetable is stationary and has to rely for the satisfaction of its hunger and reproductive needs on what is present in the soil and what comes to it or falls to it (in the way of pollen or rain), while the animal, through the power of motion, seeks its food and its mate by the exploration of a wide region. It was Professor Mead, I believe, who defined the animal as a mechanism for utilizing a non-nutrient environment as means of reaching a nutrient environment.

If now the experimenter takes an animal as subject, say the rat, brings him to the proper point of hunger and places him before a box containing food, the actions of the animal become frantic; he pushes, climbs over, burrows under, bites the box until his random movements strike the combination and he solves the problem—perhaps by pulling a string and standing at the same moment on a platform inserted in the floor. Similarly, if the rat is placed before a maze containing food and representing one chance in twenty of going right, he will begin the same frantic and random pursuit, finally locating the food through the elimination of errors. Or if you follow him into the open the dominant activity will be pursuit, varied by flight.

And in this connection I think we must conclude that just as the whole physical mechanism of the animal is adapted largely to motion, to pursuit, so the dominant interest is a pursuit interest, and the mental pattern or schema is essentially a hunting . . . [or] pursuit pattern. And we must note that the reproductive activities fall into this scheme also, for pairing among animals and human marriage are a process of pursuit and capture.

Turning now abruptly from the rat to the creative man, any one who studies the history of a practical invention or a scientific discovery will be impressed with the resemblance between the activities of the human being before his problem and those of the rat before his box or maze. For some years, in fact, I have been in the habit of pointing out that scientific pursuit is precisely of the hunting pattern. The intensity [of] interest on the part of the discoverer or experimenter, his random and frenzied movements, his following of every scent, his abandonment of false trails, his elation when he has got his result, remind us of the animal in quest of his prey and after he has made his kill. The whole scientific life of such men as Pasteur, Goodyear, Helmholtz, Mayer, is a pursuit of ideas, either a series of quests or one long quest, ending perhaps with success and exhaustion. Permit me to cite a single illuminating example from the life of Pasteur.

Pasteur's first scientific success was in the study of crystallization, and in this connection he became particularly interested in racemic acid. But this substance, produced first by Kestner in 1820 as an accident in the manufacture of tartaric acid, had in 1852 ceased to appear, in spite of all efforts to obtain it. Pasteur and his friend Mitscherlich suspected that the failure to get it was due to the fact that the present manufacturers of tartaric acid were using a different tartar. The problem became then to inspect all the factories producing tartaric acid and finally to visit the sources from which the tartars came. This was the quest, and the impatience which Pasteur showed to begin it reminds us of a hound tugging at the leash. He asked Biot and Dumas to obtain for him a commission from the Ministry, or from the Academie, but exasperated by the delay he was on the point of writing directly to the President of the Republic. "It is," he said, "a question that France should make it a point of honor to solve through one of her children." Biot counselled patience and pointed out that it was not necessary to "set the government in motion for this." But Pasteur would not wait. "I shall go to the end of the world," he said. "I *must* discover the source of racemic acid," and started independently. I will excuse you from following the quest in detail, but in a sort of diary prepared for Mme. Pasteur he showed the greatest eagerness to have her share the joy of it. He went to Germany, to Vienna, to Prague, studied Hungarian tartars. "Finally," he said, "I shall go to Trieste, where I shall find tartars of various countries, notably those of the Levant, and those of the neighborhood of Trieste itself. . . . If I had money enough I would go to Italy. . . . I shall give ten years to it if necessary." And after eight months he sent the following telegram: "I transform tartaric acid into racemic acid. Please inform M. Dumas and Senarmont." * He had made his kill.

Without citing further cases, I think it is apparent that the hunting activity, whether of animal or man, and the scientific activity of the creative man are singularly alike. And the point of interest for us is that no activity is interesting unless it follows the pursuit pattern. With reference to pleasurable and displeasurable work, obviously the more nearly the hunting scheme is followed the more vivid the interest. Those forms of work are irksome in which the interest of pursuit is dropped out, either because the constant repetition of the process leaves nothing of the problematical or because, through the division of labor, the problem is destroyed by breaking it into fragments. Society has become so complicated and artificial that it is hard for the individual to preserve a type of occupational activity of the naturalness, spontaneity and interest corresponding to the hunting schema. This is most perfectly preserved in the various games, which are all typical and integral pursuits, and in the favored occupations—scientific research, business enterprise, legal and medical callings—while hard labor represents the residuum after the interesting problems have been abstracted.

Now the pursuit, by both the rat and Pasteur, embodies, in my terminology, the desire for new experience and the desire for mastery. The incipient stage of the pursuit, or the general preparatory condition, is called curiosity. The animal *must* be interested in what is going on about him. If a noise, a movement, an approaching object were ignored, this might involve serious consequence of two kinds: he might miss the chance of pursuit and food, or he might, by failure

* Cf. Vallery-Radot, R., Life of Pasteur, 61ff.

to be alert, be made the object of pursuit, might be eaten. Consequently the animal is always alert, always getting information with reference to possible action. This expresses itself in the endless exploration of the situation by the child—the general exploration with the hands and eyes, putting things into the mouth, tasting and biting, attentive behavior to novel objects, cautious approach and retreat, etc.—and in adults in watching one another and gossiping, in the aimless wanderings of the vagabond, and in the useful "curiosity" of the scientific man. It is a fortunate fact that this curiosity becomes a desire for new experience in the abstract, enabling the mind to take an acute interest in any problem—whatever—in scientific pursuits.

What I have called the desire for mastery or the will to power, is one of the by-phenomena of anger or rage. The gloating over the object of successful pursuit, as shown in the playing of the cat with the mouse, and in the tendency of the child to tease, to bully, torment, pounce upon, tear to pieces; in the swagger, the strut, the glare of triumph or defiance; in gestures, yells and actual attacks; * later in the desire for ownership, the tendency to control every act of others, dictatorial, censorious and unbearable behavior—exerted by man more actively and woman more passively, by the latter to the degree of having her own way even by simulation of weakness or sickness—and finally in lust for power, tyranny, political despotism, and in "ambition," called by Milton "the last infirmity of noble mind"—the one that survives as long as he does.

The Wishes and Social Control

Just before the first two volumes of *The Polish Peasant* went to press, Thomas and Znaniecki wrote a general introduction in the form of the Methodological Note, wherein the wishes appear in their relation to the problem of social control. The following brief selection [2] is on this subject.

Throughout the Methodological Note, Thomas and Znaniecki are concerned with creating a social science which would have a practical utility

* Cf. Thorndike, E. L., The Original Nature of Man, 92, *et passim.*

[2] *The Polish Peasant,* 1927, Vol. I, pp. 71–74. *The Polish Peasant* contains another formulation of the wishes in the Introduction to the "Life-Record of an Immigrant." There, however, they are so embedded in a general theory of personality that it is impossible to wrench them from their context. This version of the wishes may be found on pp. 162–163, 176–177 infra.

in social life. Essentially, the question is whether or not the individual can be so influenced that his attitudes will correspond to desirable social values. The answer is "yes" because out of his whole fund of attitudes or wishes, there are four key ones toward which social influence can be directed in such a way that the individual must respond correctly. Thus rational social control is possible primarily because individuals do possess four fundamental wishes which must be satisfied by incorporation into social life.

It should be noted, however, that in this selection the term "wish" appears to be synonymous with "attitude," and the "four wishes," instead of being fundamental classes of attitudes, are merely four kinds of attitudes along with many other kinds. It is also apparent that at least two of the wishes, those of "mastery" and "security," are based respectively upon the "instincts" of hate and fear:

. . . The evolution of social life makes necessary continual modifications and developments of social technique, and we can hope that the evolution of social theory will continually put new and useful scientific generalizations within the reach of the social technician; the latter must therefore remain in permanent touch with both social life and social theory, and this requires a more far-going specialization than we actually find.

But, however efficient this type of social technique may become, its application will always have certain limits beyond which a different type of technique will be more useful. Indeed, the form of social control outlined above presupposes that the individual—or the group—is treated as a passive object of our activity and that we change the situations for him, from case to case, in accordance with our plans and intentions. But the application of this method becomes more and more difficult as the situations grow more complex, more new and unexpected from case to case, and more influenced by the individual's own reflection. And, indeed, from both the moral and the hedonistic standpoints and also from the standpoint of the level of efficiency of the individual and of the group, it is desirable to develop in the individuals the ability to control spontaneously their own activities by conscious reflection. To use a biological comparison, the type of control where the practitioner prescribes for the individual a scheme of activity appropriate to every crisis as it arises corresponds to the tropic or reflex type of control in animal life, where the activity of the individual is controlled mechanically by stimulations from without, while the reflective and individualistic control corresponds to the type of activity characteristic of the higher conscious organism, where the control is exercised from within by the selective mechanism of the nervous system. While, in the early tribal, communal, kinship, and religious groups, and to a large extent in the historic state, the society itself provided a rigoristic and particularistic set of definitions in the form of "customs" or "mores," the tendency to advance is associated with the liberty of the individual to make his own definitions.

We have assumed throughout this argument that if an adequate technique is developed it is possible to produce any desirable attitudes and values, but this assumption is practically justified only if we find in the individual attitudes which cannot avoid response to the class of stimulations which society is able to apply to him. And apparently we do find this disposition. Every individual has a vast variety of wishes which can be satisfied only by his incorporation in a society. Among his general patterns of wishes we may enumerate: (1) the desire for new experience, for fresh stimulations; (2) the desire for recognition, including, for example, sexual response and general social appreciation, and secured by devices ranging from the display of ornament to the demonstration of worth through scientific attainment; (3) the desire for mastery, or the "will to power," exemplified by ownership, domestic tyranny, political despotism, based on the instinct of hate, but capable of being sublimated to laudable ambition; (4) the desire for security, based on the instinct of fear and exemplified negatively by the wretchedness of the individual in perpetual solitude or under social taboo. Society is, indeed, an agent for the repression of many of the wishes in the individual; it demands that he shall be moral by repressing at least the wishes which are irreconcilable with the welfare of the group, but nevertheless it provides the only medium within which any of his schemes or wishes can be gratified. And it would be superfluous to point out by examples the degree to which society has in the past been able to impose its schemes of attitudes and values on the individual. Professor Sumner's volume, *Folkways,* is practically a collection of such examples, and, far from discouraging us as they discourage Professor Sumner, they should be regarded as proofs of the ability of the individual to conform to any definition, to accept any attitude, provided it is an expression of the public will or represents the appreciation of even a limited group. To take a single example from the present, to be a bastard or the mother of a bastard has been regarded heretofore as anything but desirable, but we have at this moment reports that one of the warring European nations is officially impregnating its unmarried women and girls and even married women whose husbands are at the front. If this is true (which we do not assume) we have a new definition and a new evaluation of motherhood arising from the struggle of this society against death, and we may anticipate a new attitude—that the resulting children and their mothers will be the objects of extraordinary social appreciation. And even if we find that the attitudes are not so tractable as we have assumed, that it is not possible to provoke all the desirable ones, we shall still be in the same situation as, let us say, physics and mechanics: we shall have the problem of securing the highest degree of control possible in view of the nature of our materials.

Final Formulation of the Wishes

The last and in many ways the most complete statement of the wishes appeared in *The Unadjusted Girl,* 1925, from which the following selection is taken.[3] Here Thomas uses that set of wishes in which the one for "mastery" is replaced by the wish for "response," the others remaining as in previous formulations. After summarizing Watson's work on the "instincts," he goes on to suggest that behavior might be studied in terms of the "forces which impel to action," namely, the wishes, which "correspond in general with the nervous mechanism."

This correspondence is indicated for three of the wishes: "new experience" is based on the instinct of "anger," with "curiosity" also entering as a basic tendency associated with it; "security" is opposed to "new experience" since it is referred to the instinct of "fear"; and "response" is related to the instinct of "love." Only the wish for "recognition" appears to lack an organic basis.

The wishes, then, are not instincts, nor are they merely casual surface attitudes. They appear to be fundamental tendencies, springing from the organic nature of man, yet related to the influences of social life. They are not the "causes" of behavior, as Thomas himself realizes. For example, behavior cannot be predicted for any single wish or combination of them

[3] Chapter I, "The Wishes," *The Unadjusted Girl* (Boston: Little, Brown, and Company, 1925), pp. 1–40.

may lead to a variety of different behavioral expressions. Contrariwise, one cannot infer from any specific behavior which wish or wishes are operating. Their utility must therefore lie in their being "constructs" which permit the observer to order human experience and help in its interpretation.

Nevertheless, the wishes became very popular in American social science as "explanatory" devices, and Thomas discarded them in favor of the situational approach to behavior. The following selection is noteworthy, then, because it contains the last important statement of the wishes in Thomas' writing, and because it clarifies the place of the wishes in his thought. It is also valuable as an example of how Thomas worked: using personal documents to illustrate his concepts and at the same time illuminating the documentary material.

It is impossible to understand completely any human being or any single act of his behavior, just as it is impossible to understand completely why a particular wild rose bloomed under a particular hedge at a particular moment. A complete understanding in either case would imply an understanding of all cosmic processes, of their interrelations and sequences. But it is not harder to comprehend the behavior of the "unadjusted" or "delinquent" person, say the vagabond or the prostitute, than that of the normally adjusted person, say the business man or the housewife.

In either case we realize that certain influences have been at work throughout life and that these are partly inborn, representing the original nature of man, the so-called instincts, and partly the claims, appeals, rewards, and punishments of society,—the influences of his social environment. But if we attempt to determine why the call of the wild prevails in the one case and the call of home, regular work, and "duty" in the other, we do not have different problems but aspects of the same general problem. It is only as we understand behavior as a whole that we can appreciate the failure of certain individuals to conform to the usual standards. And similarly, the unrest and maladjustment of the girl can be treated only as specifications of the general unrest and maladjustment.

In this connection students of psychology and education have been particularly interested in determining what the inborn tendencies really are. There was however no scientifically controlled work on the point until Watson undertook his experiments on newborn babies. At the time his work was interrupted he had found only three "instincts" present in the child at birth:

We are inclined now to believe that the fundamental emotional reactions can be grouped under three general divisions: those connected with fear; those connected with rage; those connected with what, for lack of a better term, we may call joy or love.

These at least deserve the name of major emotions. Whether or not other types of emotional reactions are present we cannot yet determine. . . . The principal situations which call out fear responses are as follows: (1) To suddenly remove from the infant all means of support, as when one drops it from the hand to be caught by an assistant. . . . (2) By loud sounds. (3) Occasionally when an infant is just falling asleep the sudden pulling of the blanket upon which it is lying will produce the fear response. (4) Finally, again, when the child has just fallen asleep or is just ready to awake a sudden push or a slight shake is an adequate stimulus. The responses are a sudden catching of the breath, clutching randomly with the hands (the grasping reflex invariably appearing when the child is dropped), blinking of the eyelids, puckering of the lips, then crying; in older children, flight and hiding.

Observations seem to show that the hampering of the infant's movements is the factor which apart from all training brings out the movements characterized as rage. If the face or head is held, crying results, quickly followed by screaming. The body stiffens and fairly well coordinated slashing or striking movements of the hands and arms result; the feet and legs are drawn up and down; the breath is held until the child's face is flushed. In older children the slashing movements of the arms and legs are better coordinated and appear as kicking, slapping, biting, pushing, etc. These reactions continue until the irritating situation is removed, and sometimes do not cease then. Almost any child from birth can be thrown into a rage if its arms are held tightly to its sides. . . . Even the best-natured child shows rage if its nose is held for a few seconds. . . .

The original stimuli for bringing out the earliest manifestations of joy or love seem to be as follows: gentle stroking and soft tickling of the infant's body, patting, gentle rocking, turning upon the stomach across the attendant's knee, etc. The response varies: if the infant is crying, crying ceases and a smile may appear; finally a laugh, and extension of the arms. In older children and in adults this emotion, due both to instinctive and habit factors, has an extremely wide range of expression.*

We understand of course that these expressions of emotion mean a preparation for action which will be useful in preserving life (anger), avoiding death (fear), and in reproducing the species (love),

* John B. Watson: "Practical and Theoretical Problems in Instinct and Habit," in "Suggestions of Modern Science Concerning Education," by H. S. Jennings, J. B. Watson, Adolf Meyer, W. I. Thomas, p. 63.

but even if our knowledge of the nervous system of man were complete we could not read out of it all the concrete varieties of human experience. The variety of expressions of behavior is as great as the variety of situations arising in the external world, while the nervous system represents only a general mechanism for action. We can however approach the problem of behavior through the study of the forces which impel to action, namely, the wishes, and we shall see that these correspond in general with the nervous mechanism.

The human wishes have a great variety of concrete forms but are capable of the following general classification:

1. The desire for new experience.
2. The desire for security.
3. The desire for response.
4. The desire for recognition.

1. THE DESIRE FOR NEW EXPERIENCE. Men crave excitement, and all experiences are exciting which have in them some resemblance to the pursuit, flight, capture, escape, death which characterized the earlier life of mankind. Behavior is an adaptation to environment, and the nervous system itself is a developmental adaptation. It represents, among other things, a hunting pattern of interest. "Adventure" is what the young boy wants, and stories of adventure. Hunting trips are enticing; they are the survival of natural life. All sports are of the hunting pattern; there is a contest of skill, daring, and cunning. It is impossible not to admire the nerve of a daring burglar or highwayman.[4] A fight, even a dog fight, will draw a crowd. In gambling or dice throwing you have the thrill of success or the chagrin of defeat. The organism craves stimulation and seeks expansion and shock even through alcohol and drugs. "Sensations" occupy a large part of the space in newspapers. Courtship has in it an element of "pursuit." Novels, theaters, motion pictures, etc., are partly an adaptation to this desire, and their popularity is a sign of its elemental force.[5]

[4] Cf. "Admiration of a lawless deed often foreruns censure of the deed in consciousness today: there are few men who do not admire a particularly daring and successful bank or diamond robbery, although they deprecate the social injury done." ("Sex and Primitive Morality," 1899, reprinted in *Sex and Society,* 1907, p. 153.)

[5] This idea of pursuit and new experience recurs more often in Thomas' writings than perhaps any other single one. In *Sex and Society,* 1907, for example, it is men-

1. When 11 years old Walter McDermott was brought to court in company with three other boys, accused of breaking a padlock on a grocery store and attempting to enter the store at four o'clock A. M., March 3, 1909, and also of breaking a padlock on the door of a meat-market and stealing thirty-six cents from the cash till. Put on probation. August 19, 1910, brought to court for entering with two other boys a store and stealing a pocket-book containing $3.00. He admitted to the officers he and his company were going to pick pockets down town. He is the leader of the gang. . . .

Sent to St. Charles. Ran away March 17, 1913. By breaking a window got into a drug store, with two other boys, and stole a quantity of cigars and $1.61. Having taken the money, he gave one boy ten cents and another five cents. He gave away the cigars—eight or nine boxes—to "a lot of men and some boys." Spent the money "on candy and stuff." Committed to John Worthy School . . . October 27. His conduct has improved greatly; released on probation . . .

December 23, 1913, accused of having broken, with an adult boy (19), into a clothing store and filled a suit case they found in the store with clothing and jewelry. Caught in shop. The officer said, "He would like to imitate Webb. He would like to kill some boy." According to his own confession, "It was six o'clock at night. I was going to confession. I met a boy and he said, 'Come out with me.' About nine o'clock we came to a clothing store, and we walked to the back, and seen a little hole. We pulled a couple of the laths off and as soon as we got in we got caught." But the officer said that previous to this they had burglarized a butcher's store and took from there a butcher's steel, and bored a hole in the wall with it. Committed to John Worthy School. Released June 26th, 1914. . . .

July 19, shot in a back alley twice at a little boy and once hit him. Broke with two other boys at night into Salvation Army office, broke everything he could and "used the office as a toilet room." Next day broke into a saloon, broke the piano, took cigars. Before this, July 14th, broke a side window of a saloon, stole $4.00 and a revolver. At the hearing Walter said about shooting the boy: "That boy was passing and I asked

---

tioned at least four times (pp. 57, 194–197) particularly as an explanation of exogamy. In that work he refers also to a "psychological demand for newness" (p. 195). Then, in *Source Book for Social Origins,* 1909, he notes "the interest of man in the unfamiliar" (p. 532). The same idea appears as the basic theme of "The Gaming Instinct," *American Journal of Sociology,* May 1901, pp. 750–763; and in "The Persistence of Primary-group Norms," 1917, it is stated that "no activity is interesting unless it follows the pursuit pattern" (p. 164). Here, too, it is related to scientific and creative activities, and curiosity is regarded as the "incipient stage of the pursuit" (p. 165). Thomas was still using a similar idea as late as 1933, for which see the unpublished "Report to the Social Science Research Council on the Organization of a Program in the Field of Personality and Culture," p. 443.

him for a match, and I heard this boy holler. I took a revolver off (his companion) and fixed a shot and hit the boy." His mother testified that he had spent only three nights at home since the time of his release from John Worthy School. He was arrested after the first offense, but escaped from the detention home. Committed to John Worthy School. . . .

Released after March 26. Committed a burglary in a grocery store, April 7th. Shot a man with a revolver in the left arm April 4th. Held up, with three other boys, a man on April 11, and robbed him of $12.00. Caught later, while the other boys caught at once. Held to the grand jury, found "not guilty" and released June 16, 1915.*

Vagabondage secures a maximum of new experience by the avoidance of the routine of organized society and the irksomeness at labor to which I will refer presently. In the constitutional vagabond the desire for new experience predominates over the other wishes and is rather contemplative and sensory, while in the criminal it is motor. But the discouraged criminal is sometimes a vagabond.

2. I have known men on the road who were tramping purely and simply because they loved to tramp. They had no appetite for liquor or tobacco, so far as I could find, also were quite out of touch with criminals and their habits; but somehow or other they could not conquer that passion for roving. In a way this type of vagabond is the most pitiful that I have ever known; and yet is the truest type of the genuine voluntary vagrant. . . . The *Wanderlust* vagrant . . . is free from the majority of passions common among vagrants and yet he is the most earnest vagrant of all. To reform him it is necessary to kill his personality, to take away his ambition—and this is a task almost superhuman. Even when he is reformed he is a most cast-down person.**

. . . . .

5. Girl states that she has been a tramp since she was 15 years old, going from one place to another, usually on freight trains, part of the time dressed as a boy. . . . She has a child, two years old, which she had illegitimately. The Court had compelled the father of it to marry her. This statement was verified at this office on its communication with the Probate Judge at Moundsville, W. Va.

She says that both her parents died when she was a little girl, that she lived with her grandmother, who worked out for her living, leaving her to run the streets. She says that from earliest childhood she has had the

* Records of the Juvenile Court of Cook County (Illinois).

** Josiah Flynt: "How Men Become Tramps," *Century Magazine*, Vol. 50, p. 944 (October, 1895).

wanderlust. She spoke of being as far west as Denver, and mentioned several army camps she had visited, always riding freight trains. Says that she never works except long enough to get what she can't beg. She says that she has no love for her child and that her grandmother takes care of it with money supplied by her husband. Her husband secured a divorce from her about three months after their marriage. The reason she asked to stay at the Detention Home over night was because she was going past the house in the alley and saw through the open door several young girls and thought it would be a nice place to stay all night.

Case was reported to office immediately after her admittance to the Detention Home. The next morning immediately after breakfast, while the Matron's back was turned, the girl escaped. The case was immediately reported to the Military and local police. The girl was picked up near camp, having had intercourse with several soldiers. Her appearance was the least attractive of any girl handled by this office. The little bundle of clothes she carried, tied in a bandanna handkerchief, was the dirtiest ever seen, and was burned at the Detention Home. At police headquarters she gave her age as 20 years but later told that she was but 17, which was verified from Moundsville. She was given $10.00 and thirty days and costs in the county jail, and while being taken from the jail to the clinic, by a policeman and Miss Ball, she, with another girl, escaped. Every effort was made to catch her, but she was as fleet as a deer.*

There is also in the hunting pattern of interest an intellectual element. Watson does not note curiosity among the instincts because it does not manifest itself at birth, but it appears later as the watchful and exploratory attitude which determines the character of action,—whether, for example, it shall be attack or flight. The invention of the bow and arrow, the construction of a trap, the preparation of poison, indicated a scientific curiosity in early man. Activities of this kind were interesting because they implied life or death. The man who constructed the poisoned arrow visualized the scene in which it was to be used, saw the hunt in anticipation. The preparation for the chase was psychologically part of the chase. The modern scientific man uses the same mental mechanism but with a different application. He spends long months in his laboratory on an invention in anticipation of his final "achievement." The so-called "instinct for workmanship" and the "creative impulse" are "sublimations" of the hunting psychosis. The making of a trap was a "problem," and any problem is interesting, whether the construction of a wireless or the

* Records of the Girls' Protective Bureau (Manuscript).

solving of a puzzle. Modern occupations or "pursuits" are interesting or irksome to the degree that they have or have not a problematical element[6] . . .

The craftsman, the artist, the scientist, the professional man, and to some extent the business man make new experience the basis of organized activity, of work, and produce thereby social values. The division of labor which removes the problematical from the various operations of the work makes the task totally unstimulating. The repudiation of work leads to the vagabondage just illustrated and to the antisocial attitudes described below:

7. We have in New York at present, and have had for some years past, an immense army of young men, boys between fifteen and twenty-six, who are absolutely determined that under no conditions will they do any honest work. They sponge on women, swindle, pick pockets, commit burglary, act as highwaymen, and, if cornered, kill, in order to get money dishonestly. How do they dispose of the vast sums they have already stolen? Gambling and women. They are inveterate gamblers.*

And similarly, among women we have the thief, the prostitute, the blackmailer, the vamp, and the "charity girl."

2. THE DESIRE FOR SECURITY. The desire for security is opposed to the desire for new experience. The desire for new experience is, as we have seen, emotionally related to anger, which tends to invite death, and expresses itself in courage, advance, attack, pursuit. The desire for new experience implies, therefore, motion, change, danger, instability, social irresponsibility. The individual dominated by it shows a tendency to disregard prevailing standards and group inter-

* Chief City Magistrate William McAdoo, in *New York World*, December 18, 1920.

[6] Thomas had written earlier: "The man of science works at problems and uses his ingenuity in making an engine in the laboratory in the same way that primitive man used his mind in making a trap. So long as the problem is present, the interest is sustained; and the interest ceases when the problematical is removed. Consequently, all modern occupations of the hunting pattern—scientific investigation, law, medicine, the organization of business, trade speculation, and the arts and crafts—are interesting as a game; while those occupations into which the division of labor enters to the degree that the workman is not attempting to control a problem, and in which the same acts are repeated an indefinite number of times, lose interest and become extremely irksome." ("The Mind of Woman and the Lower Races," 1907, reprinted in *Sex and Society*, pp. 280–281.)

A quotation from Dostoievsky has been omitted from the selection at this point; also the description of Pasteur's scientific quest, for which see pp. 113–114 supra.

ests. He may be a social failure on account of his instability, or a social success if he converts his experiences into social values,—puts them into the form of a poem, makes of them a contribution to science. The desire for security, on the other hand, is based on fear, which tends to avoid death and expresses itself in timidity, avoidance, and flight. The individual dominated by it is cautious, conservative, and apprehensive, tending also to regular habits, systematic work, and the accumulation of property.

The social types known as "bohemian" and "philistine" are determined respectively by the domination of the desire for new experience and the desire for security.[7] The miser represents a case where the means of security has become an end in itself.

8. Mamie Reilly's mother viewed with increasing regret the effect of premature care and responsibility on her daughter. Mamie had been working five years since, as a child of thirteen, she first insisted on getting a job. "She's a good girl, Mame is, but y'never seen anything like her. Every pay night reg'lar she'll come in an' sit down at that table. 'Now Ma,' she'll say like that, 'what *are* you goin' to do? How ever are y'goin' t'make out in th' rent?' 'Land sakes,' I'll say, 'one w'd think this whole house was right there on your shoulders. I'll get along somehow.' But y'can't make her see into that. 'Now, what'll we do, how'll you manage, Ma?' she'll keep askin'. She's too worrisome—that's what I tell her. An' she don't care to go out. Mebbe she'll take a walk, but like's not she'll say, 'What's th' use?' Night after night she jest comes home, eats 'er supper, sits down, mebbe reads a bit, an' then goes t' bed." *

Document 9 shows the desire for security in a person who is temperamentally inclined to new experience, but whose hardships call out the desire for security. The whole life, in fact, of this man shows a wavering between the two wishes. The desire for a "secure existence" which he expresses here finally prevails and he approaches the philistine type:

9. I had been ten weeks on the journey without finding any work, and I had no idea how long I should still be obliged to tramp about the world, and where was the end toward which I was going. . . . I should have been very glad of my visit to Stach had it not been for the thought of my wandering. If I had been going immediately to work from Mokrsko I should certainly have fallen in love with some girl, but the thought that

* Ruth True: "The Neglected Girl," p. 50.

[7] Cf. pp. 158–161 infra for another discussion of personality types.

I must tramp again about the world destroyed my wish for anything. Moreover I wanted to leave as soon as possible, for I could not look with dry eyes on how he wallowed in everything and had whatever he wanted. Everybody respected and appreciated him; everywhere doors were open for him, and he prized lightly everything he had, for he had never experienced any evil or misery. For if I had only one half of what he owned, how grateful I should be to God for his goodness. And tears flowed from my eyes when I compared his lot with mine. Fortune, how unjust you are! You drive one man about the world and you have no pity on him though he is whipped with wind and snow and cold stops his breath. People treat him worse than a dog and drive him away from their doors, without asking: "Have you eaten? Have you a place to sleep?" And when he asks for anything they are ready to beat him, like that peasant who struck me with the whip. And what for? Perhaps this mayor would have acted likewise if he had met me somewhere on my journey, and today he sets tables for this same tramp.

What a difference between us! Why, we have the same parents, the same name! And perhaps he is better considered because he is better instructed than I? In my opinion, not even for that. Or perhaps because he is nobler and handsomer? No, not for that. He merits consideration only because he has a secure existence, because he has bread. Let him wander into an unknown country; would he be better considered than I? No, a thousand times No. So if I want to merit consideration and respect, I ought first to win this [secure] existence. And how shall I win it and where? Shall I find it in tramping about the world? No, I must work, put money together and establish my own bakery. Then I can say boldly that I have [a secure existence] and even a better one than a teacher.*

In case 10 the desire for security is very strong but is overwhelmed by the desire for new (sexual) experience of the type which I shall term presently the "desire for response."

10. I am a young woman of twenty-five, married seven years. I have a good husband and two dear children; also a fine home. I was quite happy until an unexpected misfortune entered my life, destroying my happiness.

I consider it important to state that as a child I conducted myself decently; people regarded me as a blessing and my parents were very proud of me. As a young girl I strove to marry some good young man and live contentedly. I had no higher ambition. My dream was realized but unfortunately this did not last long.

Three years ago, my husband's cousin, a young man, came to us. He obtained employment in our town and lived with us. He stayed with us

* W. I. Thomas and Florian Znaniecki; "The Polish Peasant in Europe and America," in "Life Record of an Immigrant," Vol. 3, pp. 246 and 251.

four months altogether. During the first three months he was not in my thoughts at all . . . but during the last month my heart began to beat for him. It was a novel sensation for me and I did not know the meaning of this attraction; I said to myself: I love my husband and my children, why then this strange fascination for my husband's cousin? He surely must have done something to me to arouse this feeling in me, I thought. Fortunately, the young man soon lost his position and left for some distant place. I felt very happy at his departure, though I longed for him very much.

Two years passed thus, during which I resumed my former contented life with my husband until one day my husband informed me that his cousin had returned and planned to live in our town. I had a presentiment of dark clouds that would soon gather over my head, so I requested my husband to find other quarters than our own for his relative, on the pretext that I was not well enough to care for another person in the family. But as my husband reproached me and charged me with lack of interest in his relatives, I had to yield and give my permission for the man to stay with us.

I had decided to be indifferent and act as a stranger toward the boarder that was thrust upon me, so as to avoid trouble. I did not wish to ignite the feeling in my heart toward him by too close contact. I almost never spoke to him, and never came near him. God only knows how much these efforts cost me, but with all my energy I fought against the diabolic feeling in my heart. Unfortunately, my husband misinterpreted my behavior as a lack of hospitality. His resentment compelled me to assume a more friendly attitude toward his relative, as I wished to avoid quarrelling. What followed may easily be inferred. From amiability I passed to love until he occupied my whole mind and everybody else was non-existent for me. Of course no one was aware of my predicament.

One day I decided to put an end to my sufferings by confessing all to my boarder and requesting him to go away or at least leave our house and avert a scandal. Unfortunately, my hope of a peaceful life was not fulfilled, following my confession to the cousin. He remained in our home and became more friendly than ever towards me. I began to love him so intensely that I hardly noticed his growing intimacy with me and as a result I gave birth to a baby whose father is my husband's cousin. . . .

I am unable to describe to you one hundredth part of the misery this has caused me. I always considered an unfaithful wife the worst creature on earth and now . . . I am myself a degraded woman. . . . The mere thought of it drives me insane. My husband, of course, knows nothing about the incident. When the child was born he wanted to name it after one of his recently deceased relatives but . . . I felt as if this would desecrate the grave of his late relative. After oceans of tears, I finally induced him to name the child after one of my own relatives.

But my troubles did not end here. Every day in the week is a day of utter anguish for me and every day I feel the tortures of hell. . . . I can not stand my husband's tenderness toward the child that is mine but not his. When he gives the baby a kiss it burns me like a hot coal dropped in my bosom. Every time he calls it his baby I hear some one shouting into my ear the familiar epithet thrown at low creatures like me . . . and every time he takes the child in his arms I am tempted to tell him the terrible truth. . . . And so I continue to suffer. When my husband is not at home I spend my time studying the face of my child, and when I think it appears to resemble its father at such a moment I become terrified at the possibility of the baby's growing up into a real likeness to its father. What would my husband say and do when he noticed the similarity between my baby and his cousin? It is this thought that is killing me. . . . [If I should tell my husband I am sure he would drive me away.] I do not care for myself so much as for the child who would be branded with the name given all such children and this would remain a stain upon him for the rest of his life. . . . It is this fear that prevents me from revealing to my husband my crime against him. But how much longer shall I be able to bear the pain and wretchedness? *

3. THE DESIRE FOR RESPONSE. Up to this point I have described the types of mental impressionability connected with the pursuit of food and the avoidance of death, which are closely connected with the emotions of anger and fear. The desire for response, on the other hand, is primarily related to the instinct of love, and shows itself in the tendency to seek and to give signs of appreciation in connection with other individuals.

There is first of all the devotion of the mother to the child and the response of the child, indicated in the passage from Watson above, and in the following passage from Thorndike.

All women possess originally, from early childhood to death, some interest in human babies, and a responsiveness to the instinctive looks, calls, gestures and cries of infancy and childhood, being satisfied by childish gurglings, smiles and affectionate gestures, and moved to instinctive comforting acts by childish signs of pain, grief and misery. Brutal habits may destroy, or competing habits overgrow, or the lack of exercise weaken, these tendencies, but they are none the less as original as any fact in human nature.**

This relation is of course useful and necessary since the child is helpless throughout a period of years and would not live unless

* From the section entitled "A Bintel Brief" in *Forward* (a New York newspaper in the Yiddish language), April 12, 1920.

** E. L. Thorndike: "The Original Nature of Man," p. 81.

the mother were impelled to give it her devotion. This attitude is present in the father of the child also but is weaker, less demonstrative, and called out more gradually.

In addition, the desire for response between the two sexes in connection with mating is very powerful. An ardent courtship is full of assurances and appeals for reassurance. Marriage and a home involve response but with more settled habits, more routine work, less of new experience. Jealousy is an expression of fear that the response is directed elsewhere. The flirt is one who seeks new experience through the provocation of response from many quarters.

In some natures this wish, both to receive and to give response, is out of proportion to the other wishes, "over-determined," so to speak, and interferes with a normal organization of life. And the fixation may be either on a child or a member of either sex. The general situation is the same in the two cases following.

11. I am the unhappy mother of a dear little son, eight years old. You ask the cause of my unhappiness? I ought to be happy with such a dear treasure? But the answer is, I love my child too much. My love to my son is so great, so immeasurably deep, that I myself am worthless. My own person has not a trace of worth for me. I am as it were dead to all and everything. My thoughts by day and by night are turned toward my child. I see nothing in the world except my beloved child. Nothing exists for me except him. Every one of my thoughts, every desire and wish that awakens in me, turns around the child of my heart. I am nothing. I do not live, I do not exist. I forget myself as I forget all and everything in the world. I go around the whole day without eating and feel no hunger. I forget that I must eat. I go around often a whole day in my nightclothes because I forget that I have to dress. With soul and body, with mind and spirit I am wrapt up in my child. I have no thought for myself at all.

If clothes come to my mind, I am thinking of a new suit for my boy. I am nothing. And if I think of shoes, I imagine a pair of little shoes on the feet of my dear little boy. I myself am the same as dead. If I go to the country in the summer, I come home on account of my child. I myself do not exist. Every enjoyment in life, every happiness to which I give a thought is connected in my mind with my little boy. I myself am as if I were never at all in the world. The child is everything—my soul and my spirit, my breath and my life. He is the air I breathe. I am nothing. I don't consider myself, I don't think of myself, just as if I had never been in the world.

And so it is when my child is not well, when he has perhaps scratched his finger. . . . Oh, how I suffer then. No pen in the world can describe the terrible despair I feel. I live then as it were in a cloud, I cannot at all understand how my soul then remains in my body. My pain is then indescribable, greater than any can understand. . . . When my child is well again and his round, rosy cheeks bloom like the flowers in May and he is joyous and full of life and leaps and dances, then I myself look as if I had just recovered from a fever sickness.

Tell me, I beg you, dear editor, what can such a mama do that her dear child shall not become a lonely orphan. For I feel that I cannot continue long as it is. My strength is not holding out and a time must come when no strength to live will remain in me.*

12. I beg you to advise me, dear editor, how to stop loving. It is perhaps a ridiculous question but for me it is a very sad one. It is almost a question of life and death. It is so: I love a person who is not in a position to return my love. It is certain that we can never be united. . . . My love is hopeless but I cannot give it up. I run after the person I love, I follow his steps, knowing that it will do me no good. I have simply attached myself to an innocent person and distress him. My conscience tells me that it is not right. I suffer needlessly and I make suffering for another, but I simply have no inclination to stop.

I cannot live without my lover. When I don't see him at the expected moment I am wild, and I am ready to commit the greatest crime in order to accomplish my purpose. He runs away from me and I chase after him. When he goes away to another city I feel sure that I cannot live another twenty-four hours without him. I feel like throwing myself from a roof. I feel that I am capable of doing any evil deed on account of my love.

Do not think, dear editor, that I pride myself for having such a feeling. No, I do not compliment myself at all. I am provoked with myself, I am ashamed of myself and I hate myself. How can a person be such a rag? I argue with myself, how can I permit my mind to have no control over my heart? But my arguments with myself do me no good at all. It is work thrown away. I can love no one except him, the only one who has captured my heart and soul. I cannot even entertain the thought of ceasing to love him. It is simply impossible.

By what name would you call such a person as I am, dear editor? Perhaps I have gone out of my senses. So give me a word of advice as to how I may become sane again. I neglect everything in the world. Nothing remains in my thoughts except him. Without him everything is dark.

He is also unhappy on account of me. I don't let him breathe freely. He might have been happy with another, but I give him no chance. I disturb his life. I will add that this condition has gone on now for several years and there is no prospect of its ending.

* *Forward,* February 8, 1922.

Dear editor, give me an advice before I commit a deed after which marriage is impossible. I wait for your wise advice. Perhaps you will be my savior.*

The varieties of love in women are greater than in men, for we are to include here not only physical passion but parental feeling—that fund of emotion which is fixed on the child. The capacity of response to the child, mother love, is notorious and is painfully evident in document 11 . . . where the mother has no thought left for anything but the child. The mother is one who does not refuse. She does not refuse the breast to the lusty child even when she is herself ailing. And while this feeling is developed as a quality of motherhood it is present before motherhood and is capable of being transferred to any object calling for sympathy,—a doll, a man, or a cause. The women of the Malay Peninsula suckle little wild pigs when these are found motherless.[8] . . .

A touching expression of response from a man, a devotion to a parent as deep as mother love, is found in a letter of the psychologist William James, written to his father from England when the death of the latter was anticipated.

13. My blessed old Father: I scribble this line (which may reach you, though I should come too late) just to tell you how full of the tenderest memories and feelings about you my heart has for the last few days been filled. In that mysterious gulf of the past, into which the present will soon fall and go back and back, yours is still for me the central figure. All my intellectual life I derive from you; and though we have often seemed at odds in the expression thereof, I'm sure there's a harmony somewhere and that our strivings will combine. What my debt to you is goes beyond all my power of estimating—so early, so penetrating and so constant has been the influence.

You need be in no anxiety about your literary remains. I will see them well taken care of, and that your words shall not suffer from being concealed. At Paris I heard that Milsand, whose name you may remember is in the *Revue des Deux Mondes* and elsewhere, was an admirer of the *Secret of Swedenborg,* and Hodgson told me your last book had deeply impressed him. So will it be. . . .

As for us, we shall live on, each in his way—feeling somewhat unprotected, old as we are, for the absence of the parental bosoms as a refuge,

* *Forward,* March 8, 1922.

8 A paragraph omitted here concerns case 14, for which see p. 133 infra.

but holding fast together in that common sacred memory. We will stand by each other and by Alice, try to transmit the torch in our offspring as you did in us, and when the time comes for being gathered in, I pray we may, if not all, some at least, be as ripe as you.

As for myself, I know what trouble I've given you at various times through my peculiarities; and as my own boys grow up I shall learn more and more of the kind of trial you had to overcome in superintending the development of a creature different from yourself, for whom you felt responsible. I say this merely to show how my sympathy with you is likely to grow much livelier, rather than to fade—and not for the sake of regrets.

As for the other side, and Mother, and our all possibly meeting, I can't say anything. More than ever at this moment do I feel that if that were true all would be solved and justified. And it comes strangely over me in bidding you good-by how a life is but a day and expresses mainly but a single note. It is so much like the act of bidding an ordinary good-night.

Good-night, my sacred old Father! If I don't see you again—farewell! a blessed farewell. Your William.*

Usually this feeling is not so profound, as shown in these examples, and may be just sufficient to use as a tool and a play interest. But even then the life may be so schematized that it plays the main role. Document No. 14 is a single item taken from an autobiography of over three hundred closely written pages in which practically the only type of wish expressed is the desire for response from men, but this wish is never very strong.

14. At Wichita I went to school till I was about sixteen. Between ten and sixteen I had lots of little sweethearts. I have never been able to be happy without an atmosphere of love or at least flirtation. To such a degree is this true that I fear this story will be little else than the record of my loves and flirtations, happy and unhappy. I liked to kiss little boys from the start, but never cared to kiss the girls. I have had many women pals all through my life, but I never cared to kiss them, as many girls do. I suppose I am what my friend the newspaper man calls a man's woman. Certainly I am miserable unless there is a man around, and I generally want several. Until recently I have always been in love with two at the same time. But somehow since I met Harry it is different. My love for the other sex was always of an innocent kind. I loved men as the birds love sunshine. It is not a passion, but a necessity, like the air. I am light-hearted and buoyant by nature, and never thought of doing wrong. And yet the ugly side of this passion has always been forced upon me.**

* "Letters of William James," p. 218. *The Atlantic Monthly Press.*
** Hutchins Hapgood: "The Marionette" (Manuscript).

. . . . .

And in certain characters, almost invariably men, the desire for response is barely sufficient to keep them in contact with or on the fringe of humanity.

16. Many a man leads in London a most solitary, unsociable life, who yet would find it hard to live far away from the thronged city. Such men are like Mr. Galton's oxen, unsociable but gregarious; and they illustrate the fact that sociability, although it has the gregarious instinct at its foundation, is a more complex, more highly developed, tendency. As an element of this more complex tendency to sociability, the instinct largely determines the form of the recreations of even the cultured classes, and is the root of no small part of the pleasure we find in attendance at the theatre, at concerts, lectures, and all such entertainments.*

Frequently in marriage the wife provides the main fund of response and the husband is assimilated to the child. In No. 17 the wife has had a love adventure, is living with another man, but is planning to visit her husband clandestinely and look after him a bit.

17. My Own Dear Dean: So you would like to know if I am happy. Well, dear, that is one thing that will never be in my life again. It has gone from me forever. I don't want you to think that Clarence is not good to me, for he could not be better—I have a nice home that he has bought, and chickens and a lovely garden, and if Marjorie was his very own he could not be better to her. But he is terribly jealous, and it makes it very hard for me, for, God knows, I never give him cause. Oh, Dean, dear, wait until you see how I have changed. If I could only live my life over it would be so different. . . .

Now, dear, please don't feel that you have no interest in life, for you have our dear little girl, and just as soon as she is big enough to be a comfort to you—well, she is yours.

Dean, if you only knew how badly I want to see you. Now, listen—Clarence leaves here August 31 for Vancouver and will be there until September 6. . . . So, if you could send me my fare one way, why, then he could not refuse to let me go. . . . Let me know what you are planning, for I want to see you and cook you some good old meals again. . . . Yours only, Patsy.**

In No. 18 a conventional woman permits herself to have a single new experience in the field of response, as compensation for a married

* E. L. Thorndike: "The Original Nature of Man," p. 87.

** *Chicago American*, May 13, 1915.

relation which lacks everything but security, and then returns to her security.

18. American woman, forty-five years old, married. Husband is a prosperous real estate broker, a member of many clubs, a church warden, director of several corporations, a typical business man of the type termed "successful," a good citizen "without one redeeming vice."

She is a beautiful woman, albeit tired and faded. Her hair is prematurely white, her youthful face with deep-set brown eyes has a wistful contradictory appearance. Has many sides to her nature, can play ball with her boys as well as she can preside at a meeting. Is a good companion, has many friends, and leads a busy life as head of a prosperous household. Has five children, four boys and one girl. One would not guess that she is an unsatisfied woman; her friends all think her life ideal and, in a sense, she does not deny it. This in substance is her view of married life though not literally word for word:

"I suppose there can never be a school for marriage—how could there be?—yet how sad it is that every one must begin at the same place to work out the same problem. I had a good father and mother. They did not understand me but that was probably more my fault than theirs; I never confided in my mother overmuch. My father considered my mental progress at all times and I owe him much for the manner in which he made me think for myself, strengthened my views, and guided my education. When I left finishing school I played in society for two years and many of the men I met interested me, though none compelled me. I had never been given any clear conception of what marriage should be in the ideal sense. I knew vaguely that the man I married must be in my own class, good and honorable, and rich enough to maintain a dignified household. I had more of a vision of love at sixteen than at twenty-six, the year I married, though I was sure I loved my husband and I do—that is he is as much a part of my life as my religion or my household conventions. He is wholly a product of civilization and I discovered too late there is an element of the savage in most women. They wish to be captured, possessed—not in the sense the suffragists talk about; it is really a sense of self-abasement, for it is the adoration of an ideal. They wish to love a man in the open—a fighter, a victor—rather than the men we know who have their hearts in money making and play at being men. Perhaps it cannot be remedied, it is only a bit of wildness that will never be tamed in women but it makes for unhappiness just the same.

"My sex life had never been dominant. I had a commonplace adolescence with physical longings and sensations which were not explained to me and which did me no harm. My relation with my husband was perfectly orthodox, and vaguely I longed for something different. My husband was shocked at any demonstration on my part. If I was impulsive and threw myself in his arms he straightened his tie before he kissed me. Once at our cottage in the mountains I suggested that we spend the night in the woods. I saw a possibility of our getting nearer each other physically and spiritually if we could get out in the wilderness away from the restraints and niceties of our luxurious household. That was the first time I ever felt like a traitor. He told me quite sternly to go to bed, I was not a wild Indian and could not act like one. I went to the nursery for the night and snuggled close to my little boy and was glad he was young and slender and hoped he would never grow fat and complacent. I had noticed for the first time that my husband was growing stout, like any other church-warden.

"Since that time I have never been wholly happy. It was not the foolish incident, it was the fundamental principle, and underlying our civilization. Our babies came rather closely together and I was glad that the mother element in me needed to be uppermost. My husband was perfectly content with life, I satisfied him at dinner parties, I could dress well and talk well, managed the household money to advantage and was at hand—tame, quite tame, when he wished to kiss me. I do not mean to sound sarcastic and bitter. It is not what my husband is which troubles me, but what he is not; I think I speak for many women. I am more mated to the vision of what my children's father might have been than to the good kind man whom I teach them to love and respect.

"Perhaps you have guessed I am coming to a confession: I met the man in England two summers ago, but he is an American and is in this country now, a friend of ours whom we both see quite often. Something in both of us flared the very night we met. He and Lawrence (my husband) get along famously; they both believe in many of the same ideals and discuss kindred subjects, but my brain and his supplement each other in a way which is hard to explain. I did not mean to love him. It is an upper strata of myself; I love Lawrence; I mean I belong to him, am part of his very being and he of mine, but I am myself when I am with this other man and I refuse to think what a different self it might have been had I known him before. The very morning after I faced the awful fact that I was thinking of a man other than my husband, Lawrence put a bouquet at my plate at the breakfast table. It was a red geranium, a tiny pink rose, and some leaves of striped grass. Poor Lawrence.

"Our adventure in love came rapidly. He understood me perfectly and I knew that he cared. We have never told Lawrence for we do not intend to do anything more that is wrong. He has spent several evenings at the house when Lawrence was away. There was no deception about this—it just happened and we have talked and kissed and faced life in the open. We decided quite calmly, and without passion, that we would have each other entirely just once. I wanted the complete vision of what my love could mean. If it is wrong I cannot think so; at any rate I would not give up the memory of that time. It was only once and it was a year ago. We both knew there could be no continued sex relation. When I have an opportunity I kiss him and he me. Lawrence never kisses my lips, so they belong to him. He has helped me to be more patient, and understanding of my life as it has been and must be. I have my children and must live out the life for their sakes and for Lawrence who loves me, tamed and domesticated.

"If life could be—what it would mean to give him a child, but life in its entirety cannot be—for me. Probably that is the creed of many women." *

It is unnecessary to particularize as to the place of response in art. The love and sex themes are based on response, and they outweigh the other themes altogether. Religion appeals to fear, fear of death and extinction, and promises everlasting security, or threatens everlasting pain, but in the New Testament the element of response, connected with the concrete personalities of Jesus and Mary, predominates. Any hymn book will contain many versified love letters addressed to Jesus. There are on record, also, many alleged conversations of nuns with Jesus which are indistinguishable in form from those of human courtship.

19. Angela da Foligno says that Christ told her he loved her better than any woman in the vale of Spoleto. The words of this passage are fatuous almost beyond belief: "Then He began to say to me the words that follow, to provoke me to love Him: 'O my sweet daughter! O my daughter, my temple! O my daughter, my delight! Love me, because thou art much loved by me.' And often did He say to me: 'O my daughter, My sweet Spouse!' And he added in an underbreath, 'I love thee more than any other woman in the valley of Spoleto.' " To amuse and to delight Gertrude of Eisleben, He sang duets with her "in a tender and harmonious voice." The same saint writes of their "incredible intimacy"; and here, as in later passages of Angela da Foligno, the reader is revolted by their sensuality. . . . In the diary of Marie de l'Incarnation there is such an entry as *"entretien familier avec J.-C."*; and during such interviews she makes use of a sort of pious baby talk, like a saintly Tillie Slowboy.**

In general the desire for response is the most social of the wishes. It contains both a sexual and a gregarious element. It makes selfish claims, but on the other hand it is the main source of altruism. The

* Edith L. Smith, in collaboration with Hugh Cabot: "A Study in Sexual Morality," *Social Hygiene,* Vol. 2, p. 532.
** Burr: "Religious Confession and Confessants," p. 356.

devotion to child and family and devotion to causes, principles, and ideals may be the same attitude in different fields of application. It is true that devotion and self-sacrifice may originate from any of the other wishes also—desire for new experience, recognition, or security—or may be connected with all of them at once. Pasteur's devotion to science seems to be mainly the desire for new experience,—scientific curiosity; the campaigns of a Napoleon represent recognition (ambition) and the self-sacrifice of such characters as Maria Spiridonova, Florence Nightingale, Jane Addams is a sublimation of response. The women who demanded Juvenile Courts were stirred by the same feeling as the mother in document No. 11, whereas the usual legal procedure is based on the wish to have security for life and property.

4. The Desire for Recognition. This wish is expressed in the general struggle of men for position in their social group, in devices for securing a recognized, enviable, and advantageous social status. Among girls dress is now perhaps the favorite means of securing distinction and showing class. A Bohemian immigrant girl expressed her philosophy in a word: "After all, life is mostly what you wear." Veblen's volume, "Theory of the Leisure Class," points out that the status of men is established partly through the show of wealth made by their wives. Distinction is sought also in connection with skillful and hazardous activities, as in sports, war, and exploration. Playwriters and sculptors consciously strive for public favor and "fame." In the "achievement" of Pasteur (case 6) and of similar scientific work there is not only the pleasure of the "pursuit" itself, but the pleasure of public recognition. Boasting, bullying, cruelty, tyranny, "the will to power" have in them a sadistic element allied to the emotion of anger and are efforts to compel a recognition of the personality. The frailty of women, their illness, and even feigned illness, is often used as a power-device, as well as a device to provoke response. On the other hand, humility, self-sacrifice, saintliness, and martyrdom may lead to distinction. The showy motives connected with the appeal for recognition we define as "vanity"; the creative activities we call "ambition."

The importance of recognition and status for the individual and for society is very great. The individual not only wants them but he needs them for the development of his personality.[9] The lack of them and the fear of never obtaining them are probably the main source of those psychopathic disturbances which the Freudians treat as sexual in origin.

On the other hand society alone is able to confer status on the individual and in seeking to obtain it he makes himself responsible to society and is forced to regulate the expression of his wishes. His dependence on public opinion is perhaps the strongest factor impelling him to conform to the highest demands which society makes upon him.

20. The chief difference between the down-and-out man and the down-and-out girl is this. The d.-a.-o. man sleeps on a park bench and looks like a bum. The d.-a.-o. girl sleeps in an unpaid-for furnished room and looks very respectable. The man spends what little change he has—if he has any—for food and sleeps on a bench. The girl spends what little change she has—if she has any—for a room and goes without food.

Not because she has more pride than the man has. She hasn't. But because cops haul in girls who would sleep on benches, and well-meaning organizations "rescue" girls who look down and out. A pretty face and worn-out soles are a signal for those who would save girls from the perilous path, whereas an anaemic face in a stylish coat and a pair of polished French heels can go far unmolested. . . .

You will argue that any woman with an empty stomach and a fur coat ought to sell the coat for a shabby one and spend the money for food. That is because you have never been a lady bum. A fur coat gets her places that a full stomach never would. It is her entrée into hotel washrooms when she is dirty from job hunting. It gets her into department-store rest rooms when she is sore of foot. And in the last stages it gets her help from a certain class of people who would be glad to help her if she had suddenly lost her purse, but who never would if she had never had a purse.

And then, most important of all, it helps her to hang on to her last scraps of self-respect.*

* "The Lady Bum," by One of Them. *New York Times, Book Review and Magazine,* January 1, 1922.

[9] Thomas had begun to formulate this wish in his early writing. Thus, in "The Sexual Element in Sensibility," 1904, he wrote that all social life is characterized by the "sensitiveness of man to the opinion in which he is held by others"; and adds, "It is thus of advantage to act in such a way as to get public approval and some degree of appreciation; and a . . . reckoning upon this, is involved in the process of personal adjustment." (See *Sex and Society,* 1907, pp. 108–109, where this article is reprinted under the title "Sex and Social Feeling.")

21. Alice . . . wants to be somebody, to do great things, to be superior. In her good moods, she is overwhelmed with dreams of accomplishment. She pines to use good English, to be a real lady. There is pathos in her inquiry as to what you say when a boy introduces you to his mother and how to behave in a stylish hotel dining room. Such questions have an importance that is almost greater than the problem of how to keep straight sexually. Winning of social approval is an ever-present, burning desire, but she has no patterns, no habits, no control over the daily details of the process whereby this is gained. When one tries to place her in a good environment with girls of a better class, she reacts with a deepened sense of inferiority, expressed in more open, boastful wildness. She invents adventures with men to dazzle these virtuous, superior maidens. The craving for pleasures and something to make her forget increases.*

. . . . .

In many cases, both in boys and girls, particularly at the period of adolescence, the energy takes the form of daydreaming, that is, planning activity, and also of "pathological lying," or pretended activity. The wishes are thus realized in an artistic schematization in which the dreamer is the chief actor. The following, from the diary of a sixteen-year-old girl is in form a consistent expression of the desire for recognition, but very probably the form disguises a sexual longing, and the daydream is thus an example of the sublimation of the desire for response, as frequently in poetry and literature.

23. I am between heaven and earth. I float, as it were, on a dream-cloud which carries me up at times into a glorious atmosphere, and again nearer the mucky earth, but always on, always on. I see not man, I see not the children of man, the big ME lies in my head, in my hand, in my heart. I place myself upon the throne of Kings, and tramp the dusty road, care-free. I sing to myself and call me pretty names; I place myself upon the stage, and all mankind I call upon for applause, and applause roars to me as the thunder from the heavens. I reason that mine is not inevitable stage-madness which comes to all females of my pitiful age; mine is a predestined prophecy, mine is a holy design, my outcoming is a thing to be made way for.

I bathe myself in perfumed waters, and my body becomes white and slender. I clothe myself in loosened gowns, silks as soft as thistledown, and I am transported to scenes of glory. The even stretch of green, bedecked with flowers to match the color of my pale gold gown, is mine to dance and skip upon. A lightness and a grace comes into my limbs.

* Jessie Taft: "Mental Hygiene Problems of Normal Adolescence," *Mental Hygiene*, Vol. 5, p. 746.

What joy is mine! I leap and spring and dart in rhythm with nature, and music leaps from my steps and movements and before my eyes are men. Men and women and children with heads bent forward, with eyes aglow with wonder, and with praise and love for this essence of grace and beauty which is I. What more, what more! I hang upon this idol of a dream, but it is gone. The height of happiness is reached; alas, even in dreams there is an end to happiness, the bubble bursts, and the dust and noise of earth come back to me. I shut my eyes and ears to these and seek consolation among the poor. In dreams I go often among them. With my heaping purse of gold, I give them clothes and beds to sleep upon, I give them food to nourish them and me, to nourish and refresh my fame. But do I give my gold away, and does my purse cave inwards? Ah, no! Come to my aid, my imagination, for thou art very real to me today. An endless store of gold is mine in banks of state. My name is headed on the lists of all, my money does increase even as I hand it to these poor. The poor bless me, they kneel and kiss my hands. I bid them rise, and the hypocrisy of my godless soul bids them pray and in this find restoration.

I grow weary as I walk, and truth is even harder yet to bear than ever before. I am sad, I have nothing, I am no one. But I speak soothingly to myself, bidding me treat my hungry self to food, and I promise that the night shall be long and the dreams and journeys many.*

On the contrary, 24 is in form a desire for response, but the details show that the girl feels keenly the lack of recognition.[10] The response is desired not for itself alone but as a sign and assurance of comparative worth.

24. I am in despair, and I want to pour out my bitter heart. When I have once talked out my heart I feel better afterwards.

Dear editor, why can I not find a boy to love me? I never make a hit with young people. I never have any success with them. I associate with young people, I like them, they like me, but nobody ever runs after me. No boy is crazy about me. All my girl friends are popular with young men. Every single one has a boy or more who is in love with her and follows her steps. I alone have no luck. Do not think, dear editor, that I am burning to marry; it is not yet time for that. But the thought that I am

* Jessie Taft: "Mental Hygiene Problems of Normal Adolescence," *Mental Hygiene*, Vol. 5, p. 750.

[10] In 1926 Thomas remarked: "I doubt, I may say, whether the recognition, as I have called it, and response are different. I separate them for convenience, but I think response is basic." Then he added that recognition is "the response which you can provoke from an unfriendly world." (Unpublished minutes of the Social Science Research Council Hanover Conference, August 23 – September 2, 1926, Vol. II, p. 331.)

left out makes me very wretched. It distresses me and it hurts me to my soul's marrow to know that no one desires me, that people are indifferent toward me. Oh how happy I should be if somebody would love me, if somebody would come to see me. It must be such a sweet pleasure to feel that some one is interested in you, that some one comes to see you, comes to you especially, on account of yourself. Oh, why can I not have this happiness!

When I go to a party and when I come back I feel so low and so fallen. Young men crowded around my companions like flies around honey. I alone was an exception. I have not a jealous nature, but no other girl in my place would feel otherwise. Can you show me a way to win a boy's heart? What sort of quality must a girl possess in order to attract a young man?

It is true I am no beauty. But what do all the girls do? They fix themselves up. You can buy powder and paint in the drug stores. My companions are not more beautiful than I. I am not sleepy. When I am in the company of young people I am joyous, I make myself attractive, I try my best to attract attention to myself. But this is all thrown to the dogs.

Dear editor, if you only knew with how much care I make my clothes. I go through the great stores to select out the most beautiful materials. I annoy the dressmaker to death until she suits me exactly. If it happens that a hook somewhere on the dress is not in the right place, or a buttonhole has a single stitch more or less than it should have, I have the greatest distress, and sharpest heartache.

When I go somewhere to a dance I am full of hopes, my heart is beating with excitement. Before leaving the house I take a last look in the mirror. When I return home I have the blues, I feel cold. My teeth grind together. So much exertion, so much strength lost, all for nothing. A boy has talked to me, another boy has given me a smile, still another boy has made me a little compliment, but I feel that I am not near and dear to any one. I feel that my face has not been stamped on the heart of any one.*

From the foregoing description it will be seen that wishes of the same general class—those which tend to arise from the same emotional background—may be totally different in moral quality. The moral good or evil of a wish depends on the social meaning or value of the activity which results from it. Thus the vagabond, the adventurer, the spendthrift, the bohemian are dominated by the desire for new experience, but so are the inventor and the scientist; adventures with women and the tendency to domesticity are both expres-

* *Forward*, September 30, 1921.

sions of the desire for response; vain ostentation and creative artistic work both are designed to provoke recognition; avarice and business enterprise are actuated by the desire for security.

Moreover, when a concrete wish of any general class arises it may be accompanied and qualified by any or all of the other classes of wishes. Thus when Pasteur undertook the quest described above we do not know what wish was uppermost. Certainly the love of the work was very strong, the ardor of pursuit, the new experience; the anticipation of the recognition of the public, the scientific fame involved in the achievement was surely present; he invited response from his wife and colleagues, and he possibly had the wish also to put his future professional and material life on a secure basis. The immigrant who comes to America may wish to see the new world (new experience), make a fortune (security), have a higher standing on his return (recognition), and induce a certain person to marry him (response).

The general pattern of behavior which a given individual tends to follow is the basis of our judgment of his character. Our appreciation (positive or negative) of the character of the individual is based on his display of certain wishes as against others and on his modes of seeking their realization. Whether given wishes tend to predominate in this or that person is dependent primarily on what is called temperament, and apparently this is a chemical matter, dependent on the secretions of the glandular systems. Individuals are certainly temperamentally predisposed toward certain classes of the wishes. But we know also . . . that the expression of the wishes is profoundly influenced by the approval of the man's immediate circle and of the general public. The conversions of wild young men to stable ways, from new experience to security, through marriage, religion, and business responsibility, are examples of this. We may therefore define character as an expression of the organization of the wishes resulting from temperament and experience, understanding by "organization" the general pattern which the wishes as a whole tend to assume among themselves.[11]

The significant point about the wishes as related to the study of

[11] Cf. pp. 152–154 infra for another discussion of character and temperament.

behavior is that they are the motor element, the starting point of activity. Any influences which may be brought to bear must be exercised on the wishes.[12]

We may assume also that an individual life cannot be called normal in which all the four types of wishes are not satisfied in some measure and in some form.

[12] As we have seen, Thomas did not long maintain the same conception of the wishes. In 1926 he referred to them as "a convenience in seeing how experiences arrange themselves and come into conflict, and how it may be possible to develop one dominant, socially inclined set of interests." (Unpublished minutes of the Hanover Conference, *op. cit.*, p. 331.) In 1927 the wishes became "classes" or "fields" of values, "objects of desire" (see p. 196, n. 4, infra). Finally, in 1938 Thomas said: "They are not four wishes; they are four fields, regions within which the wishes fall." (Unpublished "Proceedings" of the Committee on Appraisal of Research, December 10, 1938, p. 79.)

9 A THEORY OF SOCIAL PERSONALITY

The following selection is from Thomas and Znaniecki's Introduction to "Life-Record of an Immigrant," a conspicuous feature of *The Polish Peasant,* 1918–20. Previously in this work the authors had sketched the recent evolution of Polish society in objective, cultural terms. By means of the autobiography of a somewhat "typical" Polish peasant, they hoped to catch the corresponding subjective view which they considered so essential to the discovery of social laws. Indeed, in the Introduction, they assert that the "personal life-record" is the "*perfect* type of sociological material."

In order for such material to be relevant to a general social science, however, there must be a theory of social personality to provide a standpoint from which human experience can be interpreted. The purpose of the Introduction was to supply such a theory.

It is, of course, impossible to summarize this theory in a few lines, but its central features may at least be indicated. To Thomas personality is not a static phenomenon; rather it is personal organization in evolution. Consequently, if the study of personality is to contribute to a general social science, certain "constants" must be specified and then treated developmentally. Such concepts as "temperament" (original nature), "character" (conscious attitudes), "life organization" (rules organizing character), and the "four desires" (fundamental tendencies) supply these constants. Also, the idea of "typical lines of genesis" enables the authors to postulate certain uniformities in personality development.

In the social process individuals evolve by "defining situations," that is, by interpreting them and applying previous experience in their solution. In this way character evolves out of temperament, and life organization becomes the discovery and application of rules to concrete situations. Since there are factors in both the individual and society which make for "typical lines of genesis" [1] in personality formation, it is possible to distinguish three "types" of personality: the philistine, bohemian, and the creative individual. These are differentiated on the basis of character stability and the degree of flexibility they manifest in the rules organizing their behavior.

This selection, in brief, is a very elaborate analysis of the patterns of

[1] Cf. "Nevertheless, there are certain general correspondences in human nature to begin with, and society by its institutions, teachings, rules, rewards, and penalties does establish a degree of regularity and probability. It is able to condition its material to a certain degree and secure, on the whole, expected behavior." ("Comment by W. I. Thomas," in Blumer, *An Appraisal of . . . The Polish Peasant,* p. 84.)

interaction between the individual and society. On the subjective side the individual originally has temperament and wishes; on the objective side there are the demands of society, embodied in social rules attached to situations. Out of the interaction of these factors individuals attain their own definitions of situations and, accordingly, different kinds of character and different forms of life organization. The result is an internally consistent and highly dynamic theory of personal evolution.

At the same time this selection re-emphasizes Thomas' estimate of the utility of the life history in personality study. The life history is indispensable because it supplies the longitudinal view of personal evolution, thus supplementing and clarifying whatever may be learned from the cross-sectional personality "test." In the present disordered state of personality theory, this interpretation with the methods of study it demands is a challenging one, worthy of recall and further exploration.

Introduction to Life-Record of an Immigrant [2]

The study of human personalities, both as factors and as products of social evolution, serves first of all the same purpose as the study of any other social data—the determination of social laws.[3] . . . Whether we draw our materials for sociological analysis from detailed life-records of concrete individuals or from the observation of mass-phenomena, the problems . . . are the same. . . . The ultimate aim . . . is . . . to use as few general laws as possible for the explanation of as much concrete social life as possible. And since concrete social life is concrete only when taken together with the individual life which underlies social happenings, . . . social science cannot remain on the surface of social becoming, where certain schools wish to have it float, but must reach the actual human experiences and attitudes which constitute the full, live and active social reality beneath the formal organization of social . . . phenomena [4] . . . A social institution can be fully understood only if we do not limit ourselves to the abstract study of its formal organization, but analyze the way in which it appears in the personal experience of various members of the group and follow the influence which it has upon their lives. . . .

[2] *The Polish Peasant,* 1927, Vol. II, pp. 1831–1907.

[3] Cf. the Methodological Note, pp. 40–58 supra, particularly pp. 55–56.

[4] In their emphasis upon understanding the subjective aspects of experience Thomas and Znaniecki were, of course, reacting to the "sociologism" of Durkheim—as the reference to "certain schools" and their study of "surface" phenomena indicates. For a similar statement see *The Polish Peasant,* 1927, Vol. I, p. 44, n. 1.

The development of sociological investigation . . . , particularly the growing emphasis which . . . is being put upon special and actual empirical problems as opposed to the general speculations of the preceding period, leads to the growing realization that we must collect more complete sociological documents than we possess.[5] And the more complete a sociological document becomes the more it approaches a full personal life-record. . . . We are safe in saying that personal life-records, as complete as possible, constitute the *perfect* type of sociological material,[6] and that if social science has to use other materials at all it is . . . a defect, not an advantage, of our present sociological method.[7] . . .

But in order to be able to use adequately personal life-records . . . social science must have criteria permitting it to select at once from a mass of concrete human documents, those which are likely to be scientifically valuable for the solution of a given general problem.[8] We cannot study the life-histories of all the individuals participating in a certain social happening, for then our task would be inexhaustible. We must limit ourselves, just as the natural scientist does, to a few *representative* cases whose thorough study will yield results as nearly applicable as possible to all other cases concerned. But the problem of selecting representative cases is much less easy in social

[5] As early as 1912 Thomas had recognized that "undesigned records" should be used as much in sociological research as "designed records." These undesigned records included letters, diaries, newspapers, and the like—the same kind of material used in *The Polish Peasant.* See Thomas' "Race Psychology: Standpoint and Questionnaire with Particular Reference to the Immigrant and the Negro," *American Journal of Sociology,* May 1912, pp. 770 ff.

[6] This discussion of the life history opened up a new field for theory and research, leading to various critical studies and further clarification. In addition to Blumer's *An Appraisal of . . . The Polish Peasant,* the following works may be cited as examples: Louis Gottschalk, Clyde Kluckhohn, and Robert Angell, *The Use of Personal Documents in History, Anthropology, and Sociology* (Social Science Research Council Bulletin 53, 1945); John Dollard, *Criteria for the Life History* (New Haven: Yale University Press, 1935). The latest statement is from an anthropologist: Clyde Kluckhohn, "Needed Refinements in the Biographical Approach," in S. S. Sargent and M. W. Smith, eds. *Culture and Personality* (New York: The Viking Fund, 1949), pp. 75–92.

[7] These first two paragraphs have been rearranged from the opening pages of the Introduction to "Life-Record of an Immigrant."

[8] For a discussion of the role of research problems in scientific advance, see pp. 83–85 supra.

than in natural science because the greater complexity and variety which human personalities present as compared with natural things makes their classification more difficult. When . . . [the social scientist] has studied the process of the appearance of a certain attitude or a certain value in the life-history of one social personality he is taking a serious risk when he provisionally assumes that this case is representative of a certain general class—that the process is the same, for example, in all the individuals who belong to a certain community, nation, profession, religious denomination, etc. Of course any error which he commits can be corrected by further research, but the question is, how to diminish in advance the chances of such errors, how to find criteria which will permit us, after having investigated one human being, to tell more or less exactly to what class of human beings the results of this investigation are applicable.

Such criteria can be given only by a theory of human individuals as social personalities. The use of individual life-records as material for the determination of abstract social laws must be supplemented by a sociological study of these individuals themselves in their entire personal evolution, as concrete components of the social world. . . .

Before proceeding, therefore, . . . we must discuss the standpoint from which every . . . study of a human individual as social personality should be made. This implies a complete revision of the problem of *type* [9] . . . Our present discussion will be, of course, merely formal and methodological; we do not aim to establish in advance a complete classification of human personalities—this must be the result of long studies—but to show in what way such a classification can be reached. We shall be forced, indeed, to characterize several ideal types which social personalities tend to assume,[10] but our characterization will be purely formal and based upon relations between the individual and his social environment whose essential

[9] This fundamental problem is still with us. See Gordon Allport, *The Use of Personal Documents in Psychological Science* (Social Science Research Council Bulletin 49, 1942), p. 146: "Much work remains to be done before the typing of documents can be considered satisfactory. The whole question of types in social and psychological science urgently calls for investigation and clarification. When this is accomplished the handling of personal documents will improve."

[10] See pp. 158–161 infra for a description of these types.

features are the same in all societies, whatever may be the content of the personal and social life. Our classification will, therefore, claim to be only a starting-point for researches whose aim must consist in a synthetic characterization of human types precisely with regard to the content of the attitudes and values which constitute their social personalities.

The essential points, which cannot be . . . sufficiently emphasized, are that the social personality as a whole manifests itself only in the course of its total life and not at any particular moment of its life, and that its life is . . . a continuous evolution in which nothing remains unchanged.[11] This evolution often tends toward a stabilization as its ultimate limit, but never attains this limit completely; and even then it is not this limit as such, but the very course of evolution tending to this limit, that constitutes the main object-matter of socio-psychological synthesis.

If we wish, therefore, to use the concept of type as applied to social personalities, we must, first of all, extend this concept to the process of personal evolution. Now this implies a special problem. A personal evolution taken in its totality is certainly a unique occurrence; no individual develops in the same way as any other individual. On the other hand, from the standpoint of nomothetic social science this total development should be entirely analyzable into elementary facts, each indefinitely repeatable and subordinated to a general law.[12] . . . We must, therefore, assume—and social observation certainly corroborates this assumption—that not only single attitudes and values, not only single elementary facts, but more or less complete combinations, series of facts, present a certain similarity from

[11] Cf. "The personality as we used to see it was what you got out of a case history brought up to and focussed on the present. Personality was considered a sort of snapshot as Bergson would have said. . . . But more and more we find that neglecting the individual's *perpetually changing* emphases gets us into insoluble problems." (Gardner Murphy, "The Relationships of Culture and Personality," in Sargent and Smith, *op. cit.*, p. 14.)

See also Clyde Kluckhohn and Henry A. Murray, eds. *Personality in Nature, Society, and Culture* (New York: Alfred A. Knopf, 1948), p. 4: "Personality is process: it will not stop and allow itself to be examined repeatedly and at leisure by the experts."

[12] Cf. the discussion of nomothetic vs. idiographic uses of personal documents in Allport, *op. cit.*, pp. 53–64.

individual to individual.[13] This similarity cannot be assumed to go as far as absolute identity; the identity is always only approximate. . . . But the concept of type, unlike the concept of law, needs only an approximate identity of individual cases, and a class is supposed to possess only a relative generality.

The application of sociological generalization to social personalities requires thus, first of all, the admission of what we may call *typical lines of genesis.* A line of genesis is a series of facts through which a certain attitude is developed from some other attitude (or group of attitudes), a value from some other value (or group of values), when it does not develop directly, and the process cannot be treated as a single elementary fact. For example there is probably no social influence that could produce directly an attitude of appreciation of science from the parvenu's pride in his wealth, no intellectual attitude that could directly lead an untrained individual to produce a scientifically valid concept from the data of common-sense observation; but by a series of intermediary stages the parvenu can become a sincere protector of science, by a more or less long training in theoretic research a student learns to produce scientific values. In such a series every single link is a fact of the type: attitude—value—attitude, or: value—attitude—value . . . but the series as a whole cannot be subject to any law, for there are many possible ways in which an attitude can be developed out of another attitude, a value out of another value; all depends on the nature of the intermediary data. . . . To take well-known examples, there is probably usually one and the same primary attitude—a particular form of the desire for excitement . . . out of which habitual drinking develops, and yet there are many possible ways of becoming a drunkard. The history of inventions shows that many inventors working independently on the same practical problem may produce the same invention, but their procedure may be completely different. And of course it is hardly necessary to say that from a given attitude or value many different lines of evolution may start and reach quite different

[13] Cf. "In personal relations . . . this uniqueness of personality usually is, and should be, accented. But for general scientific purposes the observation of uniformities, uniformities of elements and uniformities of patterns, is of first importance. This is so because without the discovery of uniformities there can be no concepts, no classifications, no principles, no laws." (Kluckhohn and Murray, *op. cit.*, pp. 37–38.)

results, and that a given attitude or value may have been reached from many different starting points by different lines of evolution. Moreover in the development of a human personality there are many and various divergent lines of genesis, since at any moment of his life the individual not only presents many attitudes acquired during his past development and produces many values which he has learned to produce, but this acquired set of attitudes and abilities is more or less different from moment to moment. Viewed therefore from the standpoint of particular lines of genesis the human personality in its total evolution might appear as too complex to be the object-matter of scientific generalization. But the theoretically limitless variety of lines of genesis is really limited in practice. . . . When the individual has acquired a more or less rich stock of stabilized attitudes, a certain influence may not be accepted because in disagreement with this stock. Therefore the way in which a given new attitude can develop is limited, and it may be difficult, sometimes even practically impossible, to produce it because the necessary influences to which the individual would react in the desired way may not be available. Thus the stabilization of individual attitudes diminishes the probability that his future development will assume an unforeseen direction.

And there is a further limitation of the possible lines of genesis in the stability and limited variety of external conditions. First of all there is a general negative limitation of external influences by the fact that the milieu in which the individual lives includes only a limited variety of values. But much more important is the positive limitation of evolution which society imposes upon the individual by putting him into a determined frame of organized activities which involves in advance a general succession of influences—early family education, beginning of a definite career with determined openings, marriage, etc.—establishes a regularity of periodical alternations of work and play, food and sleep, etc., and with the help of economic, legal and moral sanctions prescribes and excludes certain forms of behavior. The more uniform and steady this frame, the greater the relative parallelism of evolution between individuals; similar lines of genesis repeat themselves in many members of the group, for the individual cannot find around him influences which would make him take a course different from other members of the group in acquiring a new attitude.[14] Of course this means also a limitation of the variety of possible attitudes or values that can develop from a given starting-point; given a certain material in the form of an individual disposition or of a social value, it is probable that the group will make of it something very definite, and the same in every case, particularly where the social framework is little varied and flexible.

Still more extensive uniformities of development are found in connection with temperament and character.[15] . . . *Temperament* and *character* are the concepts in which has been expressed the common-sense realization that there are always a few organized groups of attitudes in a personality which play a predominant part in its activity, so that for practical purposes any attitudes outside of those groups can be neglected as inconspicuously manifesting themselves in personal behavior. The concept of individual *life-organization* may be used to indicate the existence, within the sphere of experience of an individual, of a limited number of selected and organized groups of social values which play a predominant part in his life both as partial causes and partial effects of his more or less organized attitudes.

We must here investigate the methodological significance of these concepts and attempt to give them more exact and more productive meanings than those they have had in popular psychology and in half-literary reflection about human life. It must be remembered in particular that the fundamental problems of the synthesis of human personalities are not problems of a personal *status* but problems of personal *becoming,* that the ultimate question is not what temperaments and characters there are but what are the ways in

14 "Study of socialization in a comparative perspective is . . . demonstrating that there are important elements of uniformity in the 'character structure' of those who have been socialized in the same cultural and institutional system, subject to variations according different roles within the system." (Talcott Parsons, "The Present Position and Prospects of Systematic Theory in Sociology," in Gurvitch and Moore, *Twentieth Century Sociology,* p. 64.)

15 Cf. Thomas' early statement: "There is much reason to think that temperament . . . is quite as important as brain-capacity in fixing the *characteristic lines of development* followed by a group." ("The Province of Social Psychology," *American Journal of Sociology,* January 1905, p. 452; italics ours.)

which a definite character is developed out of a definite temperament, not what life-organizations exist but by what means a certain life-organization is developed. It is relatively easy to classify temperaments and characters, but this classification is entirely unproductive unless it is used as a mere preparation for the study of their evolution, where the aim is to determine human types as *dynamic* types, as types of development. Similarly with regard to personal life-organization, we find in any society ready models of organization with which individuals are expected to comply; but the analysis of these models does not constitute a study of personalities—it is merely its starting-point. After learning what models the group proposes to its members, we must learn by what typical means those members gradually realize or fail to realize these models. In other words the concepts of temperament, character, life-organization, mark only the starting-point and the limit of the evolution which is the real object-matter of the study of human personalities. It becomes, therefore, a point of essential importance to frame definitions of temperament, character and life-organization which may be used in the study of personal evolution.

We may call temperament the fundamental original group of attitudes of the individual as existing independently of any social influences; we may call character the set of organized and fixed groups of attitudes developed by social influences operating upon the temperamental basis. The temperamental attitudes are essentially instinctive, that is, they express themselves in biological action but not in reflective consciousness; the attitudes of the character are intellectual, that is, they are given by conscious reflection. . . .

. . . A group of temperamental attitudes either finds its expression at a given moment by pushing others aside, or is pushed aside by some other group and is not expressed at all. Thus, hunger and sexual desire, fear and anger manifest themselves independently of each other without any conscious attempt at coordination. In character, on the contrary, attitudes are more or less systematized; their continuity through many manifestations makes this indispensable. Thus, hunger or sexual desire becomes a permanent basis of a conscious and systematic organization of a large group of economic, social, hedonistic, intellectual, aesthetic attitudes, and this organization works continuously, independently of the actual association of these attitudes from case to case; the attitudes organized for the permanent satisfaction of hunger or sexual desire manifest themselves even while no hunger or sexual desire is actually felt and while the actual material conditions do not suggest them in any way. . . .

These differences between temperament and character find their expression on the objective side in matters of life-organization. But in order to understand this side of the question we must get rid of the whole schematic conception of the world assimilated from common-sense reflection and from science. We must put ourselves in the position of the subject who tries to find his way in this world, and we must remember, first of all, that the environment by which he is influenced and to which he adapts himself, is *his* world, not the objective world of science—is nature and society as he sees them, not as the scientist sees them. The individual subject reacts only to his experience, and his experience is not everything that an absolutely objective observer might find in the portion of the world within the individual's reach, but only what the individual himself finds. And what he finds depends upon his practical attitudes toward his environment, the demands he makes upon it and his control over it, the wishes he seeks to satisfy and the way in which he tries to satisfy them. His world thus widens with the development of his demands and his means of control, and the process of this widening involves two essential phases—the introduction of new complexities of data into the sphere of his experience and the definition of new situations [16] within those complexities.

The first phase is characterized by an essential vagueness. The situation is quite undetermined; even if there are already in the individual wishes which will give significance to the new data, they are not sufficiently determined with regard to these data, and the

[16] It should be noted here that Thomas used the concept "definition of the situation" in at least two ways. On the subjective side it refers to the way individuals perceive their environment and interpret it; on the objective side it refers to the social norms and rules which embody "common" definitions of the situation. This dual sense of the concept seems especially useful for a theory of "social personality." See "The Primary Group and the Definition of the Situation," pp. 226–231 infra, for the objective formulation.

complexity is not ordered, values are not outlined, their relations are not established. In the second phase the situation becomes definite, the wish is crystallized and objectified, and the individual begins to control his new experience. Now, the sphere of experience in which new situations can be defined by the temperament alone does not include social life at all. It includes only internal organic processes and such external experiences as are directly connected with the satisfaction of organic needs and the avoidance of physical danger. Of course this sphere is also continually extended, chiefly during the period between birth and maturity, and its extension, as we know from observation and from direct consciousness of such processes as the development and satisfaction of sexual instincts, has also the two periods of vague perception of a chaos of new data and gradual definition of new situations. But all the material with which the temperament deals has one essential limitation: it includes only natural objects, whose significance for the individual is determined by their sensual content. Meanwhile the social values are significant as much or more because of the meaning they have for other individuals or for the group. For example, a material object outside of social life and in relation to organic needs may be significant on account of its sensual qualities, as foods, as shelter, as source of possible pain, etc. In social life it acquires through its meaning for others ideal qualities which make it an economic value (object of exchange), a source of vanity, a weapon in a fight for some other value, etc. A word outside of social life is a mere sound, perhaps helping to foresee possible danger or satisfaction; in social life it has a meaning, it points to experiences common to many individuals and known as common by all of them. . . . An individual of the other sex is naturally chiefly a body, object of physical satisfaction; socially it is also a conscious being with an experience of its own and a personality which has to be adapted to the subject's own personality or to which the subject has to adapt himself. And so on. This is why social psychology, while rejecting the old conception of individual consciousness as closed receptacle or series of conscious data or happenings, cannot accept as its methodological basis the principles recently developed by the behavioristic school. The behavior of an individual as social personality is not scientifically reducible to sensually observable movements and cannot be explained on the ground of the direct experience of the observing psychologist; the movements (including words) must be interpreted in terms of intentions, desires, emotions, etc.—in a word, in terms of attitudes—and the explanation of any particular act of personal behavior must be sought on the ground of the experience of the behaving individual which the observer has indirectly to reconstruct by way of conclusions from what is directly given to him. We cannot neglect the meanings, the suggestions which objects have for the conscious individual, because it is these meanings which determine the individual's behavior; and we cannot explain these meanings as mere abbreviations of the individual's past acts of biological adaptation to his material environment—as manifestations of organic memory—because the meanings to which he reacts are not only those which material things have assumed for him as a result of his own past organic activities, but also those which these things have acquired long ago in society and which the individual is taught to understand during his whole education as conscious member of a social group.

The biological being and his behavior represent therefore nothing but the limit dividing natural from social life . . . Therefore this limit itself must be defined by social psychology in terms of attitudes, and the concept of temperamental attitudes serves precisely this purpose. An individual with nothing but his biological formation, or—in social terms—with nothing but his temperamental attitudes, is not yet a social personality, but is able to become one. In the face of the world of social meanings he stands powerless . . . Such is the position of the animal or the infant in human society; and a similar phenomenon repeats itself on a smaller scale whenever an individual on a low level of civilization gets in touch with a higher civilized environment, a worldling with a body of specialists, a foreigner with an autochthonic society, etc. In fact, human beings for the most part never suspect the existence of innumerable meanings—scientific, artistic, moral, political, economic—and a field of social reality whose meanings the individual does not know, even if he can observe its sensual contents, is as much out of the reach of his practical experience as the other side of the moon.

In order to become a social personality in any domain the individual must therefore not only realize the existence of the social meanings which objects possess in this domain, but also learn how to adapt himself to the demands which society puts upon him from the standpoint of these meanings and how to control these meanings for his personal purposes; and since meanings imply conscious thought, he must do this by conscious reflection, not by mere instinctive adaptations of reflexes. In order to satisfy the social demands put upon his personality he must reflectively organize his temperamental attitudes; in order to obtain the satisfaction of his own demands, he must develop intellectual methods for the control of social reality in place of the instinctive ways which are sufficient to control natural reality. And this effective reorganization of temperamental attitudes leads, as we have seen, to character, while the parallel development of intellectual methods of controlling social reality leads to a life-organization, which is nothing but the totality of these methods at work in the individual's social career.

The practical problem which the individual faces in constructing a life-organization . . . [resembles biological adaptation only in so far as both imply] a certain stabilization of individual experiences . . . But the nature of this stability . . . is essentially different in both cases—a difference which has been obliterated by the indistinct use of the term "habit" to indicate any uniformities of behavior. This term should be restricted to the biological field.[17] A habit, inherited or acquired, is the tendency to repeat the same act in similar material conditions. . . . This tendency is unreflective; reflection arises only when there is disappointment, when new experiences cannot be practically assimilated to the old ones. But this form of stability can work only when the reality to which the individual has to adjust is entirely constituted by sensually given contents and relations. It is evidently insufficient when he has to take social meanings into account, interpret his experience not exclusively in terms of his own needs and wishes, but also in terms of the traditions, customs, beliefs, aspirations of his social milieu. Thus the introduction of any stable order into experience requires con-

[17] It is not entirely clear why Thomas and Znaniecki should have recommended this, inasmuch as Thomas had continually stressed habits as "learned" behavior, without any necessary reference to biological heredity.

tinual reflection, for it is impossible even to realize whether a certain experience is socially new or old without consciously interpreting the given content—an object, a movement, a word—and realizing what social meaning it possesses. However stable a social milieu may be, its stability can never be compared with that of a physical milieu; social situations never spontaneously repeat themselves, every situation is more or less new, for every one includes new human activities differently combined. The individual does not find passively ready situations exactly similar to past situations; he must consciously define every situation as similar to certain past situations, if he wants to apply to it the same solution applied to those situations.[18] And this is what society expects him to do when it requires of him a stable life-organization; it does not want him to react instinctively in the same way to the same material conditions, but to construct reflectively similar social situations even if material conditions vary. The uniformity of behavior it tends to impose upon the individual is not a uniformity of organic habits but of consciously followed *rules*. The individual, in order to control social reality for his needs, must develop not series of uniform reactions, but general *schemes* of situations; his life-organization is a set of rules for definite situations, which may be even expressed in abstract formulas. Moral principles, legal prescription, economic forms, religious rites, social customs, etc., are examples of schemes.

The definiteness of attitudes attained in character and the corresponding schematization of social data in life-organization admit, however, a wide scale of gradation with regard to one point of fundamental importance—the range of possibilities of further development remaining open to the individual after the stabilization. This depends on the nature of the attitudes involved in the character and of the schemes of life-organization, and also on the way in which both are unified and systematized. And here three typical cases can be distinguished.

The set of attitudes constituting the character may be such as practically to exclude the development of any new attitude in the given conditions of life, because the reflective attitudes of an indi-

[18] As late as 1949 Gardner Murphy was lamenting that "in discussing personalities we often fail to specify the *situation* in which they appear." ("The Relationships of Culture and Personality," in Sargent and Smith, *op. cit.*, pp. 21–22.)

vidual have attained so great a fixity that he is accessible to only a certain class of influences—those constituting the most permanent part of his social milieu. The only possibilities of evolution then remaining open to the individual are the slow changes brought by age in himself and by time in his social milieu, or a change of conditions so radical as to destroy at once the values to whose influence he was adapted and presumably his own character. This is the type which has found its expression in literature as the "Philistine." It is opposed to the "Bohemian," whose possibilities of evolution are not closed, simply because his character remains unformed. Some of his temperamental attitudes are in their primary form, others may have become intellectualized but remain unrelated to each other, do not constitute a stable and systematized set, and do not exclude any new attitude, so that the individual remains open to any and all influences. As opposed to both these types we find the third type of the individual whose character is settled and organized but involves the possibility and even the necessity of evolution, because the reflective attitudes constituting it include a tendency to change, regulated by plans of productive activity, and the individual remains open to such influences as will be in line of his preconceived development. This is the type of the creative individual.[19]

A parallel distinction must be made with regard to the schemes of social situations constituting the life-organization. The ability to define every situation which the individual meets in his experience is not necessarily a proof of intellectual superiority; it may mean simply a limitation of claims and interests and a stability of external conditions which do not allow any radically new situations to be noticed, so that a few narrow schemes are sufficient to lead the individual through life, simply because he does not see problems on his way which demand new schemes. This type of schemes constitutes the common stock of social traditions in which every class of situation is defined in the same way once and forever. These schemes harmonize perfectly with the Philistine's character and therefore the Philistine is always a conformist, usually accepting social tradi-

[19] Compare this discussion of "personality types" with the earlier one by Thomas in "The Persistence of Primary-groups Norms" in Jennings and others, *Suggestions of Modern Science Concerning Education,* 1917, pp. 178–180. A more elaborate analysis of the "creative individual" will be found infra, pp. 203–211.

tion in its most stable elements. Of course every important and unexpected change in the conditions of life results for such an individual in a disorganization of activity. As long as he can he still applies the old schemes, and up to a certain point his old definition of new situations may be sufficient to allow him to satisfy his claims if the latter are low, although he cannot compete with those who have higher claims and more efficient schemes. But as soon as the results of his activity become unsuccessful even in his own eyes, he is entirely lost; the situation becomes for him completely vague and undetermined, he is ready to accept any definition that may be suggested to him and is unable to keep any permanent line of activity. This is the case with any conservative and intellectually limited member of a stable community, whatever may be his social class, when he finds himself transferred into another community or when his own group undergoes some rapid and sudden change.

Opposed to this type we find an undetermined variation of schemes in the life of all the numerous species of the Bohemian. The choice of the scheme by a Bohemian depends on his momentary standpoint, and this may be determined either by some outburst of a primary temperamental attitude or by some isolated character-attitude which makes him subject to some indiscriminately accepted influence. In either case inconsistency is the essential feature of his activity. But on the other hand he shows a degree of adaptability to new conditions quite in contrast with the Philistine, though his adaptability is only provisional and does not lead to a new systematic life-organization.

But adaptability to new situations and diversity of interest are even compatible with a consistency of activity superior to that which tradition can give if the individual builds his life-organization not upon the presumption of the immutability of his sphere of social values, but upon the tendency to modify and to enlarge it according to some definite aims. These may be purely intellectual or aesthetic, and in this case the individual searches for new situations to be defined simply in order to widen and to perfect his knowledge or his aesthetic interpretation and appreciation; or his aims may be "practical," in any sense of the term—hedonistic, economical, political, moral, religious—and then the individual searches for new situations in order to widen the control of his environment, to adapt to his purposes a continually increasing sphere of social reality. This is the creative man.[20]

The Philistine, the Bohemian and the creative man are the three fundamental forms of personal determination toward which social personalities tend in their evolution. None of these forms is ever completely and absolutely realized by a human individual in all lines of activity; there is no Philistine who lacks completely Bohemian tendencies, no Bohemian who is not a Philistine in certain respects, no creative man who is fully and exclusively creative and does not need some Philistine routine in certain lines to make creation in other lines practically possible, and some Bohemianism in order to be able to reject occasionally such fixed attitudes and social regulations as hinder his progress, even if he should be unable at the time to substitute for them any positive organization in the given line. But while pure Philistinism, pure Bohemianism and pure creativeness represent only ideal limits of personal evolution, the process of personal evolution grows to be more and more definite as it progresses, so that, while the form which a human personality will assume is not determined in advance, either by the individual's temperament or by his social milieu, his future becomes more and more determined by the very course of his development; he approaches more and more to Philistinism, Bohemianism or creativeness and thereby his possibilities of becoming something else continually diminish.

These three general types—limits of personal evolution—include, of course, an indefinite number of variations, depending on the nature of the attitudes by which characters are constituted and on the schemes composing the life-organization of social individuals. . . .

[20] The research utility of these personality types may well be questioned, as Thomas himself indicated in "The Configurations of Personality" (see pp. 194 ff. infra). It is interesting to note, however, that their parallel has recently appeared, though with many qualifications as to application. Kluckhohn and Murray suggest these types: the "undersocialized," "oversocialized," and "adequately socialized"—which are obviously similar to the Bohemian, Philistine, and creative man types of Thomas. Similarly, the same authors make a distinction between the "innovator" (whose activity is constructively toned) and the "rebel" (whose activity is destructively toned)—again a conception paralleling Thomas' creative man, and Bohemian. See Kluckhohn and Murray, *op. cit.*, pp. 27, 29.

But, as we have seen, the problem is to study characters and life-organizations not in their static abstract form, but in their dynamic concrete development. And both character and life-organization—the subjective and the objective side of the personality—develop together. . . . In the continual interaction between the individual and his environment we can say neither that the individual is the product of his milieu nor that he produces his milieu; or rather, we can say both. For the individual can indeed develop only under the influence of his environment, but on the other hand during his development he modifies this environment by defining situations and solving them according to his wishes and tendencies. . . . In various cases we may find various degrees of dependence upon the environment, conditioned by the primary qualities of the individual and the type of social organization. The individual is relatively dependent upon society in his evolution, if he develops mainly such attitudes as lead to dependence, which is then due both to his temperamental dispositions and to the fact that the organization of society is such as to enforce by various means individual subjection; he is relatively independent if in his evolution he develops attitudes producing independence, which again results from certain primary tendencies determined by a social organization which favors individual spontaneity. And thus both dependence and independence are gradual products of an evolution which is due originally to reciprocal interaction; the individual cannot become exclusively dependent upon society without the help of his own disposition, nor become independent of society without the help of social influences. The fundamental principles of personal evolution must be sought therefore both in the individual's own nature and in his social milieu.

We find, indeed, two universal traits manifested in all individual attitudes, instinctive or intellectual, which form the condition of both development and conservatism. In the reflex system of all the higher organisms are two powerful tendencies which in their most distinct and explicit form manifest themselves as curiosity and fear. Without curiosity, that is, an interest in new situations in general, the animal would not live; to neglect the new situation might mean either that he was about to be eaten or that he was missing his chance for food.[21] And fear with its contrary tendency to avoid certain experiences for the sake of security is equally essential to life. To represent these two permanent tendencies as they become parts of character in the course of the social development of a personality we shall use the terms *"desire for new experience"* and *"desire for stability."* . . . The desire for stability extends to a whole period of regular alternations of activity and rest from which new experiences are relatively excluded; the desire for new experience finds its expression in the break of such a whole line of regulated activities. And the range and complexity of both stability and change may have many degrees. Thus, for example, stability may mean the possibility of a single series of satisfactions of hunger in a certain restaurant, of a week's relation with an individual of the other sex, of a few days' stay in one place during travel, of a certain kind of work in an office; or it may lie in the possibility of such an organization of money-affairs as gives the certainty of always getting food, of a permanent marriage-relation, settling permanently in one place, a life career, etc. And new experience may mean change of restaurant, change of the temporary sexual relation, change of the kind of work within the same office, the resuming of travel, the acquiring of wealth, getting a divorce, developing a Don Juan attitude toward women, change of career or specialty, development of amateur or sporting interests, etc.

On the individual side, then, alternation of the desire for new experience and of the desire for security is the fundamental principle of personal evolution, as including both the development of a character and of a life-organization. On the social side the essential point of this evolution lies in the fact that the individual living in society has to fit into a pre-existing social world, to take part in the hedonistic, economic, political, religious, moral, aesthetic, intellectual activities of the group. For these activities the group has objective *systems,* more or less complex sets of schemes, organized either by traditional association or with a conscious regard to the greatest possible efficiency of the result, but with only a secondary, or even with no interest in the particular desires, abilities and experiences

[21] See "The Persistence of Primary-group Norms," *op. cit.,* p. 165, for the same view in almost exactly the same words.

of the individuals who have to perform these activities. . . . The gradual establishment of a determined relation between these systems which constitute together the social organization of the civilized life of a group, and individual character and life-organization in the course of their progressive formation, is the central problem of the social control of personal evolution. . . .

There is, of course, no pre-existing harmony whatever between the individual and the social factors of personal evolution, and the fundamental tendencies of the individual are always in some dis-accordance with the fundamental tendencies of social control. Personal evolution is always a struggle between the individual and society [22]—a struggle for self-expression on the part of the individual, for his subjection on the part of society—and it is in the total course of this struggle that the personality—not as a static "essence" but as a dynamic, continually evolving set of activities—manifests and constructs itself.[23] The relative degree of the desire for new experience and the desire for stability necessary for and compatible with the progressive incorporation of a personality into a social organization is dependent on the nature of individual interests and of the social systems. . . . For every system within a given group and at a certain time there is a maximum and a minimum of change and of stability permissible and required. The widening of this range and the increase of the variety of systems are, of course, favorable to individual self-expression within the socially permitted limits. Thus, the whole process of development of the personality as ruled in

[22] "The whole problem of culture hinges on the relation of the individual to society. Each is an indispensable value to the other. . . . But the nature of the individual, demanding a maximum of new experience, is in fundamental conflict with the nature of society, demanding a maximum of stability, and it would be interesting to analyze the various particular effects of the repressive action of society on the individual." ("The Persistence of Primary-group Norms," *op. cit.*, p. 177.)

[23] Floyd N. House in *The Range of Social Theory* (New York: Henry Holt and Company, 1929), p. 169, n. 30, cites Ellsworth Faris to the effect that Thomas defined personality as "the subjective aspect of culture." Neither House nor Faris were able to find a citation to that effect, nor has the present editor. The statement above does not easily lead to any such definition, nor does the following: "We must mention, however, that the community does not determine the character of its members as completely as . . . [some cases] would indicate. It gives the member those attitudes which are necessary to the common life, but outside of these he may be individualistic, even obstinate and incalculable." (*Old World Traits Transplanted*, 1921, p. 33, n. 2.)

various proportions by the desire for new experience and the desire for stability on the individual side, by the tendency to suppress and the tendency to develop personal possibilities on the social side, includes the following parallel and interdependent processes: [24]

(1) Determination of the character on the ground of the temperament;

(2) Constitution of a life-organization which permits a more or less complete objective expression of the various attitudes included in the character;

(3) Adaptation of the character to social demands put upon the personality;

(4) Adaptation of individual life-organization to social organization.

1. We know already that the development of temperamental attitudes into character-attitudes can assume many different directions, so that, if the proper influences were exercised from the beginning, a wide range of characters, theoretically any possible character, might be evolved out of any temperament. . . .

But in actual social life . . . the possible attitudes which the members of the group wish to suppress are usually those whose direct expression in action would, in the social opinion, be harmful, rather than those which are contrary to the development of other useful ones. The control exercised by the group is negative much more than positive, tends to destroy much more than to construct . . . And even when it wishes to construct, it often assumes, implicitly or explicitly, that when an undesirable attitude is suppressed, the contrary desirable one will develop. And, of course, if there is in individual temperament a possibility of the desirable attitude, this supposition may be true. But the point is that by suppressing an attitude . . . we suppress at the same time all the possible lines of a further evolution that may have started from the suppressed attitude and resulted in something very desirable. The earlier the suppression, the greater the number of possibilities destroyed and the greater the resulting limitation of the personality. Well-known

[24] Cf. the determinants of personality suggested by Kluckhohn and Murray: constitutional, group-membership, role, and situational (*op. cit.*, pp. 38–46).

examples are the suppression of the adventurous spirit and of the critical tendency in children.

The mechanism of suppression is double. A temperamental possibility not yet conscious is suppressed if given no opportunity to manifest itself in any situation, for only through such manifestations can it become explicit and be evolved into a character-attitude. This form of suppression is attained by an isolation of the individual from all experiences that may give stimulation to endeavors to define situations by the undesirable tendency. The suppression of sexual attitudes and of free thought in religious matters are good examples of this mechanism. The second course, used when an attitude is already manifested, in order to prevent its further development and stabilization, is suppression by negative sanction; a negative value—punishment or blame—is attached to the manifestation of the attitude, and by lack of manifestation the attitude cannot evolve. But both mechanisms are in fact only devices for postponing the development of the undesirable attitude until a character is fixed including the contrary attitudes, and it is only this fixation which does suppress the undesirable attitude definitively.[25]

But suppression is not always a necessary consequence of the evolution of character from temperament. Attitudes need to be suppressed only when they are inadequately qualified and thus interfere with more desirable ones when meeting in the same field of social experience. For example, unqualified spirit of adventure and a tendency to regulated life, unqualified sexual desire and claims of social respectability, unqualified wish for pleasures and recognition of

[25] A clarification of the role of suppression in personality development may be found in another part of *The Polish Peasant:* "This makes it clear why violent repression of anti-social acts often fails to prevent similar acts by other individuals, or even by the individual punished. Repression does, indeed, develop the attitude of fear which efficiently counterbalances anti-social tendencies, but only if a situation *similar* to that which resulted in punishment presents itself; in other words, it prevents the repetition of similar anti-social acts. [Cf. the psychological concepts of discrimination and repetition.] But it does not prevent the individual from satisfying his socially undesirable tendencies by constructing *new* situations in which he will try to avoid social repression. In order to have the individual conform in his behavior with definite social rules, it is not enough to frighten him away from certain forms of behavior conflicting with these rules, but it is indispensable to make him positively want to conform." (Vol. II, 1927, pp. 1257–1258.)

familial obligations are, indeed, more or less irreconcilable with each other. . . .

The principle that permits the harmonizing of opposite attitudes without impairing the consistency of character is, in general, distinction of applicability of attitudes. The situations involved must, of course, be classed in advance so that certain features of a given complex of values may be a sufficient criterion for the application of one attitude or another. Many criteria are given by social tradition; the conventionalization [26] of certain attitudes in certain circumstances permits their preservation together with others to which they are opposed. The criteria are of various kinds. They may consist, for example, in a time-limitation. Vacation is considered a time when some of the spirit of adventure suppressed during the year may be expressed. Or it may be a limitation in space, as when certain behavior is permitted at a certain place, like the dropping of social forms and the relative freedom of relations between the sexes at bathing resorts. Sometimes the occasion is ceremonial, as in the hilarity of evening parties and the drinking at social meetings. On other occasions a certain attitude is assumed to be excluded from situations to which without the conventionalization it would apply. Thus, the sexual attitude is theoretically not applied to passages in the Bible bearing on sexual questions, or to an artist's model, or in medical studies and investigations and in legal works. More important cases of conventionalization are found when a whole line of organized activities, with the corresponding attitudes, is permitted under circumstances carefully circumscribed and usually designated by some social symbol. Thus, marriage is a conventionalization of the woman's—to some extent also the man's—system of sexual attitudes, besides being a familial organization. War is the conventionalization of murder, plundering and arson, diplomacy a conventionalization of cheating and treachery. Freedom of theoretic investigation has attained a social conventionalization in the physical sciences but not yet in human sciences . . .

In every case the dividing line between the fields of applicability

[26] Cf. William G. Sumner, *Folkways* (Boston: Ginn and Company, 1906), pp. 68–70, for the development of the idea of "conventionalization."

of two contrary attitudes can be drawn by or for the individual even if no general rules of division are laid down by society. The only difficulty is that every attitude if allowed to develop freely tends to an exclusive domination of the whole field of experience to which it can be applied. Of course this is not true of every attitude of every individual, but there is probably not a single attitude which does not in somebody tend to assume such an importance as to conflict with others. . . . But it is evident that with a proper limitation no attitude needs to be suppressed and all the temperamental possibilities can be allowed to develop without leading to internal contradictions and impairing the consistency of character. The principle through which any attitude can be made not only socially harmless but even useful, is *sublimation*.[27] It consists in turning the attitude exclusively toward situations that have in them an element endowed with social sacredness. . . . At present it is enough to point out that an object is socially sacred when it provokes in members of the group an attitude of reverence and when it can be profaned in the eyes of social opinion, by being connected with some other object.[28] There are many degrees of social sacredness; an object that may appear as sacred in comparison with another may be itself a source of profanation of a third. Thus, business has a feature of sacredness which becomes manifest when it is interfered with by frivolous things like drinking or the company of women of the demi-monde; but its sacredness is not very high since it can easily appear as profane when it interferes with scientific or religious interests. . . . And of course the degree of sacredness attached to different objects varies from group to group and from time to time . . . But in spite of all these variations of sacredness there are, from this point of view, higher and lower forms possible for every attitude, dependent on the relative degree of sacredness of the situations which it defines. Thus, the spirit of adventure may manifest itself in a criminal's career, in a cow-boy's or trapper's life, in the

[27] This is one of the few concepts that Thomas seems to have borrowed more or less directly from psychoanalysis, without altering the meaning. See pp. 196 ff. infra where Thomas considerably transforms the meaning of "unconscious" as used by the Freudians.

[28] Cf. Émile Durkheim, *The Elementary Forms of the Religious Life* (tr. Joseph W. Swain; London: Allen & Unwin, 1915), Book I, chap. 1, for the distinction between "sacred" and "profane."

activity of a detective, in geographical or ethnographical exploration; the desire for money, in stealing, gambling, "living by one's wits," commercial activity, great industrial organization; the sexual attitude may manifest itself in association with prostitutes, in relations, short but not devoid of individualization, with many girls and married women, in an ordinary marriage for the sake of the regulation of sexual life; in romantic love, in artistic creation, in religious mysticism. Even such attitudes as seem essentially harmful, as the desire of shedding blood, may become sublimated; the butcher's activity represents a lower degree of sublimation, surgery the highest. . . .

The principles of discrimination of situations [29] to which contrary attitudes should be applied and of sublimation of socially forbidden attitudes allow a rich and consistent character to develop without suppressions from any source, temperamental or social. The individual spontaneously tries to preserve his temperamental attitudes, and as he can do this only by removing contradictions between attitudes contending for supremacy and by sublimating attitudes that can find no expression in his milieu, and since society never gives him all the ready conventions and the whole hierarchy of sacredness that he needs, he is naturally led to create new discriminations and new valuations, and becomes a creative type simply by fully developing all of his possibilities. The only task of . . . culture is to prepare him for this creation by teaching him the mechanism of discrimination and sublimation in general, and not interfering with his efforts to preserve all that he is able to preserve of his individuality. It is the suppression that produces the two other fundamental characters, the Philistine and the Bohemian. If society is successful in repressing all the possibilities that seem directly or indirectly dangerous until a character is formed which excludes them once and forever, then the product tends to be an individual for whom there are no prob-

[29] This phrase obviously invites comparison with the principle of "discrimination" as formulated more systematically in the learning theory of Hull and his followers. E. R. Hilgard (*Theories of Learning,* New York: Appleton-Century-Crofts, 1948) has classified learning theories under two heads: the "associational" (of which Hull's is an example), and the "field," the former stressing past accumulation of habits, the latter the present situation. Since there has been some rivalry between adherents of the two schools, it is appropriate to recall Thomas' view that "Our behavior is historically, as well as contemporaneously, conditioned." ("The Problem of Personality in the Urban Environment," *Publications of the American Sociological Society,* Vol. 20, p. 32.)

lems of self-development left, no internal contradictions to solve, no external oppositions to overcome—a limited, stable, self-satisfied Philistine. If, on the contrary, the suppression is unsuccessful and the rebellious attitudes break out before a sufficiently stable set of contrary attitudes is formed, the individual is unprepared to meet the problems that arise, unable to discriminate or to sublimate, and an inconsistent, non-conformist, Bohemian type develops, which in its highest form, as artist, thinker, religious reformer, social revolutionist, may even succeed in producing, but whose products will always lack the internal harmony and social importance of the true creative type.

2. The construction of a life-organization in conformity with individual character may go on in two typically different ways. There may be ready social schemes which are imposed upon the individual, or the latter may develop his schemes himself, in agreement or non-agreement with those prevailing in his social environment. In the first case the scheme is usually given to the individual in an abstract form or through concrete examples, and then he is taught to apply it to the various situations which he meets by chance or which are especially created for him. In the second case he works out himself a definition of every new situation in conformity with his existing attitude, which grows in definiteness as the solved situation acts back upon it, and out of these definitions he gradually constructs a schematism.

Education gives us many examples of the first method. The inculcation of every moral norm, precept of behavior, logical rule, etc., follows this course. The formula or example is easily communicated; the difficulty begins with its application. It may happen that the individual has already defined situations spontaneously as the rule demands; then he accepts gladly the formulation of his own behavior which solves in advance the problem of reconciling this part of his life-organization with the social organization of the group. The well-known educational device is precisely to find among the individual's own actions such as are in accordance with the rule and then to state the rule as an induction from his own behavior. This is really an introduction of the second method, the one of spontaneous development, into the field of education. More frequently it happens that the individual has the attitude necessary to define situations in accordance with the rule, but the attitude lacks the determination that it needs to express itself in action, has not attained the consciousness of its social object enabling it to pass from the sphere of temperament into that of character. If then the individual has one or two situations defined for him it is enough to make him imitate this definition in the future and accept the scheme as a rule of behavior.

But the most common case is the one where the individual lacks the attitude which the social scheme demands. This is very general in the education of youth, where attitudes are developed progressively and the social group does not wait—and frequently cannot wait—for their spontaneous development, but forces the process so as to fit young people promptly into a social framework and have as little trouble with them as possible. Another general cause of the frequent failure of the social schemes to find ready response in the individual is their uniformity and stiffness. The social schematism is not adapted to the variety of individuals but to the artificial production of a minimum of uniformity. And even when this is successful the attitudes tend to evolve, not only in single individuals but also in the whole group, and this evolution is continuous, while the schemes can be changed only discontinuously, and so they remain behind—occasionally run ahead of—the social reality which they tend to express. From all these causes comes the continual and in a large measure fruitless effort to adapt the content of social life to its form—to produce attitudes to fit the schemes, while the contrary and more important process must be left largely to the individuals themselves.

The adaptation of attitudes to schemes may be pursued by two methods. The representatives of the social environment [30] can try to develop the attitude on the basis of some existing attitude by applying such social laws as may be known. This would be the normal and successful method, but though it is sometimes applied, its success

[30] Cf. "In the concrete, the individual personality is never directly affected by the group as a physical totality. Rather, his personality is molded by the particular members of the group with whom he has personal contact and by his conceptions of the group as a whole. . . . Concretely, not the group but group agents with their own peculiar traits determine personality formation." (Kluckhohn and Murray, *op. cit.*, p. 42.)

is now quite accidental, because, as we have indicated . . . social technique is at present in a purely empirical stage, for there are scarcely any social laws definitely demonstrated.[31] . . . By the second and more usual method the individual is forced to define situations according to the imposed scheme, because to every situation coming under the scheme some sanction is added, some value which appeals to an existing attitude of the individual. But if the sanction is a more or less successful device in suppressing temporarily the manifestation of undesirable attitudes until character is formed, it proves quite unsuccessful in developing desirable ones. The situation to which the sanction is added is quite different from what it would have been without the sanction; the scheme accepted is really not the scheme that society wanted to impose, but a different one, consisting fundamentally in an adaptation to the sanction, and the individual develops not the attitude demanded, but another one, a modification of the attitude provoked by the sanction. Thus—to take a familiar type of cases—by inducing the individual to comply with a moral norm through the fear of punishment or the hope of reward the idea of punishment or reward is added to every situation which demands the application of the moral norm. Then the situation is not the moral situation as such, but the moral situation *plus* the idea of punishment or reward; the scheme is not a moral scheme, but a scheme of prudence, a solution of the problem of avoiding punishment or of meriting reward; the attitude developed is not the moral attitude, but the fear of punishment or the hope of reward qualified by the given moral part of the situation.

When the individual constructs his life-organization himself instead of having it imposed upon him by society, his problem always consists, as we have already seen, in the determination of the vague. Any new situation is always vague and its definition demands not only intellectual analysis of the objective data but determination of the attitude itself, which becomes explicit and distinct only by manifesting itself in action. The definition of the new situation is therefore possible only if a new corresponding attitude can directly arise out of some preceding one, as its qualification or modification in view of the new values, and this determination of the attitude is in

[31] Cf. the Methodological Note, pp. 40 ff. supra.

turn possible only if the new situation can be defined on the ground of some analogy with known situations—as an old problem viewed from a new standpoint. . . . There is still a lingering of the past, a conscious or unconscious effort to interpret the new in terms of the old, to consider the recently formed type of behavior as a mere variation of the pre-existing type. The constitution of a new scheme at once makes conscious the evolution that has been accomplished—sometimes even makes the subject exaggerate its importance. In its light the recent changes appear as examples of a new general line of behavior, acquire an objectivity that they did not possess, for the scheme can be communicated to others, compared with social rules of behavior and can even become a social rule of behavior—for such is the source of every social reform.

The factor making the individual perceive and define new situations is always his own, conscious or subconscious, desire for new experience. There is no external power capable of forcing him to work out a new definition. . . . The usual doctrine that new ways of behavior, new definitions, appear as a result of adaptation to new external conditions is based upon a quite inadequate conception of adaptation. The common idea is that adaptation marks a certain fixed limit to which the individual has to approach, because as long as he has not reached it he is misadapted, and various calamities force him to adapt himself. But where is such a limit? It must be different for various individuals. Napoleon was adapted to the conditions of French life after the revolution, and so was any one of his guards; the honest and solid real estate owner is well adapted to the conditions of city life as is the successful pick-pocket. And it must change for every individual; the errand-boy who becomes a millionaire is no less adapted to his environment during his youth than in his later life. If adaptation means anything, it can be only a harmonious relation between individual claims and individual control of the environment; the harmony can be perfect whatever the range of claims and of control. But then the concept of readaptation to a changed environment loses its seeming precision. By an analogy with biological theories, the meaning that is given to readaptation in sociology is usually this, that the individual attains in the new conditions a range of control and claims relatively equal to those he had in the old conditions. This equality is not particularly difficult to determine in biology where for every organism a certain minimum can be fixed and the living being seldom goes far beyond this minimum. But how shall we fix a minimum of claims and control in social life? And without this the meaning of equality of range of adaptation becomes very unclear.

The real point is not adaptation as a state reached at a certain moment, but the process of the widening or narrowing of the sphere of adaptation. And this depends essentially upon the individual himself, not upon his environment. If the individual is satisfied with what he can get out of the given conditions he will not try to set and solve new problems, to see more in the situations he meets than he used to see or to find in his environment a greater complexity of situations than he used to find.[32] The dissatisfaction which the individual feels with what he can get out of given conditions arises frequently, indeed, when an external change makes it impossible to get the same results with the same efforts, but even then the individual may as well resign the results as increase his efforts.[33] The course he selects depends on the prevalence of the desire for new experience over the desire for stability, the first pushing him to find new methods and to widen the sphere of activity in order to preserve the old claims, the second tending to preserve the old form and range of activity in spite of the changed conditions and to be satisfied with the results that can be obtained in this way. . . .

With the formation of schemes it is different. A new scheme which the individual finds to express his new way of defining situations is not the result of the desire for new experience, but, on the contrary, the result of the desire for stability. Behavior that is not schematized . . . provokes a desire for a settlement. Moreover there are always plans to be made for the future requiring a conscious stabilization

[32] In this connection see the growing literature on "levels of aspiration"; for example, Kurt Lewin, Tamara Dembo, Leon Festinger, and Pauline S. Sears, "Level of Aspiration," in J. McV. Hunt, ed. *Personality and the Behavior Disorders* (New York: The Ronald Press Company, 1944), Vol. I, pp. 333–378.

[33] Taking a more explicit "functional" view, Kluckhohn and Murray suggest that one of the functions of personality is the "reduction of aspiration tensions" *(op. cit.,* pp. 20–21).

of the individual's own activity.[34] And thus . . . the individual, after a longer or shorter period during which new forms of behavior are developed, wants to fix his acquisition in a stable formula. And when such a moment comes, if the individual is unable to create his own scheme, he is ready to accept any one that is given to him and expresses more or less adequately his new way of defining situations. This explains such striking cases as the sudden "conversion" of individuals whose intellectual level is much above the doctrine to which they are converted, the influence that people of a limited intellectual power but of strong convictions can occasionally exercise over much more profound, but doubting personalities, and the incomprehensible social success of self-satisfied mediocrities during periods of intellectual unrest. Anything may become preferable to mental uncertainty.

Although there seems to be little difference between the schemes spontaneously created or selected by the individual and the schemes imposed by society, in the sense that both correspond to the way in which the individual actually does define situations, the different processes of development lead to the formation of quite opposite life-organizations. It is clear that if the individual learns to adapt his attitudes to the schemes given him he will always be dependent upon society and its ready schemes, and if society succeeds in imposing upon him a complete life-organization and in adapting his character to this, no further development will be possible for him unless his environment works out some new scheme; but even then it will be difficult for him to adapt himself to this new scheme in the degree that his life-organization and character have become stabilized. Or if he is temperamentally inclined to change he will pass from one form of behavior to another according to the schemes that actually happen to come in his way. A Philistine or Bohemian life-organization is thus the necessary result of this process in which schemes are imposed and attitudes are made to fit them. Bolshevism is really nothing but the disorganization of a society that was organized exclusively for

[34] Cf. Kluckhohn and Murray's concept of "serial programs," i.e., "one of the important functions of personality is the temporal arrangement of the sub-goals which must be attained in order to arrive at . . . destinations" (*ibid.*, p. 16).

Philistinism. On the contrary the individual who has learned to work out new schemes spontaneously will not be stopped in his evolution by the non-existence of a ready scheme nor disorganized at periods of social crisis, but will be able to construct progressively better schemes to suit his spontaneous evolution. . . . Thus an organization of life in view of creation is the result of the spontaneity of the process in which the individual elaborates schemes to fit his developing attitudes.

3. We pass now to the social aspect of the problem of personal evolution. We have seen that the social group tends to fit the individual perfectly into the existing organization and to produce a definite character as rapidly as possible. This character must also be stable, so that no surprises need be anticipated from its future development; simple, so that any member of the group, however limited his mental capacities, can understand it at once; presenting a perfect unity, in spite of the multiplicity of individual activities; based on attitudes common to all members and socially desirable, so that each member shall appreciate it positively. In other words, in its demands upon personal character society aims to stop individual evolution as early as possible, to limit the complexity of each personality as much as is compatible with the variety of interests which it is required to possess, to exclude all real or apparent irrationality of its manifestations in different fields of social civilization, to reduce the differences between personalities to a minimum compatible with the social division of classes and professions.

The tendency of society to produce such characters in its members is most efficient when the social environment is a primary group in which all his activities are enclosed. In such a group, as, for instance, a peasant community, all the individual interests are supposed to be subordinated to the predominant social interest, because all the values—hedonistic, economic, intellectual, aesthetic—which are within the reach of the individual are included in the stock of civilization of his primary group and controlled by it. . . . Every situation is first of all treated as a social situation and only secondarily as an economic, religious, sexual, aesthetic intellectual one.

The adaptation of the individual to the primary group requires, therefore, that all his attitudes be subordinated to those by which the group itself becomes for him a criterion of all values. These fundamental social attitudes are the *desire for response,* corresponding to the family system in the primary group-organization, and the *desire for recognition,* corresponding to the traditionally standardized systems of social values upon which the social opinion of the community bases its appreciations. The desire for response is the tendency to obtain a direct positive personal reaction to an action whose object is another individual; the desire for recognition is the tendency to obtain a direct or indirect positive appreciation of any action, whatever may be its object.[35] The desire for response is the common socio-psychological element of all those attitudes by which an individual tends to adapt himself to the attitudes of other individuals—family affection, friendship, sexual love, humility, personal subordination and imitation, flattery, admirative attachment of inferior to superior, etc. Of course each of the attitudes indicated by these terms is usually more or less compound and contains other elements besides the desire for response. . . . and yet the desire for response as such and independently of its further consequences is hardly ever absent even in the most radical examples of these contradictory attitudes. It is clearly an egotistic attitude and yet it contains a minimum of altruistic considerations. Its egotistic side makes it the most general and on the average the strongest of all those attitudes by which harmony is maintained and dissension avoided between the members of a group; it may be qualified, therefore, as representing the lowest possible, and yet precisely, therefore, in the large mass of mankind, the most efficient positive type of *emotional morality.*

The desire for recognition is the common element of all those attitudes by which the individual tends to impose the positive appreciation of his personality upon the group by adapting his activities to the social standards of valuation recognized by the group. It is found, more or less connected with other attitudes, in showing-off, pride, honor, feeling of self-righteousness, protection of inferiors, snobbishness, cabotinism, vanity, ambition, etc. It is the most com-

[35] It is interesting to note that Parsons has recently specified these two "wishes" or "desires" as components of the general motive of "self interest" and "satisfaction." See "The Motivation of Economic Activities," in his *Essays in Sociological Theory Pure and Applied* (Glencoe: The Free Press, 1949), pp. 208–209.

mon and most elementary, and probably the strongest factor pushing the individual to realize the highest demands which the group puts upon personal conduct, and, therefore, constitutes probably the primary source of *rational morality*.

These two fundamental social attitudes supplement each other, in normal conditions, in producing the general basis for a unified character, such as is needed in and demanded by the primary group.[36] If they sometimes conflict—as when the desire for recognition impels the individual to ignore the attitudes of his family when its standing in the community is low—the existence of a conflict usually shows a certain disorganization of the primary group itself; as long as the latter is consistent and strong the two fundamental social attitudes are more apt to strengthen each other than to conflict; for instance, family solidarity in the peasant community is one of the grounds of recognition, and a high recognition shown to a member by the community may produce in the relatives of this member a readiness to respond to him proportionate to the degree in which they are influenced by social opinion.

It is clear that an individual dominated by these attitudes, if he stays permanently within a primary group, can develop the very kind of character which society requires. His personality will be relatively stabilized at an early period . . . his character will be relatively simple, because primarily constituted by attitudes on the ground of which he can get response and recognition of many

[36] The relation between these wishes and social change is elaborated upon in another part of *The Polish Peasant:* "In order to induce the individual to accept a certain socially sanctioned definition . . . an appeal is made to the fundamental social attitudes on which the whole primary group system rests—the desire for response and the desire for recognition. The community implicitly assumes that these attitudes are an inexhaustible source from which, whenever necessary and under any circumstances, active tendencies to conform with socially sanctioned definitions can be derived. . . .

"This method is very well adapted to the average psychology of primary-group members . . . But when its only object is to help maintain the traditional rules, its limitations are evident. Its results, and often the very possibility of its application, depend on precisely those conditions which the process of disorganization tends to destroy or modify. It presupposes that the community is still solidary and coherent enough to organize for the defense of the old system, that the fundamental primary-group attitudes are still vital and strong in the members who are to be reformed and that the satisfaction of their desires for response and recognition cannot be adequately obtained outside of the community." (Vol. II, 1927, pp. 1258–1259.)

members of the group; *i.e.*, by the most average and commonplace attitudes; it will present few, if any, important conflicts, for conflicts appear when the individual has many incompatible interests, whereas here all interests are subordinated to the social interest; finally, it will be positively appreciated by the whole group, since all the members of the latter possess and want to possess in a large measure similar tendencies.

But such a stabilization and unification of character on the ground of the desires for response and recognition becomes more and more rare with the progress of civilization. Even in the still existing primary groups it tends to diminish as members of these groups get in contact with the external world. Every attempt of a member of such a group to define his situations from the standpoint of his hedonistic, economic, religious, intellectual, instead of his social attitudes is in fact a break in his character, and such attempts become more and more frequent as, through extra-communal experiences, the individual finds before him situations that are not connected with the primary group—for example, when in the city he has the opportunity of drinking without any ceremonial occasion, when he earns money by hired labor instead of working on the family farm, when he can have a sexual experience without passing through the system of familial courtship, when he learns anything alone by reading and not in common with the whole village from a news-bearer, etc.[37] But since the educational factors of his new environment which might replace those of the old are not at first given him, and he is unable to develop a character by his own efforts, such new experiences destroy the old unity of character without constructing a new one, and we witness partial disorganization from which only gradually new types emerge—the economic climber, the student, etc. And then the problem assumes a new form.

A complex modern society is no longer in all its parts in immediate touch with its members. It is composed, indeed, of small groups whose members are in personal interrelations; but none of these groups can enclose all the interests of the individual, because each one has only a limited and specialized field. Therefore individual character can be no longer unified upon the basis of the general

[37] Cf. "The Individualization of Behavior," pp. 238–258 infra.

desires for response and recognition, for even if these desires always remain fundamental for social relations, they must be differently qualified in different groups. The kind of response and recognition the individual gets in his family, in his church, in his professional group, in his political party, among his companions in pleasure, varies within very wide limits. It is based now upon the special activities which constitute the object of interest of every special group. Therefore the ground of the unity of character must now be sought in attitudes corresponding to these activities; the character of the social personality can no longer be unified by a reduction of all special attitudes to a general social basis but by an organization of these attitudes themselves.

But the difficulty is that each limited and specialized social group tends to impose upon every member a specific character corresponding to its particular line of common interests,[38] wants him to be mainly, if not exclusively, a family member, a religious person, a professional, a political party member, a sportsman, a drunkard, etc., and expects his other attitudes to be subordinated to one particular kind of attitude. . . .

But precisely because of the growing specialization of occupational groups, cases of character formed exclusively by adaptation to one occupational group are becoming less and less frequent.[39] The modern individual usually belongs to different groups, each of which undertakes to organize a certain kind of his attitudes. But it remains true that the way in which these various complexes of attitudes are combined usually shows a complete lack of organization. An individual of this type is a completely different man in his shop, in his family, with his boon campanions, preserving his balance by distributing his interests between different social groups, until it is impossible to understand how such a multiplicity of disconnected, often radically conflicting characters, can co-exist in what seems to be one

[38] Cf. Ralph Linton, "Problems of Status Personality," in Sargent and Smith, eds. *Culture and Personality,* pp. 163–174.

[39] It might be of interest to compare this analysis with that of Durkheim in *The Division of Labor in Society* (tr. George Simpson; Glencoe: The Free Press, 1947). In the Preface to the first edition Durkheim wrote: "This work had its origins in the question of the relations of the individual to social solidarity." (*De la division du travail social,* Paris: F. Alcan, 1893, p. 37.)

personality. This is a new style Philistinism—the Philistinism of the dissociated personality, amounting to a sort of stabilized Bohemianism. And a striking feature of modern society . . . is the fact that society does not notice this chaotic and mechanical stabilization of the character of its member, provided he shows himself properly adapted to the minimum demands of each of the special groups to which he belongs, and does not give an undue prevalence to one of his particular characters at the expense of others. . . . We may even make a more general supposition: The "moral unrest" so deeply penetrating all western societies, the growing vagueness and indecision of personalities, the almost complete disappearance of the "strong and steady character" of old times, in short, the rapid and general increase of Bohemianism and Bolshevism in all societies, is an effect of the fact that not only the early primary group controlling all interests of its members on the general social basis, not only the occupational group of the mediaeval type controlling most of the interests of its members on a professional basis, but even the special modern group dividing with many others the task of organizing permanently the attitudes of each of its members, is more and more losing ground.[40] The pace of social evolution has become so rapid that special groups are ceasing to be permanent and stable enough to organize and maintain organized complexes of attitudes of their members which correspond to their common pursuits. In other words, society is gradually losing all its old machinery for the determination and stabilization of individual characters.

. . . The center of pedagogical and ethical attention must, therefore, be entirely shifted; not attainment of stability, but organization of the very process of personal evolution for its own sake should be the conscious task of social control. At the present moment society not only lacks any methods by which it could actually and continuously organize the change of attitudes of its members, but it is only beginning (in our experimental schools) to search consistently for methods of education by which the individual can be trained in his youth to organize his later evolution spontaneously and without social help. At present the individual who succeeds in producing

[40] Cf. Robert K. Merton, "Social Structure and Anomie," in his *Social Theory and Social Structure,* pp. 125–149.

for himself such a dynamic organization has to do it by his own devices, is forced to invent for himself all the methods of self-education which he needs without profiting by the past experiences of others, and must consider himself lucky if his environment does not interfere with him too efficiently by trying to impose upon him a stable character.

4. The chief social problem arising with reference to the relation between individual life-organization and social organization is the reconciliation of the stability of social systems with the efficiency of individual activities, and the most significant feature of social evolution in this line is the growing difficulty of maintaining a stable social organization in the face of the increasing importance which individual efficiency assumes in all domains of cultural life.

In early societies we find individual efficiency entirely subordinated to the demand for social stability.[41] All the social schemes of the group are connected, are parts of one whole, one large complex of social tradition . . . The individual must make each and all of these schemes his own in order to be a full member of the group. If for the formation of his character the important point is that all his interests are satisfied within the group and therefore are supposed to be founded on his social interest, the essential thing about his life-organization is that he is supposed to share in all the interests of his group and to adopt all social schemes as schemes of his personal behavior. There may be some differentiation between individuals as to the relative importance which certain particular interests assume in their lives, but no specialization in the sense of an absorption by some particular interests to the exclusion of others. Each member of a primary group is by a gradual initiation introduced into all the domains which compose the civilization of the group and is as all-sided in his activities as the stage of civilization which his group has reached permits him to be.

. . . When [then] . . . the primary group is brought rapidly into contact with the outside world with its new and rival schemes, the entire old organization is apt to break down at once, precisely because all the old schemes were interconnected in social consciousness; and the individual whose life-organization was based on the

[41] Cf. "The Primary Group and the Definition of the Situation," pp. 226–231 infra.

organization of his primary group is apt also to become completely disorganized in the new conditions, for the rejection of a few traditional schemes brings with it a general negative attitude toward the entire stock of traditions which he has been used to revere, whereas he is not prepared for the task of reorganizing his life on a new basis. . . .

But with the growing social differentiation and the increasing wealth and rationality of social values, the complex of traditional schemes constituting the civilization of a group becomes subdivided into several more or less independent complexes. The individual can no longer be expected to make all these complexes his own; he must specialize. There arises also between the more or less specialized groups representing different more or less systematic complexes of schemes a conscious or half-conscious struggle for the supremacy of the respective complexes or systems in social life, and it happens that a certain system succeeds in gaining a limited and temporary supremacy. . . .

. . . Moreover each of the broad complexes which we designate by the terms "religion," "state," "nationality," "industry," "science," "art," etc., splits into many smaller ones and specialization and struggle continue between these. The prevalent condition of our civilization in the past and perhaps in the present can thus be characterized as that of a plurality of rival complexes of schemes each regulating in a definite traditional way certain activities and each contending with others for supremacy within a given group. The antagonism between social stability and individual efficiency is under these circumstances further complicated by the conflicting demands put upon the individual by these different complexes, each of which tends to organize personal life exclusively in view of its own purposes.

Whenever there are many rival complexes claiming individual attention the group representing each complex not only allows for but even encourages a certain amount of creation, of new developments, within the limits of the traditional schemes . . . Therefore the conservative groups which support any existing schematism want it to be alive, to be as adaptable to the changing conditions of life as is compatible with the existence of the traditional schemes. The amount of efficiency which a scheme makes possible varies, of course, with the nature of the scheme itself, with the rigidity with which the group keeps the mere form, with the rapidity of the social process. . . .

But such a traditional fixation of special complexes of schemes within which efficiency is required with the condition that all schemes remain recognized does not correspond at all with the spontaneous tendencies of individuals. First of all, the scheme represents for the evolving individual either the minimum of stability which he reaches after a period of changing active experiences, or the minimum of new active experiences which he reaches after a period of passive security. . . . The individual may indeed oscillate, so to speak, from relative passivity to relative creativeness without going far enough in the first direction to become entirely inefficient, and without becoming so efficient as to have to reject the scheme; the less radical these oscillations, the more the individual's conduct approaches the average prescribed by the scheme. . . . Frequently, however, the individual goes on with a progressively intense and efficient activity, tries continually to find and to define new situations; his efficiency becomes then increasingly dangerous to the scheme, because even if activity begins in perfect conformity with the scheme, the accumulating novelty of experience sooner or later makes the scheme appear insufficient. . . .

The second difficulty concerning the adaptation of individual life-organization to the social complexes is the fact that while a complex has to be accepted or rejected in its entirety, since the group does not permit the individual to accept some schemes and to reject others, the individual in his spontaneous development tends to make a selection of schemes from various complexes, thus cutting across social classifications of schemes, and often including in his dynamic life-organization successively, or even simultaneously, elements which from the traditional standpoint may seem contradictory. . . . The individual who has a complex imposed upon him or accepts it voluntarily is expected to show the prescribed amount of efficiency—neither more nor less—in all activities regulated by the schemes belonging to the complex, and is not expected to perform any activities demanded by a rival complex, or to invent any new schemes which may seem to disagree with the accepted ones. More than this, he is often required to abstain from activities which, even if they do not contradict directly the existing schematism, may take his time and energy from the performance of the prescribed activities.

It is obvious that this type of social organization disregards entirely the personal conditions of efficiency. . . . The organization of activities demanded by a social complex is both impersonal and changeless, whereas an organization which would fulfill the conditions of the highest individual efficiency would have to be personal and changing.

An unavoidable consequence of the now prevalent social organization is that the immense majority of individuals is forced either into Philistinism or Bohemianism. An individual who accepts any social system in its completeness, with all the schemes involved, is necessarily drifting toward routine and hypocrisy. A part of the system may satisfy his personal needs for a time, particularly as long as he is gradually assimilating and applying certain of its schemes, but the rest of the system will not correspond to his predominant aspirations and may be even opposed to them. . . . In order to remain socially adapted, to avoid active criticism of the group, the individual has then to display in words interests which he does not possess and to invent all kinds of devices in order to conceal his lack of efficiency. This tendency to hypocrisy and pretense is greatly facilitated in such cases by the fact that the majority of the group is in a similar situation and is not only willing to accept any plausible pretension designed to cover individual inefficiency but even often develops a standardized set of "conventional lies" to be used for this purpose, which every one knows to be lies but tacitly agrees to treat as true.

If, on the contrary, the individual either refuses to accept certain of the schemes included in a social complex or develops some positive form of behavior contradicting in the eyes of society some of the schemes of the complex, he is forced to reject the complex in its entirety, and becomes thus, voluntarily or not, a rebel. His situation is then rather difficult, for society has not trained him to develop a life-organization spontaneously and the social organization of the type outlined above opposes innumerable obstacles to such a development. With rare exceptions, he can do nothing but adopt some other ready system instead of the rejected one. But then the same problem repeats itself, and every successive attempt at complete adaptation to a new system after rebellion is usually more difficult than the preceding ones, both because the personal demands of the individual become better and better defined in opposition to social regulation and because each particular rebellion undermines the prestige of social systems in general. The usual consequence of rebellion is thus Bohemianism, a permanent tendency to pass from one system to another, attracted at first by the personally interesting sides of a system and soon repelled by the personally uninteresting ones. The result is again unproductivity. . . .

It is clear that these new characters of modern social evolution require an entirely new standpoint with reference to individual life-organization. The individual must be trained not for conformity, but for efficiency, not for stability, but for creative evolution. And we cannot wait until new educational methods are developed by the slow and groping way of unorganized and unreflective empirical trials. We must realize that social education in the past, viewed from the standpoint of the human personality, has always been a failure and that whatever social progress and whatever personal development has ever been achieved was due to the spontaneous constructive power of individuals who succeeded, not thanks to social help but in spite of social hindrances. The best that society has ever done for its members was to put at their disposal materials for creative development by preserving values produced by the past. The task of future society will be not only to remove obstacles preventing spontaneous personal development but to give positive help, to furnish every individual with proper methods for spontaneous personal development, to teach him how to become not a static character and a conformist, but a dynamic, continually growing and continually creative personality. And such methods can be found only by socio-psychological studies of human individuals.

10 PERSONALITY AND THE CONTEXT OF THE FAMILY

In August 1926 the Social Science Research Council held a conference of members of its advisory committees at Hanover, New Hampshire. Thomas, a member of a committee on personality traits and community factors in juvenile delinquency, was a participant and the speaker at an evening session. The following selection is taken from the informal paper which he gave on this occasion. It has not been published before.

After reviewing his general position that the meaning of an experience is given only by a knowledge of the context in which it appears, Thomas emphasized the importance of knowing the extent to which a person has been conditioned by critical incidents or by the steady habitual influence of the social environment. In this connection the family, as the "primary conditioning agency," is introduced as a cultural influence on personality.

Formerly, the family was a large kin group, practically coterminous with the community. It formed the major context in which individuals developed, and their integration into this wider group was such that the influence of the family was regular and decisive. Now, however, the family is not coterminous with the community; it is not a large kin group, but a married pair and their offspring, and this creates new problems of individual adjustment. In our typical small family group, emotions are exaggerated, and the child is not prepared for the hostile or indifferent larger community of which the family is but a segment. Critical experiences multiply with the result that personality disorders are increased rather than lessened.

Within the broad outline of Thomas' thought, this selection emerges as a brief study of the influence of a specific institution on personality development. It also touches upon the importance of critical experiences in individual lives, and the way in which changed situations lead to altered behavior and new problems of adjustment. Thus it represents several features of Thomas' theories.

Methods of Approaching the Problem of Child Study with Particular Reference to the Delinquent [1]

I have become interested in the adequacy and inadequacy of available materials for the study of personality development in the nor-

[1] Unpublished minutes of the Social Science Research Council Hanover Conference, August 23 – September 2, 1926, Vol. II, pp. 322–327.

mal, abnormal, and the criminal. My own interest in behavior is somewhat from the standpoint of what would now be called the Gestalt psychology—the meaning always emerges in a context.[2] The isolated experience has no psychological meaning. It is necessary to know something of the total experience of the individual in order that the particular behavior manifestation, whether crime or other activity, some ambitious scheme or creative activity, may, as an item, be understood in a context.

In the same connection, there is no logical separation between the normal and the abnormal. They should be studied together for completeness and because of the context. Certain children, for example, behave in perfectly normal ways in socially abnormal situations. The ideal would be, so far as materials are concerned, records of a large variety of behavior reactions displayed in total situations, in the whole life experience representing normal, pathological, and delinquent subjects. . . .

You will understand also that I do not find exactly in the records the materials which I should desire to have in some of my own pursuits, and that I do not expect you to organize a scheme for preparing them. At the same time, I would present my general behavior standpoint as if I had in view the documentation of behavior.

First of all, I will take a somewhat dogmatic general standpoint. Since Pavlov's first experiments on the conditioned reflex, the conditioned reaction has had growing recognition, and to some of us, the characteristic behavior traits of individuals, races, and nationalities appear so largely a result of a series of conditionings that the questions of biological heredity, germ plasm, and constitutional differences recede greatly in importance; they are practically . . . negligible. The behavior patterns seem to be essentially fashions, dif-

[2] The Gestalt concept in psychology goes back to Ehrenfels in 1890, but its influence in social psychology, at least in America, was not felt until the 1920's through the early writings of Köhler, Koffka, and Wertheimer. Markey has suggested that Thomas' insistence on the "situation," or the total context, as a factor in behavior diminished the direct contributions of Gestaltism to social psychology. See J. F. Markey, "Trends in Social Psychology," in George A. Lundberg and others, eds. *Trends in American Sociology* (New York: Harper & Brothers, 1929), p. 153. More recently, of course, the work of Sherif and Lewin, among others, has made new contributions in this direction.

fering from fashions in dress only in the fact that they are not seasonal but developed rather through decades and centuries, and so the changes are more imperceptible. . . .

At any rate, if we proceed from the standpoint of conditioning, having some study and documentation in view, it is important to note to what extent the factors which determine personality are due to one of two factors: first, the steady, habitudinally impressed influence of the social environment, the family, community, and other institutions, which influences are not acutely felt but are pressed in constantly; and on the other hand, how far to certain critical experiences.[3] That is, a common body of habit is developed in children always and everywhere beginning with the reflexes, automatisms, relation to parents, Ten Commandments or their equivalent. The ordinary run of daily experience in a given situation, geographical environment, social environment, tends to make a type of a certain kind—Englishman, Bostonian, Mississippian, Puritan, Pagan—but I suspect that certain critical experiences tend to form the traits differentiating the individual from the others in his community or family.[4]

It is the experience of many, perhaps all of us, that our life directions, our general projects, have turned upon the influence of personalities. I remember two winters ago the scenic artist Bakst gave some account of his own artistic development. He said when a child of four, he was taken by his parents to hear Patti sing in what was then St. Petersburg. It was necessary in the opera (which was La Sonnabula) for the prima donna to drink poison and die. At that point, the child made an outcry. He wouldn't have it. After the play, he was taken to Patti's dressing room. She took him on her lap and reassured him, and she took her make-up materials and drew red lines, lengthened his eyebrows in black, and made his face

[3] Cf. pp. 298–299 infra for a later, more detailed formulation of these problems.

[4] Cf. "Obviously, the institutions of a society, beginning with the family, form the character of its members almost as the daily nutrition forms their bodies, but this is for everybody, and the unique attitudes of the individual and his unique personality are closely connected with certain incidents or critical experiences particular to himself, defining the situation, giving a psychological set, and often determining the whole life-direction." ("The Problem of Personality in the Urban Environment," *op. cit.*, p. 31.)

up. When he got home, the nurse attempted to wash him but he wouldn't have it. Psychologically, that never washed out. It was the base of his artistic set.

In other words, I mean that we should take note in our studies, first, of the total milieu and, second, of the particular psychological set, which is again context.

Any scheme of study and documentation should also provide data for determining how far, as over against a single critical incident or series of them, the causes of any behavior pattern, say delinquency, are multiple and cumulative. Burt,[5] the English criminologist, has emphasized the point that a child may have one or two deficiencies, but that the accumulation of those is an important matter to observe. This information about multiple and cumulative causation would put us in position to form welfare programs that would avoid the particularistic schemes of social welfare. It is notorious that specialists in medicine tend to look for and find the cause of the disease in the line of their specialty whether they are liver specialists, kidney specialists, heart specialists, surgeons, or internalists. Similarly, programs of welfare tend to fix on a particular influence—bad homes, bad mother fixation, bad sex habits, inferior I.Q., lack of religious influence, and so forth.

A general question of great importance arises at once in connection with any scheme of this sort, that is, of the social norms and values, and how far these and the institutions representing them correspond with the spontaneous behavior tendencies of the young. Obviously, they do not completely and cannot, because we have to regulate behavior. The disparity between the generations at the present moment is very striking. Children differ in behavior from their parents as widely as races and nationalities differ among themselves. Rabbi Wise is reported as saying recently, he was happy to say his son still spoke to him. How far do institutions and their representatives represent present realities, the present trend of evolution? What is essential and not essential to moral life in the traditional codes? Too great a divergence from reality in the preceptual code causes total loss of control. No boy could live by the Old Testament; no girl could live by the code of her grandmother. The salvationists among

[5] Cyril Burt, *The Young Delinquent* (New York: D. Appleton and Company, 1925).

social workers (and there are many) would attempt to impose norms that are really not used.

In this connection, the family as the primary conditioning agency, definer of norms, calls for the most scrupulous and extensive analysis and documentation. The main behavior trends are determined here, and we do not even know at all how extensive may be the remodeling which the larger society may be able to make later. Watson thinks very little; I think more.[6] It would appear that the modern family, generally speaking, is very weak, totally inadequate. In former times, before the development of communication and print and crowded populations, the family and community did succeed in remarkable degree in subordinating the wishes of its members to given norms, that is, the wishes of the group as a whole. Almost the whole life of the savage and peasant was predetermined by his society. It is true this was accomplished at the sacrifice of what we prize very highly—individual variation and initiative.

It may be said the main idea at this stage was as early and complete a fixation of character as possible. The young person should work, be married, and settled as soon as possible. It meant the sacrifice of new experience to security, prevalence of utility selection of interests over hedonistic selection. This task was accomplished almost as thoroughly as the living organism is integrated by the participation of all its members in a common work.

But there is, I think, a general misapprehension as to the function of the family in this situation historically. The family was not a married pair and their offspring, but a relatively large kinship group, including marriage kin. In making a study of the Polish peasant, I found it impossible to use the word "family" for the married pair and children. It was necessary to call this the "marriage pair," and reserve the term "family" for the larger kinship group.[7]

In such a group as that, the family in our sense, both parents and

[6] No doubt Watson did emphasize early conditioning, but for evidence that he did not neglect later learning see his "Practical and Theoretical Problems in Instinct and Habit," in Herbert S. Jennings and others, *Suggestions of Modern Science Concerning Education,* especially pp. 91–95. In this connection see also the concept of "enculturation" as developed by Herskovits, *Man and His Works,* pp. 40–41.

[7] Cf. p. 201 infra where this distinction is attributed to the problems encountered in translating the Polish materials.

children, was largely controlled by the larger group. It had a context outside of itself, that is, the larger group would be the kin and community.[8] These large families were in competition. The norm of marriage, for instance, was not love but respect and status, and the preservation of that in marriage. The parents of the married pair interfered to see that that was true. At present, we do not know our neighbors, we do not associate intensively with our kin. The small family never was, in the history of the world, an agency which formed alone the character of children. That is, the task which we are claiming it cannot perform now, it never did perform. It is true we have the church and the school and other institutions, but the face-to-face relation and the gossip and the taboo of a larger group are gone.

As to the present disabilities of the family, in this situation, unfortunately human nature unless conditioned by some experiences and ideals does not tend to be altogether sweet in small groups. Men do not get along together on arctic expeditions in small groups, and it is the same in the West with herders; and it is only in groups where the wishes of the individual are limited by the fear of the reaction of a larger censoring group that we have regulated emotional behavior.

I refer to the fact men tend to be cruel, sadistic, diabolical, when placed in positions of unlimited power. I will not elaborate this point; I am thinking of the atrocities, the development of blood-lust, among the representatives of superior races when placed among inferior races, the brutalities to children reported in the English Society for the Prevention of Cruelty to Children, and Moll's *Sexual Life of the Child* has a lot of very sad stuff on the way parents are able to treat children. On the other hand, there is in the family love, parental love, reciprocal love from children. This is idealized and sublimated, and often tends to be as bad as the other because it is

[8] Cf. "Causes that counteract individualization within the family are chiefly influences of the primary community of which the family is a part. If social opinion favors family solidarity and reacts against any individualistic tendencies, and if the individual keeps in touch with the community, his desire for recognition compels him to accept the standards of the group and to look upon his individualistic tendencies as wrong. But if the community has lost its coherence, if the individual is isolated from it, . . . there are no social checks important enough to counterbalance disorganization." (*The Polish Peasant,* 1927, Vol. II, p. 1168.)

over-determined. Between domination and love, parents spoil and distort the development of their children to an astonishing degree. They demand forms of behavior representing fixity, conformity to norms that are a remnant of older family organization, not represented really in the lives of the parents themselves, but heritages, like the dead hand in law—not justified from the standpoint of utility, but rationalized as good for the children by the parents.

Adjustment to modern life demands not fixed but plastic forms of behavior, not uniformity but diversity of development. The proper ideal of development is continuous change or evolution, so that the cessation of growth would not coincide with physical maturity but more nearly with the point of death.

There is thus a sort of antinomy between the family ideals and the evolution of the personality of the child. Furthermore, parents tend to use their children for the realization of their own wishes and relief of their own infirmities. Only this month, the New York newspapers recorded a case in which a mother shot her two-year old child and herself and left a note for her husband, saying, "The only way I could spite you was to kill the child." On the other hand, the pride of parents in a precocious child may lead to such sheltering and pampering as to make it queer, timid, awkward, and finally throw it out of adjustment with the school and society. Too much love and too much hate are generated in family relations, and it often appears the family is the worst possible place for the child.[9]

[9] Cf. "The Configurations of Personality," pp. 201–203 infra, for a further statement of this position.

11 THE CONFIGURATIONS OF PERSONALITY

The final selection of Part II contains Thomas' last published work in personality theory. Entitled "The Configurations of Personality," it appeared in *The Unconscious: A Symposium,* published in 1927 with an Introduction by Mrs. W. F. Dummer.

Here Thomas is primarily concerned with analyzing the creative process in terms of the "unconscious." Approaching the concept of the "unconscious" from a sociological standpoint, Thomas finds that it is manifested in several ways: as "visceral unconscious," "lapsed memory," and the "creative imagination." Presumably these represent configurations which all individuals have in varying degrees, but Thomas merely illustrates the first two and concentrates on the third.

Using Coleridge and his poetry as a case in point, Thomas analyzes the dynamics of the creative process: what takes place between the point of initial stimulation and the final product. This process is marked by three stages. First there is a more or less ordinary human experience; second this experience is elaborated and proliferated in the unconscious; and finally there is the conscious transformation of the experience into the desired image. Thus Coleridge's reading supplied the material with which the unconscious had to work, and out of this emerged conscious poetical form.

Several features of this selection are noteworthy. In addition to the penetrating analysis of Coleridge which it contains, it reveals clearly how Thomas was not a mere passive borrower of concepts. Rather, he took over the idea of the "unconscious" and creatively endowed it with new meanings and applications, thereby adding to our knowledge of the human personality. Thomas suggests that the *force créatrice* is not the unique possession of a few individuals, but is common in human experience. What differentiates the ordinary from the extraordinary individual is the extent to which the creative configuration is encouraged and exercised, and the social value which is placed upon the creative product.

THE UNCONSCIOUS—CONFIGURATIONS OF PERSONALITY [1]

I

The classification of personalities by psychological types on the basis of extravert and introvert tendencies has a certain value. . . .

[1] From C. M. Child and others, *The Unconscious: A Symposium* (New York: Alfred A. Knopf, 1927), Chapter VI, pp. 143–177. By permission.

It is plain, however, that persons are usually extravert at one moment and introvert at another, and the same person may be disposed in one direction at one age level and stage of maturation and in the other direction at another, and we further have no data as to the role played by conditioning factors, which is certainly a very great one.

At any rate, instead of taking this line of approach, I am assuming, at least for the initial standpoint for the study of the formation of the personality, that there are certain satisfactions, objects of desire, which men always and everywhere want and seek to secure, and we may speak of these satisfactions as values. These values will be found also to fall into classes or fields, corresponding partly with instinctive or unlearned action tendencies and partly with learned or conditioned tendencies. We may speak of the action tendencies as attitudes and of the values as stimuli.

From this standpoint a personality would be regarded as an organization of attitudes,[2] and personalities would be distinguished among themselves by their greater or less tendency to seek their satisfactions, play their roles, in this or that field of the values.[3] But we have to make the same remark here as with reference to extravert and introvert types—a few will be found characterized by a preponderance of this or that attitude and value, while the many will represent a mingling of all of them. Moreover, it will appear that in connection with stages of physical and mental and emotional maturation the personality will be weighted differently with the different attitudes and values, and questions will always arise with reference to constitutional traits as against habit formation.

Viewed, then, as a configuration, a personality would be a background of attitudes and values common to everybody, upon which

[2] In 1948, discussing trends in personality conceptions, Kluckhohn and Murray state that one such trend "is towards some idea of an *organization*, rather than a sum, of responses and action systems. This constitutes a decided improvement." (*Personality in Nature, Society, and Culture*, pp. 7–8.)

[3] Cf. Thomas' definition of personality in American Psychiatric Association and Social Science Research Council, *Proceedings: Second Colloquium on Personality Investigation* (Baltimore: Johns Hopkins Press, 1930), p. 155: "Assuming that 'attitudes' are tendencies to act, and that 'values' are objects or goals desired, a personality represents an organization or configuration of attitudes as related to values. The preponderance of certain attitudes and values in the configuration will determine the role the person plays or attempts to play in a society, and will distinguish also the 'person' from the 'individual.' "

certain attitudes and values, or constellations of attitudes and values, assume a prominent or perhaps a dominant position.[4] . . .

But assuming that these attitudes and values are represented in every person in some proportions and that the type of personality depends on the character of their organization among themselves, we still have only a description, a possible classification or schedule, while we are here interested in the selection and arrangement of preferences as represented in a concrete personality. This must be understood, if at all, in connection with the experience[5] of the individual, the kind of materials he has in consciousness, and the organization of these materials into his unique habit system and stimulus system will have to be related also to the habit systems and stimulus system of the groups with which he has more or less intimacy.

With reference to the unconscious in this connection, it is not my intention to speak of this psychologically but sociologically. And from the standpoint of the problems with which I have to deal, I seem to meet with not one but several manifestations of the unconscious. For my purpose here also, the conscious and the unconscious represent simply more and less awareness of what is going on.

II

There is a phase of habit formation and the unconscious which could be compared rather extensively with Professor Child's data on the structuralization of the organism by the operation of the stimuli of the environment.

[4] Six paragraphs are omitted here since they are devoted to summarizing the "four wishes"—only now the term "wish" has been dropped in favor of "classes of values." The general ambiguity which surrounds the terms "attitudes," "values," and "wishes" is nowhere better demonstrated than here. As Blumer has remarked of the use of "attitude" and "value" in *The Polish Peasant:* "Frequently, the authors refer to essentially the same thing by either attitude or value; in other places, either term might be substituted for the other without changing the meaning of the discussion." (*An Appraisal of . . . The Polish Peasant,* p. 25.)

The point is especially significant when it is recalled that the wishes were originally regarded by Thomas as fundamental classes of attitudes.

[5] Cf. "The Problem of Personality in the Urban Environment," *op. cit.,* p. 32, where the organization of experiences is called "an experience complex." Here Thomas also remarks: "You can never know, under a given stimulus, which experience complex will come to the front and determine the behavior reaction" (p. 37).

An observer in California, for example, visited a family of fruit-pickers and noticed a boy of twelve tossing in his sleep and picking here at the coverlet and in the air. The mother explained that he was going through the movement of picking prunes. . . . The repetition of the activity had tended to structuralize the organism of the boy.* . . .

Something of this kind appears in connection with the attempts of Stefansson to break the dogs of his arctic teams of their food habits. He found that his dogs would not eat anything they were not accustomed to eating. Dogs brought up on a diet of seal, caribou meat and fish were taken to a region where nothing was obtainable except geese and "for several days all the dogs in the team refused to eat, and one dog persisted for more than a week before eating at all, although he had to work part of the time." On another occasion Stefansson's party happened to kill a wolf, and as the dogs of this team had never tasted wolf meat, he took occasion to break the dogs of this food prejudice, thinking he might later be in a situation where only wolf meat was available. "We did not," he says, "know exactly the ages of our dogs, but could judge them roughly by the teeth. One of the dogs was presumably two or three years older than any other member of the team. There were six dogs altogether. We offered them the meat for three or four days before any of them ate any of it. Then they began to eat it . . . in the order of their age, the youngest being the first to give in. The oldest dog went for two weeks without swallowing any of the wolf meat, although he occasionally took a piece of it in his mouth and dropped it again." This particular dog never gave in. He became skin and bones and it was necessary to feed him with caribou meat to save his life. On the other hand, Stefansson mentions that dogs accustomed to foraging about ships on the coast had no food prejudices whatever. The same writer had a similar experience with a tribe of Eskimo in Coronation Gulf who had never eaten a berry known as the "salmon berry," and appreciated by all other tribes whom he had met. The children tried this food readily, the men without much resistance, but the women not at all.** In the same connection it is notorious that the European

* Arthur Gleason, "Little Gypsies of the Fruit," *Hearst's International,* Feb., 1924.
** V. Stefansson, "Food Tastes and Food Prejudices of Men and Dogs," *Scientific Monthly,* 11:540–543.

peasant will not readily taste food to which he is not accustomed. "Was der Bauer nicht kennt, isst er nicht."

Up to this point we have a determination of preferences and the assumption of roles, so to speak, without awareness, without conscious choice, without reference to persons, an environmental imposition, dependent on the consistent repetition of stimulus.

On the other hand, we have in much the same situations the possibility of quite the contrary. The dogs who foraged about ships became cosmopolitan in taste; the gourmet, as over against the peasant, makes the selection of foods a leading role. The repetition of stimulus leads also to aversion. Pairs of men get on each other's nerves. Madame de Maintenon said: "I have always observed that our great aversions have their birth in the repetition of trivialities." There are situations where married people grow alike and the more frequent ones where they acquire quick aversions. . . .

The repetition of stimulus hampers movements . . . on the one hand and gives heightened stimulation on the other. This is seen in those situations called ambivalent and represented in the relation of mother and child. Bleuler reports of one of his patients who had poisoned her child that she was later in great despair, but he noticed that during her moaning and crying she smiled quite perceptibly. And in one of his sketches Anatole France represents a little boy who when his mother came to kiss him good-night put his arm around her neck and gave her a hug, but wished that he could strangle her. . . .

This region I am in the habit of calling the "visceral unconscious." I give one more example involving a conflict between this unconscious and the region of the conscious. A white woman loves poetry, reads the poems of Dunbar and seeks an occasion to meet him. She knows he is black, but she is conditioned by such phrases as "equality," "fraternity," and prepared to be very cordial to a black poet. During the interview she holds up very well, but afterwards, on her return home, she is nauseated.*

III

This is the region of the formation of aversions and preferences and evidently furnishes some of the basic factors in the structuraliza-

* Communicated to me by Professor R. E. Park.

tion of persons and societies. There is another region of the unconscious which may be described as the "lapsed conscious." [6] It occupies a large and useful place in every life but simple and primitive societies are more heavily weighted with it. There the action systems tend to become stable, universal and invariable. There is harmony between the habit system and the stimulus system. This statement is an oversimplification, but it holds in principle.[7] . . .

In this situation, the verbalization of behavior, the voices of the living and the voices of the dead, the laws and the prophets, result in a body of collective habit—the "collective representations" of Durkheim and Lévy-Bruhl and the "collective unconscious" of Jung.[8] But for the individual it is a "lapsed consciousness," structuralized, shall we say, in the habit system, but not structuralized in the sense of organically inheritable, merely as a body of habit traditionally perpetuated.

What we call individuation means that the habit system [culture] of the group is not changing as fast as the stimulus system of the individual. The nature of the change of a stimulus system may be seen by comparing the varieties of new experience presented to the young today in connection with commercialized pleasure, newspaper stories, going into the city to work, etc., with the attitudes and values, the norms of the older generations. These norms were once formed by words and gestures, often by bitter processes of consciousness, and then lapsed into habit, into the unconscious. Habit is a definition of a situation. And new stimuli, rival stimuli suggest new definitions of situations. Consciousness seems to appear in just this connection.

In our present society, where the evolution of the stimuli systems is more rapid than the evolution of the habit systems, I have noticed from the reading of cases a number of types of the behavior reactions to the habit system, and I will mention three of these. In one the behavior corresponds to the habit system, in another the habit

[6] Cf. *Primitive Behavior,* p. 23, where Thomas in 1937 identifies the levels of consciousness (or the unconscious) as "unlearned," "lapsed memory" (automatic), and "involuntary" (physiological).

[7] Cf. "The Primary Group and the Definition of the Situation," pp. 226–231 infra.

[8] Durkheim, *The Elementary Forms of the Religious Life;* Lucien Lévy-Bruhl, *Primitive Mentality* (tr. Lilian A. Clare; London: George Allen & Unwin, 1923); C. G. Jung, *Psychology of the Unconscious* (tr. Beatrice M. Hinkle; New York: Moffat, Yard and Company, 1916).

system is largely ignored, which amounts to anti-social behavior, and in the third a new organization of the personality is effected by the repudiation of the old habit system and the personal selection of stimuli.

In Philadelphia (a case recorded by the White-Williams Foundation) there are two girls, the father dead or removed, the mother very poor. They were given a dime at school to buy milk, but they returned a nickel, explaining that one of them did not drink her milk. Attractive enough, they were followed in the street, but never picked up. The extensive record shows all the features which we usually think of as producing delinquency, but no delinquency.

On the other hand, in Chicago there is a very admirably kept record, in the Institute for Juvenile Research, of a girl who for about nine years has been doing almost everything that is good and bad, but nothing vicious. I call her the "polymorphous normal" girl, with apologies to Freud. She gets up in the night to give the younger children a drink, scrubs the floors and cleans the house. She runs away, steals from home, kicks up a pile of refuse in the street, cries, and tells a pedestrian that she has lost a bill and her mother will punish her. She gets the money, buys sweets, goes to the movies, but always shares with the children of the neighborhood. Beaten, she stays out all night, and sleeps under the steps. She has been sent here and there, I am told, on vacations and into homes as many as twenty-seven times. She follows all pleasing stimuli.

A Boston girl (one of Dr. Healy's cases) was brought to the court by her mother who complained that there "must be something wrong with her head." She detested her father who was petulant, unclean, locked up the music box when he was not at home, read the Polish paper aloud evenings and would have no comments. Now it appeared that the girl, when she was about eight, had lied about her age in order to get a library card. She read a great many fairy tales and day-dreamed a good deal, imagining she was a princess. At about twelve she became interested in love stories, and read them so much she became sick of them and went over to mystery stories. Later she left home, went into a publishing house, sent part of her wages home, associated with a nice set of girls, and joined them in dramatic performances, dances and debates. She had no sex experiences, but married well. After leaving home she went up, and the family went down. A visitor reported: "The house itself was dirty, the floors strewn with papers and bits of cloth, the bathroom so neglected it seemed impossible to use, and the beds were covered with dirty linen. The mother said that since Stasia had left no one had cared whether the place was orderly or not." The reading was the critical experience [9] through which she had selected the behavior patterns not in the family system. But what had put her up to the reading?

It is precisely because children, with about the same family situations, organize their interests in so diverse ways that students of the child are making their records as minute and complete as possible. Sometimes a critical experience, as in the case of Stasia, comes to the front and dominates the configuration.

The degrees of intimacy and distance in connection with various types of relationship to groups, and the effect of this on personality patterns is something I cannot dwell on. It would be best illustrated by cases. But I will single out one example to illustrate what I mean. It has to do with what I regard as a gross exaggeration of intimacy in modern family life. The modern small family of three or four or more is something that has never before existed, as a general thing. Formerly the family was a kinship group of forty, sixty, a hundred or more persons. When Dr. Znaniecki was translating Polish materials he found it impossible to use the term "family" as we use it. He called the kinship group the "family," and our conception of family he called the "marriage-group." [10] That meant that formerly the parents and children were themselves incorporated in a larger regulating group. Now (without pausing to describe how this has come about) with the dissolution of the large group the small family has become introverted, turned upon itself, and has taken a pathological trend in the direction of demanding and conferring response. Love in the family is the only pleasure seeking to which no limits are set by the moral code, short of incest. I will point out one of the effects of this situation on the configuration of personalities.

[9] Cf. Thomas' use of the concept "crisis," pp. 218–220 infra.

[10] Cf. the distinction between "conjugal" and "consanguine" kinship types in Linton, *The Study of Man,* chap. 8.

Both mother love and child love are built originally on a rather slender instinctive basis. I was reading in a paper by Dr. L. Pierce Clark [11] that the new-born child does not grasp the mother's breast because he is hungry but in the last struggle not to be removed from the womb he holds on with his teeth, so to speak—that the milk is not appreciated as nourishment but as a libido stream. Now this is pure mythology, autistic thinking. Probably the first attitude of the child toward the mother, the tendency to grasp the breast, is not different from the attitude of the newly hatched chick toward the grain of wheat—it is something in each case to peck at and secure, a nutritive value. The new-born child does not prefer his mother's face or footstep. . . . But if the mother feeds and warms and cuddles him he will within a few weeks recognize her, prefer her, select out her voice and footstep. He is conditioned to her. This intimacy is then cultivated by language and gestures and more love response provoked. At any rate, these intimacies become most dangerous for the personality configuration of the child. You know what happens—the spoiled child, tantrums, negativism, exactions going so far that in one case the child would sleep only on the body of his mother in a certain position. . . .

Response and recognition are the same thing in different fields of application.[12] They both seek appreciation. But response operates in relations of intimacy and where you are permitted to have, in the main, what you want when young. The family, and friendship groups and marriage and the gang all represent response. The gang is an organization which will help you get what you want. . . . The public, on the other hand, is an enmity group. Not even a profession, as Professor Park has pointed out to me, is an intimate group. It wishes you to honor the profession but does not wish you honored. The public makes heroes but it is even more pleased to unmake them. Corbett relates that when he entered the ring at New Orleans to fight Sullivan he realized that everybody wanted to see him killed. When he drew blood from Sullivan he realized that everybody

[11] Since Dr. Clark wrote so many psychoanalytic papers, it is difficult to say precisely which one inspired the remark quoted. It is probably "A Tentative Formulation of the Origin of Sadomasochism," *Psychoanalytic Review,* 14:85–88 (1927).

[12] Cf. p. 141, n. 10, supra.

wanted to see Sullivan killed. The cries of "Kill him" when a fighter is groggy are one of the most appalling expressions of mass psychology. To overcome the public, force recognition is very sweet to some. The actor has a full measure when he "stops the show."

In this general situation I have seen, and no doubt you have seen, young persons, and old, who bring to everybody an urgent expectation of that pattern of response from the public which they got from an indulgent mother. The feeling of inadequacy arising in the transition from the intimacy situation to the enmity situation, the inability to get the reaction to which they have been conditioned, the consequent feeling of inferiority, play a large role in the psychoneuroses. The regressions of psychopathology seem, from the cases, to some extent a resignation of recognition and a retreat to response.

IV

We may now turn to that manifestation of the unconscious which I take to be one of the main interests of this meeting—the synthetizing force, *force créatrice,* which participates in, or perhaps we may say, does the work of the creative imagination. For the sake of completeness we may call this the "cortical unconscious," though it is in fact cortical + visceral + lapsed. And, of course, I can only describe what it does, not determine what it is. The region of phantasy, of the elaboration of the materials of memory, psychic intimacy with self, detachment from persons and groups and time and place, give the most favorable situation for the development of unique personalities and products. And in this respect the daydreamer, the lunatic, the mathematician and the creative artist are alike. The social values are different but the process is the same. . . .

If we attempt to analyze this process, to see what is its mechanism, we may note, first, that the material for elaboration may be furnished by an incident, a critical experience. In the dream the initiation of the theme may be some intra-organic stimulation, some posture on the bed. The neck twisted on the pillow may initiate a dream of strangulation by a burglar and the elaboration may result in a drama of money, women, life and death. A physiologist has recently produced elaborate dreams by changing the tension of the skin through the application of adhesive tape.* Or the experience may be social. . . . Oliver Caswell, deaf, dumb and blind, was under the care of Dr. Howe, who developed Laura Bridgman.[13] Oliver was a murderous little beast. In his fights with boys he drew his finger across his throat, making horrible sounds. It developed that before he lost his senses, at the age of three, he had witnessed the slaughter of a hog. Circumstances then shut him off from experience, and he had evidently greatly elaborated this simple theme. Miss Mateer has some materials illustrating the early fixation on materials. A child of three and a half centered all his energies for months on the fear that the world's supply of paper would give out before he grew up, and another of five spent his time in such chants as,

Life is a dark hole,
Life is a dark hole,

where we seem to have a tendency toward schizophrenic autism.** Bleuler, illustrating the imaginings of his schizophrenic patients, gives the case of an escaped inmate, who enters an inn, goes to bed and announces that he is waiting for the queen of Holland, who wants to marry him. Commenting on the case Bleuler points out that the man's life is not disturbed in other respects. He works and behaves regularly, but here he is *living* a fairy tale, not *reading* a fairy tale, not *telling* a fairy tale, but *living* one.*** This particular retreat from reality gives opportunity to play any role you wish with none of the checks encountered either in the intimate group or in the enmity group. You can have response, recognition, new experience in whatever proportion you want, with security. Bleuler claims that his patients always choose a role endowing them with the qualities in which they are most hopelessly lacking.

The difference between the schizophrene or the day-dreamer and the artist is that the artist selects his materials and elaborates them with regard to social patterns and social values. We are not concerned here with what the values are, or what is the importance of art,

* A. J. Cubberley, "Bodily Tension Effects upon the Normal Dream," *British Journal of Psychology*, January, 1923, 243–265.
** Florence Mateer, *The Unstable Child*, 50.
*** E. Bleuler, "Autistic Thinking," *American Journal of Insanity*, 69:873–878.

13 S. G. Howe, *Annual Reports of Perkins Institution and Massachusetts Asylum of the Blind*, 1838, 1841.

merely with the process of the artist. The artist seeks materials appropriate for elaboration. He may have them in his own experience, he may go out to get new experience, atmosphere, or he may explore the experiences of others in this connection. . . .

Let us . . . [turn] to Coleridge as creative artist, as it happens the man whose poetry is supposed to be the product of opium dreams, and examine the sources of his materials for elaboration and their relation to the "unconscious," the *"force créatrice."* Fortunately we are able to do this with rather astonishing completeness because eight days ago there fell from the press a volume of 639 pages called *The Road To Xanadu,* by Professor Lowes of Harvard, on precisely this point, and the details which I shall mention are taken from this remarkable study. I assume that not many of you have as yet seen the volume.

Probably we should all agree that *The Rime of the Ancient Mariner, Kubla Khan* and *Christabel* are representative of what we have in mind when we speak of "works of the imagination." They are weird, phantasmagorical, apparently unrelated to a background of concrete personal experience. But let us see what is going on in the mind of Coleridge, limiting ourselves to *The Rime of the Ancient Mariner.*

Coleridge began this poem on a walking trip with Wordsworth and Wordsworth's sister Dorothy. They agreed to write a poem together and sell it for five pounds, to pay the expenses of the trip, but Wordsworth relates that he soon withdrew, since the development of the theme was not in the line of his talents. At this time, and until he finished the poem, Coleridge had never been down to the sea in ships. He had not even crossed the Channel. But he was a voracious reader. He said himself that he had read everything. He was looking for materials. Especially he steeped himself in the narratives of the old voyagers and explorers, and the accounts of the Jesuit missionaries represented now in the collection called *Jesuit Relations,* edited by Professor Thwaites in seventy-three volumes. And we must note at this point several items. Coleridge had planned a great work, a *Hymn to the Elements,* starting with Thales, probably, and what he had to say about water. He was also nursing the idea of an epic on the Wandering Jew theme. Incidentally we see the Wandering Jew transformed into a sea-faring Wandering Jew in the person of the Ancient Mariner, but this was not the original plan. Further, Coleridge kept a note-book, now preserved in the British Museum, in which he jotted down passages and phrases for future use and elaboration. Moreover, he read all the books mentioned in the text or the notes of any book he had been reading. This enabled Professor Lowes to track him. For example, Coleridge read Priestly's *Optics,* or more exactly, his *History and Present State of Discoveries Relating to Vision, Light and Colours,* containing a chapter on "Light from Putrescent Substances," and an account of fishes which "in swimming left so luminous a track behind them that both their size and species might be distinguished by it." We are here already on the track of the origin of the water-snakes in the Ancient Mariner which "moved in tracks of shining white." But pass that over for a moment. Priestly appended a foot-note to a certain passage referring to the *Philosophical Transactions of the Royal Society (Abridged),* Volume V, page 213. Coleridge read in this volume a letter from Father Bourzes, containing a passage about "artificial light in the water," but he read further, and another passage, something not in Father Bourzes, caught his eye, namely: "He says, there is a tradition among them that in November, 1668, a star appeared below the body of the moon within the horns of it." Looking for the source of this information we find it in a letter dated Boston, November 24, 1712, communicated to Mr. Waller of the Royal Society, and signed, "Cotton Mather." So the lines of the Ancient Mariner:

> Till clomb above the eastern bar
> The hornèd moon, with one bright star
> Within the nether tip,

lead back to Beacon Hill.*

This will show how Coleridge worked and how Professor Lowes worked. And I cannot refrain from calling your attention to the fact that Coleridge is evidently having one grand rigadoon of new experience, of the pursuit pattern. He is like a hunter tracking game.[14]

* J. L. Lowes, *The Road to Xanadu,* 38–41.

[14] Cf. the wish for new experience, pp. 124–125 supra.

But let us examine in more detail how the conscious and unconscious mind worked in the creation of a poem.

Coleridge's memory was egregious, and in *The Friend* he speaks of what he calls the "hooks-and-eyes of memory." When, for example, the reading of a picturesque passage from one of the old voyagers has left in his mind a constellation of concrete images on a background, and the reading of another old voyager presents another set of images, he hooks some of the newer images into the older background, and gradually also transforms the background. Without, then, following the critical procedure by which Professor Lowes establishes the fact that he did read first one author and then another, let us take some lines from the *Ancient Mariner* and note how this transformation and fusion go on:

> Beyond the shadow of the ship,
> I watched the water-snakes;
> They moved in tracks of shining white,
> And when they reared, the elfish light
> Fell off in hoary flakes.
>
> Within the shadow of the ship
> I watched their rich attire;
> Blue, glossy green, and velvet black,
> They coiled and swam; and every track
> Was a flash of golden fire.

In his letter Father Bourzes had written: "In my voyage to the Indies . . . we often observed a great light in the wake of the ship. . . . The wake then seemed like a river of milk. . . . Particularly, on the 12th of June, the wake of the vessel was full of large vortices of light [which] appeared and disappeared again like flashes of lightning. Not only the wake of a ship produces this light, but fishes also in swimming leave behind 'em a luminous track. . . . I have sometimes seen a great many fishes playing in the sea, which have made a kind of artificial fire in the water that was very pleasant to look on."

Coleridge took this picturesque passage as material and background but changed the imagery somewhat. He introduces water-snakes instead of fishes, and they are not merely luminous; they have vivid hues—blue, glossy green and velvet black. Following Coleridge's reading further, we find the vivid hues in the voyages of Captain Cook: "Some small sea animals . . . that had a white or shining appearance . . . put in a glass cup with some salt water . . . emitted the brightest colors of the most precious gems. . . . They assumed various tints of blue . . . which were frequently mixed with ruby or opaline redness; and glowed with a strength sufficient to illuminate the vessel and water. . . . But by candle light the color was chiefly a beautiful, pale green, tinged with a burnished gloss; and in the dark it had the appearance of glowing fire." Here we have all the color used by Coleridge except "velvet black":

> Blue, glossy green, and velvet black,
> They coiled and swam; and every track
> Was a flash of golden fire.

Reading further in Bartram's *Travels,* familiar to Coleridge, "The whole fish," he says, "is of a pale gold (or burnished brass) color . . . the scales are powdered with red, russet, blue and green specks [while at the gills is] a little spatula, encircled with silver, and velvet black." The "powdered" color might well fall off in "flakes," and Professor Lowes thinks the word "hoary" was lifted from Falconer's *Shipwreck.*

But what about the water-snakes, and the "coiled" movement? *Purchas his Pilgrimages* was one of Coleridge's "midnight darlings," and there we read in a record of Sir Richard Hawkins, becalmed in the Azores, of a sea, "replenished with several sorts of jellies and forms of serpents, adders and snakes, green, yellow, black, white, and some parti-colored, whereof many had life, being a yard and a half or two yards long. And they could hardly draw a bucket of water clear of some corruption withal." And in Dampier's *Voyages and Adventures,* quoted and admired by Coleridge, we read: "This day we saw two water-snakes. . . . The snake swam away . . . very fast, keeping his head above water." In *The History of the Bucaniers in America* (and it is not established that Coleridge had read this) the water-snakes, like Coleridge's, are many colored: "As we sailed we saw . . . water-snakes of divers colors." That is to say, first snakes, the water-snakes, and finally colored water-snakes. There was also another volume, Norwegian and Latin in parallel columns. Leemius,

De Lapponnibus (how much Coleridge had used this you can see in Professor Lowes' volume) in which a *serpens marinus* (sea-serpent or water-snake?) is described: "In dog-days, when the sea lies unruffled by the winds, the sea-serpent is wont to emerge, arched into all sorts of coils *(in varias spiras sinuatus),* of which some project from the water, while the rest are hidden under it." *

We have had a picture of water so full of life, of slime and corruption that "they could scarce draw a bucket of water clear of [it] withal," and with snakes gyrating on its surface, that we should not be surprised to see some of the creatures of these "pestful calms" climb upon the water and walk. And so they do:

> The very deep did rot: O Christ!
> That ever this should be!
> Yea, slimy things did crawl with legs
> Upon the slimy sea.

The Mariner himself speaks elsewhere of "a million, million slimy things," and in Martens' *Voyage into Spitzbergen and Greenland,* a book which Coleridge had read, we have a description of these "million, million slimy things." A whole chapter is devoted to the varieties of the "Slime-fish." Of the Snail Slime Fish he says: "It is very remarkable that out of the utmost part of him come two stalks, like unto the beam of a pair of scales. . . . With these stalks he moves himself up and down. . . . The seamen take these small fish for spiders. . . . They swim in great numbers in the sea, as numerous as the dust in the sun." And of the star-fish, in another chapter: "Where the legs come out of the body they spread themselves double into twigs, and . . . are . . . like unto the feet of a spider. When they swim in the water they hold their legs together, and so they row along." These were arctic creatures, in fact, but Coleridge, with his imagination, simply swept them down into the tropics. "And from that amazing carnival of miniature monsters," says Professor Lowes . . . "with an artistic restraint, which must none the less have cast a longing look behind [he] seized upon the one touch which for sheer uncanny realism is unsurpassed: "Yea, slimy things did crawl *with legs* upon the slimy sea."

And if you take *Kubla Khan,* which was based directly on an

* Lowes, *op. cit.,* 42–52.

opium dream, you find the same thing. Word for word the images are taken from the old writers. In *Purchas his Pilgrimages* we read: "In Xamdu did Cublai Cann build a stately palace . . . ," and in the poem:

> In Xanadu did Kubla Khan
> A stately pleasure-dome decree. . . .

Coleridge, in fact, fell asleep over *Purchas* and dreamed his dream. These facts are not to be taken in disparagement of either the poem or the unconscious. They show that the poem was not something created by the unconscious out of nothing. The man worked and the unconscious worked also. As to the nature of the creative process involved and the operation of the unconscious, Coleridge himself has this to say: "In that shadowy half-being, that state of nascent existence in the twilight of imagination and just on the vestibule of consciousness [there is] a confluence of our recollections [through which] we establish a center, as it were, a sort of nucleus in [this] reservoir of the soul." *

It will be interesting to compare this with what Henri Poincaré says of the unconscious in his attempt to show "what happens in the very soul of a mathematician," and I will then leave Professor Lowes' fascinating volume to you. "This unconscious work," says Poincaré, "is not possible, or in any case not fruitful, unless it is first preceded and then followed by a period of conscious work. . . . All that we can hope from these inspirations which are the fruits of unconscious work, is to obtain points of departure for [our] calculations. As for the calculation themselves, they must be made in the second period of conscious work which follows the inspiration. . . . They demand discipline, attention, will, and consequently consciousness. In the subliminal ego, on the contrary, there reigns what I would call liberty, if one could give this name to the mere absence of discipline and to disorder born of chance. Only, this very disorder permits of unexpected couplings." **

Thus in the most formal procedures, as in mathematics, and in the most inspirational, as in art, the creative process is partly elaborated by the unconscious and then completed and given some

* Lowes, *op. cit.,* 55–60.
** Henri Poincaré, *Science and Method,* quoted by Lowes, *op. cit.,* 62.

systematization by the conscious. It would be a great psychological undertaking to work out this relation of the unconscious and of the creative imagination to the social backgrounds and psychic configurations of different historical periods, with their emphasis on the different fields of values.[15]

[15] Since this selection utilizes psychoanalytic terminology, perhaps Thomas' general view of this school of thought should be indicated. In historical perspective there can be no doubt that Thomas studied and appreciated the contributions of Freud and his followers. But, and this is typical of Thomas, he never became doctrinaire. He was influenced by various schools of thought, but became a disciple of none.

In his later development, particularly the mid-twenties and after, Thomas became a rather severe critic of psychoanalysis. See, for example, *The Child in America,* 1928, chap. x. Again, in an unpublished undated paper he wrote: "The psychoanalytic technique is also a method of obtaining a life-history but its employment up to the present has most frequently had the vicious feature of indoctrinating the subject by suggesting, consciously or unconsciously, replies corresponding with the particular theory of the analyst." See p. 297 infra for a similar statement.

On a more general level, in 1937 he classed Freudian theory with that of Nordic superiority in degree of error. See *Primitive Behavior,* p. 730.

In general, then, Thomas developed and changed with reference to psychoanalysis, just as he did with other "particularistic" schools of thought. But it was only after thorough exposure and understanding that he rejected this approach—at least as a single explanation of behavior.

Part III

SOCIAL BEHAVIOR AND CULTURAL DYNAMICS

12 THE PSYCHOLOGY OF CULTURE CHANGE

Part III contains five selections depicting the way Thomas looked at society in operation. Society, like the individual, must meet events requiring adjustment and is neither static nor mechanical. Change is a characteristic feature of society, and culture is social life in process, just as personality is individual life in process.

One thing should be noted, however, about the selections in Part III. They represent a merging of two distinct interests on Thomas' part: a preoccupation with the cultural process itself (stability and change), and social disorganization (the accompaniment of change). These are closely related in his thought, but received different emphases at different times and in connection with different problems.

Thomas' basic conception of society as process is to be found in the Introduction to *Source Book for Social Origins,* 1909, from which the first selection in Part III is taken. The *Source Book* itself is a compilation of various anthropological studies—the best of the time—so arranged and classified as to be of use to students in social science. The Introduction is presented as an aid in the interpretation of the diverse materials therein contained.

After a preliminary section on the impact of evolutionary doctrines on social thought (which has been omitted here) Thomas develops his theory of society in terms of three essentially psychological concepts: control, attention, and crisis. These are related, on one hand, to individual habits and, on the other, to the presence of extraordinary individuals in society, the level of culture, and the character of the culture. For Thomas these variables constitute the major factors in culture change. Finally, he criticizes certain "particularistic" theories of culture.

This selection is of crucial importance in understanding Thomas' social thought. Appearing in 1909, it foreshadowed many of the developments contained in *The Polish Peasant,* 1918–20, and included a penetrating analysis of the "crisis" concept. Its over-all importance and influence is illustrated by the fact that Ogburn drew upon it for his classic *Social Change,* 1922.[1]

However, it should be pointed out that Thomas was a victim of his time so far as terminology is concerned. Thus he speaks, for example, of the "lower races" and "savages." Indeed, the Introduction to the *Source Book*

[1] William F. Ogburn, *Social Change with Respect to Culture and Original Nature* (New York: B. W. Huebsch, 1922; Viking Press, 1928).

was also published in the *American Journal of Sociology* under the title "Standpoint for the Interpretation of Savage Society." A more misleading title would be hard to find. The important point, though, is that Thomas' ideas should not be judged on the basis of occasional lapses into a now discarded terminology.

Source Book for Social Origins—Introduction [2]

There have been many notable attempts to interpret the social process in terms of so-called elemental or dominant social forces. Among these may be mentioned Tarde's "imitation," Gumplowicz's "conflict," Durkheim's "constraint," de Greef's "contract," and Giddings' "consciousness of kind." [3] Now it is evident that the social process is a complex, and cannot be interpreted by any single phrase. It includes all of the forces mentioned above, and more. "Imitation" is a powerful social factor, but it is hardly more important than inhibition. The "thou shalt nots" have played a large role in the life of the race, as they do still in the life of the individual. Similarly "conflict" and "contract" offset each other, and "consciousness of kind" is hardly more conspicuous as a social force than consciousness of difference. . . .

There is, however, a useful concept into which all activity can be translated, or to which it can at least be related, namely, *control.* Control is not a social force, but is the object, realized or unrealized, of all purposive activity. Food and reproduction are the two primal necessities, if the race is to exist. The whole design of nature with

[2] The selection is from the fourth edition (Boston: Richard G. Badger, 1909), pp. 13–26.

[3] G. Tarde, *Les lois de l'imitation* (3rd ed.; Paris: F. Alcan, 1900), or *The Laws of Imitation* (tr. Elsie C. Parsons; New York: H. Holt and Company, 1903).

Ludwig Gumplowicz, *Der Rassenkampf* (Innsbruck: Wagner, 1883); *Grundriss der Sociologie* (Vienna: Manz, 1885), or *The Outlines of Sociology* (tr. F. W. Moore; Philadelphia: American Academy of Political and Social Science, 1899), among other works.

E. Durkheim, *Les regles de la methode sociologique* (2nd ed.; Paris: F. Alcan, 1901), or *The Rules of Sociological Method* (tr. Sarah A. Solovay and John H. Mueller; Chicago: University of Chicago Press, 1938).

Guillaume de Greef, *Introduction à la sociologie* (2 vols.; Brussels: G. Mayolez, 1886–89); *Le transformisme social* (2nd ed.; Paris: F. Alcan, 1901).

Franklin H. Giddings, *The Principles of Sociology* (New York: The Macmillan Company, 1896).

reference to organic life is to nourish the individual and provide a new generation before the death of the old, and the most elementary statement, as I take it, which can be made of individual and of social activity is that it is designed to secure that control of the environment which will assure these two results. I will illustrate my meaning by applying the concept of *control* to some of the steps in organic and social development.

. . . In man the principle of motion and consequent control is extended through the use of animals and the various means of mechanical transportation which he has developed. With the use of free hands man immensely increased his control, through the ability to make and use weapons and tools. Fire is a very precious element in control, since through its use man was able to transform inedible into edible materials, to smelt and forge iron, and to enlarge the habitable world by regulating the temperature of the colder regions. Mechanical invention is to be viewed as control. It utilizes new forces or old forces in new ways, making them do work, and assist man in squeezing out of nature values not before suspected, not within reach, or not commonly enjoyed. The gregariousness of animals and the associated life of men are modes of control, because numbers and cooperation make life more secure. Language is a powerful instrument of control, because through it knowledge, tradition, standpoint, ideals, stimulations, copies, are transmitted and increased. Forms of government are aids to control, by providing safety and fair play within the group and organized resistance to intrusions from without. Religion assists control, reinforcing by a supernatural sanction those modes of behavior which by experience have been determined to be moral, i.e., socially advantageous. Art aids control by diffusing admirable copies for imitation, with the least resistance and the maximum of contagion. Play is an organic preparation and practice for control. Marriage secures better provision and training to children than promiscuity. Medicine keeps the organism in order or repairs it. Liberty is favorable to control, because with it the individual has opportunity to develop ideas and values by following his own bent which he would not develop under repression.[4]

[4] Cf. the argument in Bronislaw Malinowski, *Freedom and Civilization* (New York: Roy Publishers, 1944).

The human mind is pre-eminently the organ of manipulation, of adjustment, of control. It operates through what we call knowledge. This in turn is based on memory and the ability to compare a present situation with similar situations in the past and to revise our judgments and actions in view of the past experience. By this means the world at large is controlled more successfully as time goes on.[5] Knowledge thus becomes the great force in control, and those societies are the most successful and prosperous in which the knowledge is most disseminated, most reliable, and most intensive. This is the sense in which knowledge is power. And as to morality, if we should single out and make a catalogue of actions which we are accustomed to call laudable and virtuous, we should see that they can all be stated from the control standpoint. But I will not multiply instances, and I need not point out that all conflict, exploitation, showing off, boasting, gambling, and violation of the decalogue, are designed to secure control, however unsuccessful in the end.

There is, however, a still more serviceable standpoint for the examination of society and of social change, and that is *attention.* This is by no means in conflict with the category of *control.* Control is the end to be secured and attention is the means of securing it. They are the objective and subjective sides of the same process.[6] Attention is the mental attitude which takes note of the outside world and manipulates it; it is the organ of accommodation. But attention does not operate alone; it is associated with habit on the one hand and with crisis on the other. When the habits are running smoothly the attention is relaxed; it is not at work. But when something happens to disturb the run of habit the attention is called into play and devises a new mode of behavior which will meet the crisis. That is,

[5] Later, in *The Polish Peasant,* there is a parallel to this view: "social situations never spontaneously repeat themselves, every situation is more or less new . . . The individual does not find passively ready situations exactly similar to past situations; he must consciously define every situation as similar to past situations." (Vol. II, 1927, p. 1852.)

[6] This discussion of the "objective" and the "subjective" in social life would appear to be a foreshadowing of the conceptual scheme employed later in *The Polish Peasant.* In that work, "values" are substituted for "control" (goal of purposive behavior) and "attitudes" for "attention." See pp. 49–55 supra.

the attention establishes new and adequate habits, or it is its function to do so.[7]

Such conditions as the exhaustion of game, the intrusion of outsiders, defeat in battle, floods, drought, pestilence, and famine illustrate one class of crisis. The incidents of birth, death, adolescence, and marriage, while not unanticipated, are always foci of attention and occasions for control. They throw a strain on the attention, and affect the mental life of the group. Shadows, dreams, epilepsy, intoxication, swooning, sickness, engage the attention and result in various attempts at control. Other crises arise in the conflict of interest between individuals, and between the individual and the group. Theft, assault, sorcery, and all crimes and misdemeanors are occasions for the exercise of attention and control. To say that language, reflection, discussion, logical analysis, abstraction, mechanical invention, magic, religion, and science are developed in the effort of the attention to meet difficult situations through a readjustment of habit, is simply to say that the mind itself is the product of crisis. Crisis also produces the specialized occupations. The medicine-man, the priest, the law-giver, the judge, the ruler, the physician, the teacher, the artist and other specialists, represent classes of men who have or profess special skill in dealing with crises.[8] Among the professions whose connection with crisis is least obvious are perhaps those of teacher and artist. But the teacher is especially concerned with anticipating that most critical of periods in the life of the youth when he is to enter manhood and be no longer supported by others; and art always arises as the memory of crisis.

Of course a crisis may be so serious as to kill the organism or destroy the group, or it may result in failure or deterioration. But crisis, as I am employing the term, is not to be regarded as habitually

[7] The similarity between this formulation and the one recently popularized by Toynbee as "challenge and response" is striking. See Howard Becker, "Historical Sociology," in Harry E. Barnes, and Howard and Frances B. Becker, eds. *Contemporary Social Theory* (New York: Appleton-Century Company, 1940), p. 512.

The vitality of the crisis concept is also indicated by Muzafer Sherif, *An Outline of Social Psychology* (New York: Harper & Brothers, 1948), chap. 16, "Men in Critical Situations."

[8] In *Primitive Behavior,* 1937, Thomas referred to these as "special definers of the situation." See p.108 supra.

violent. It is simply a disturbance of habit, and it may be no more than an incident, a stimulation, a suggestion. It is here that imitation plays a great role. But it is quite certain that the degree of progress of a people has a certain relation to the nature of the disturbances encountered, and that the most progressive have had a more vicissitudinous life. Our proverb "Necessity is the mother of invention" is the formulation in folk-thought of this principle of social change.

The run of crises encountered by different individuals and races is not of course, uniform, and herein we have a partial explanation of the different rate and direction of progress in different peoples. But more important than this . . . is the fact that the same crisis will not produce the same effect uniformly.[9] And in this connection I will briefly indicate the relation of attention and crisis to (1) the presence of extraordinary individuals in the group, (2) the level of culture of the group, and (3) the character of the ideas by which the group-mind is prepossessed:

1. Whatever importance we may attach to group-mind[10] and mass-suggestion, the power of the attention to meet a crisis is primarily an individual matter, or at least the initiative lies with the individual.[11] The group, therefore, which possesses men of extraordinary mental ability is at an advantage. The fleeing animal, for instance, is always a problem, and the resilience of wood is probably always observed, but the individual is not always present to relate the two facts, and invent the bow and arrow. If he is present he probably . . . raises his group to a higher level of culture by producing a new food epoch. The relation of the "great man" to crisis is indeed one of the most important points in the problem of progress. Such men as Moses, Mohammed, Confucius, Christ, have stamped the whole character of a civilization. . . . Similar cases of

[9] In the Methodological Note of *The Polish Peasant,* this idea is treated somewhat differently. There, the belief that "men react in the same way to the same influences" is regarded as a fallacy of social practice. See p. 44 supra.

[10] Thomas had rejected this idea some years before. See "The Province of Social Psychology," *Congress of Arts and Science Universal Exposition, St. Louis, 1904* [Proceedings], Vol. 5, pp. 860–868.

[11] Thomas was certainly among the first of social scientists to realize the importance of the individual in promoting change. This is reflected not only here, but also in his emphasis on the "creative personality" type. Also, see p. 237 infra.

the reconstruction of the habits of a whole people by the dominating attention of a great man are found among the lower races.[12] Dingiswayo and Chaka converted pastoral Zululand into a military encampment, as a result of witnessing the maneuvers of a regiment of European soldiers in Cape Colony. And Howitt's *Native Tribes of South East Australia* has interesting details on the influence of extraordinary men in a low race.

2. The level of culture of the group limits the power of the mind to meet crisis and readjust. If the amount of general knowledge is small and the material resources scanty, the mind may find no way out of an emergency which under different conditions would be only the occasion for further progress. If we could imagine a group without language, numbers, iron, fire, and without the milk, meat, and labor of domestic animals, and if this group were small, as it would necessarily be under those conditions, we should have also to imagine a very low state of mind in general in the group. In the absence of mathematics, fire, and iron, for example, the use of electricity as a force would be out of the question. The individual mind cannot rise much above the level of the group-mind, and the group-mind will be simple if the outside environmental conditions and the antecedent racial experiences are simple. On this account it is just to attribute important movements and inventions to individuals only in a qualified sense.[13] The extraordinary individual works on the material and psychic fund already present, and if the situation is not ripe neither is he ripe. From this standpoint we can understand why it is almost never possible to attribute any great modern invention to any single person. When the state of science and the social need reach a certain point a number of persons are likely to solve the same problem.[14]

12 That Thomas was aware of the fallacy involved in referring to the "lower races" or "primitive man" is evident in the following statement: ". . . we should once for all discard the habit of thinking of the lower races *en bloc*. There is as much difference between the North American Indian and the Australian as between the Indian and the white man." (*Source Book for Social Origins,* p. 133.)

13 For a similar statement see "The Province of Social Psychology," *op. cit.,* p. 862. It is interesting to see how Thomas avoids the extreme position often taken by "great men" theorists.

14 It has been noted that Ogburn drew upon this essay for his classic discussion of social change. The above paragraph makes it particularly clear. What Thomas calls

3. The character of the accommodations already made affects the character of the accommodation to the new crisis. When our habits are settled and running smoothly they much resemble the instincts of animals. And the great part of our life is lived in the region of habit. The habits . . . are safe and serviceable. They have been tried, and they are associated with a feeling of security. There consequently grows up in the folk-mind a determined resistance to change. And there is a degree of sense in this, for while change implies possibilities of improvement it also implies danger of disaster, or a worse condition. It must also be acknowledged that a state of rapid and constant change implies loss of settled habits and disorganization. As a result, all societies view change with suspicion, and the attempt to revise certain habits is even viewed as immorality. Now it is possible under these conditions for a society to become stationary, or to attempt to remain so. The effort of the attention is to preserve the present status rather than to reaccommodate.[15] This condition is particularly marked among the savages. In the absence of science and a proper estimation of the value of change, they rely on ritual and magic, and a minute, conscientious, unquestioning and absolute adhesion to the past. Change is consequently introduced with a maximum of resistance. Some African tribes, for example, have such faith in fetish that they cannot be induced to practice with firearms. If, they say, the magic works, the bullet will go straight; otherwise it will not. Similarly, oriental pride in permanence is quite as real as occidental pride in progress, and the fatalistic view of the Mohammedan world, the view that results are predetermined by Allah and not by man, is unfavorable to change. Indeed, the only world in which change is at a premium and is systematically sought is the modern scientific world.[16] It is plain therefore that the nature of the

---

the "level of culture" appears in *Social Change* as the "culture base," and Ogburn gave a striking demonstration of the number of inventions and discoveries made independently but at nearly the same time.

[15] This is a clear foreshadowing of the theory of change presented in *The Polish Peasant,* particularly in the discussion of social disorganization as a regular feature of change. See pp. 233–237 infra.

[16] This point was later elaborated in "The Persistence of Primary-group Norms," 1917. See p. 231 infra.

reaction of attention to crisis is conditioned by the ideas which prepossess the mind.

It is, of course, possible to overwork any standpoint, but on the whole I think that the best course the student can follow is to keep *crisis* constantly in mind—the nature of the crisis, the degree of mental and cultural preparation a people has already attained as fitting it to handle the crisis, and the various and often contradictory types of reaccommodation effected through the attention. . . .

Finally, I wish to warn the student to be suspicious of what may be called the particularistic explanation of social change. Some years ago, when it was the habit to explain everything in terms of "the survival of the fittest," an ingenious German scholar put forth the theory that the thick crania of the Australians were due to the fact that the men treated the women with such violence as to break all the thin heads, thus leaving only thick-headed women to reproduce. A still more ingenious German offered as an explanation of the origin of the practice of circumcision the desire of certain tribes to assure themselves that there should be no fraud in the collection of trophies in battle. This was assured by first circumcising all the males of one's own tribe. Under these circumstances certitude was secured that any foreskins brought in after battle with uncircumcised enemies could not have been secured from the slain of one's own party. Lippert,[17] the great culture-historian, has argued that the presence or absence of the milk of domestic animals has sealed the fate of the different races, pointing out that no race without milk has ever risen to a high level of culture. He is also responsible for the suggestion that man took the idea of a mill for grinding, with its upper and nether mill-stones, from the upper and lower molars in his own mouth. Pitt-Rivers [18] says that the idea of a large boat might have been suggested in time of floods, when houses floated down the rivers before the eyes of men. I think that even the eminent ethnolo-

[17] Julius Lippert, *Kulturgeschichte der Menschheit in ihrem organischen aufbau* (2 vols.; Stuttgart: F. Enke, 1886–87). For Lippert's view and appropriate comment see his *The Evolution of Culture* (tr. G. P. Murdock; New York: The Macmillan Company, 1931), p. 71.

[18] A. Lane-Fox Pitt-Rivers, *The Evolution of Culture and Other Essays* (Oxford: Clarendon Press, 1906), pp. 180–227.

gists Mason and McGee[19] err in this respect when they suggest the one that "the hawks taught men to catch fish, the spiders and caterpillars to spin, the hornet to make paper, and the crayfish to work in clay" . . . and the other that plants and animals were first domesticated in the desert rather than in humid areas, because in unwatered regions plants, animals, and men were more in need of one another and showed a greater tolerance and helpfulness . . .

Some of these theories are simply imaginative and absurd, and others are illustrations of the too particularistic. Doubtless milk is a very precious possession, but so also is iron. No race ever attained a considerable level of culture in the absence of iron. And it would be possible to name a number of things which races of high culture possess and races of low culture do not possess. The idea of crushing, pounding, and rubbing is much too general to warrant us in saying that the idea of the mill is derived from the human mouth. When man has once a floating log, bark boat, or raft, he can enlarge it without assistance from floating houses. The growth of plant life and the idea of particular attention to it are too general to depend on any particular kind of accident, or on a desert environment. Animals follow the camp for food, they are caught alive in traps, and the young ones are kept as pets; and this would happen if there were no desert regions. . . .

The error of the particularistic method lies in overlooking the fact that the mind employs the principle of abstraction—sees general principles behind details—and that the precise detail with which the process of abstraction begins cannot in all cases be posited or determined. Thus the use of poison was certainly suggested to man by the occurrence of poison in nature, and in some crisis it occurred to man to use poison for the purpose of killing. And since the snake is the most conspicuous user of poison in nature it has usually been said that man gets his idea from the snake, and that the poisoned arrow-point is copied from the tooth of the poisonous snake. I have no doubt that this thing frequently happened in this way, but there

[19] Otis T. Mason, "Technogeography, or the Relation of the Earth to the Industries of Mankind," *American Anthropologist,* 7:137–161 (1894); and W. J. McGee, "The Beginning of Agriculture," *ibid.,* 8:350–375 (1895) and "The Beginning of Zooculture," *ibid.,* 10:215–230 (1897).

are also various other poisons in nature. The deadly curare with which the Guiana Indian tips his tiny arrow is a vegetable product. The Bushmen use animal, vegetable, and mineral poisons, and a mixture of all of them, and the Hottentots manufacture poisons from the entrails of certain insects and from putrifying flesh. In short, assuming poison in nature and the arrow in the hands of man, we can assume the development of a poisoned arrow-point even if there had been no such thing as an envenomed serpent's tooth.

Neither can we look too curiously into the order of emergence of inventions nor assume a straight and uniform line of development among all the races. There have been serious attempts to determine what was the first weapon used by man. Was it a round stone, a sharp-pointed stone, a sharp-edged stone, or a stick? But all we can really assume is prehensility and the general idea. The first weapon used was the object at hand when the idea occurred to man. Or, having any one of these objects in his hand, it used itself, so to speak, and the accident was afterward imitated.

The attempt to classify culture by epochs is similarly doomed to failure when made too absolutely. The frugivorous, the hunting, the pastoral, and the agricultural are the stages usually assumed. But the Indian was a hunter while his squaw was an agriculturist. The African is pastoral, agricultural, or hunting indifferently, without regard to his cultural status. And the ancient Mexicans were agricultural but had never had a pastoral period. Different groups take steps in culture in a different order, and the order depends on the general environmental situation, the nature of the crises arising, and the operation of the attention. . . .

13 THE PRIMARY GROUP AND THE DEFINITION OF THE SITUATION

While principally concerned with change, the preceding selection also introduced the idea of stability—one we now recognize as indispensable in the study of cultural dynamics. In 1917, in "The Persistence of Primary-group Norms," Thomas took up this idea of stability with particular reference to primary group organization. The following selection is from that essay.

In Cooley's conception (1909) the primary group was marked by "a certain fusion of individuals in a common whole." Here Thomas links the primary group concept with that of the "definition of the situation," thereby illuminating this entire area.

Definitions of situations in the present sense are both process and product. As process, they occur in socialization; individuals learn how to behave properly by having situations defined for them. As product, definitions are embodied in social codes, the norms of behavior. The agreement of definitions, both as process *and* product, results in the solidarity and stability so characteristic of the isolated primary group. An emotional attachment to the norms leads to general conformity and resistance to change. Definitions are agreed upon, and enforced, in common.

Thomas is careful to avoid, however, the fallacy of the idea of the changeless primitive. Change does take place but in the primary groups of the past it has been slow and local. Now, through the appliances of modern science, change is more rapid and widespread. Efficiency and individualization supplant the emotional solidarity which has been such an effective means of social control.

The following selection is significant for several reasons. It includes the first published statement of the "definition of the situation" concept; it suggests the problem of change which Thomas regarded as the major challenge of our time; and it provides a "base line" against which Thomas' other views of change may be more easily comprehended.

Primary-group Norms [1]

. . . The great common desire of a human society is . . . to remain solidary, and it accomplishes this by the formation of a code of behavior. In a society, the same act is good or bad, organizing

[1] From "The Persistence of Primary-group Norms in Present-day Society," in Jennings and others, *Suggestions of Modern Science Concerning Education,* pp. 167–187.

or disorganizing, according to its meaning for the welfare of the whole group.[2] Thus, the desire for mastery[3] may express itself in furious and sadistic rage and murder and pillage, and is immoral, disorganizing and criminal when directed against the members of one's own society, but becomes courage, patriotism, heroism and virtue when turned against outsiders, in the protection of women and children, of the state.

The code therefore represents the judgment of society on the activities of its members, it dictates the limits within which the desires may find expression, and it is developed by a method which we may call "the definition of the situation." This defining of the situation is begun by the parents in the form of ordering and forbidding and information, is continued in the community by means of gossip, with its praise and blame, and is formally represented by the school, the law, the church. Of course morality and immorality, organization and disorganization are relative terms; what would be considered disorganization in one society would not be considered so in another—it is perfectly good organization to kill your parents in Africa because they wish to reach the next world while still young enough to enjoy it—and so the code will differ widely in different communal, national and racial groups, but will usually define truthfulness, honesty, obedience, cleanliness, unselfishness, kindliness, industry, economy, politeness, courage, chastity, the ten commandments, the golden rule, "women and children first," respect to the aged, etc., in terms of positive appreciation.

Moreover, when the code has been defined, no matter what its content, its violation provokes an emotional protest from society designed to be painfully felt by the offender, and it is so felt, owing to the dependence of the member on society for safety and recognition. The epithets, "coward," "traitor," "thief," "bastard," "heretic," "scab," etc., are brief definitions designed to be felt as painful. And the effect of these definitions is deeper than we suspect. Many of our profound disgusts, for example, those connected with cannibalism and incest, are so developed—that is, they are highly emotionalized institutional products. And all codified acts, even those of no intrinsic

[2] Cf. the concept of "mores" as developed in W. G. Sumner, *Folkways.*

[3] Cf. pp. 114–115 supra for Thomas' formulation of this desire.

importance, become eventually saturated with emotion. It is a matter of no intrinsic importance whether you carry food to the mouth with the knife or the fork, but the situation has been defined in favor of the fork, with grave emotional and social consequences—disgust and social ostracism. In short, any definition, however arbitrary, that is embodied in the habits of the people is regarded as right. It was, for instance, a custom to burn women in India on the death of their husbands, and to strangle them in the Fiji islands, and any widow would demand this privilege although she did not wish it. The contrary behavior would mean social death. . . .

And we are not to regard these examples as merely curious or disgusting—slavery, duelling, burning of witches are examples of practices coming within the definition of moral acts in our own past—but as evidence of the power which the communal definitions have to control behavior. Our immigration problem and our criminal problem are not mainly questions of inherent mental and moral worth, but questions of the attitudes and norms of behavior established by definitions of the situation.

We are in the habit of calling "primary groups" [4] those societies which through kinship, isolation, voluntary adhesion to certain systems of definitions, secure an emotional unanimity among their members. By virtue of their unanimity the mob and the jury are also momentary primary groups.

Clear examples of the primary group are the South Slavonian *zadruga* and the Russian *mir*. When there arises in these communities the necessity of defining a new situation, it is not even sufficient to reach a unanimous decision; each member must voice his opinion and agreement, make it explicit. Cases are recorded where in a conflict between the traditional communal definition (say of poverty) and that of the great state, a member has appeared before the communal assembly, sustained by the confidence in a new and authoritative definition, only to wither and collapse before the white scorn of a solidary group. If a member is stubborn his family members and close friends weep, embrace, implore—beg him not to disgrace them and his community by showing the neighbors that they cannot

[4] See Charles H. Cooley, *Social Organization* (New York: C. Scribner's Sons, 1909), chap. III.

agree. It has been remarked by students of the *mir* that boys six or eight years of age speak and act like grown men. They repeat the standard definitions of "our community," "our people." . . .

The Polish peasant uses a word, *okolica,* "the neighborhood round about," "as far as the report of a man reaches," and this may be taken as the natural external limit of the size of the primary group—as far as the report of a member reaches—so long as men have only primary means of communication. But with militancy, conquest and the formation of the great state we have a systematic attempt to preserve in the whole population the solidarity of feeling characterizing the primary group. The great state cannot preserve this solidarity in all respects—there is the formation of series of primary groups within the state—but it develops authoritative definitions of "patriotism," "treason," etc., and the appropriate emotional attitudes in this respect, so that in time of crisis, of war, where there is a fight of the whole nation against death, we witness, as at this moment, the temporary reconstitution of the attitudes of the primary group.

Similarly, in the great religious systems such as Christianity and Mohammedanism, we have a systematic attempt to make the whole world a primary group, to win men away from the merely communal, human and worldly definitions (or to reaffirm these) by a system of definitions having a higher value through their divine derivation. God is the best definer of situations because he possesses more knowledge and more prestige than any man or any set of men and his definitions tend to have finality, absoluteness and arbitrariness and to convey the maximum of prepossession. . . .

But I do not wish to leave the impression that definitions are dependent for their validity on their authoritative source. All usual and habitual practices are emotionalized, become behavior norms, and tend to resist change. The iron plow-share, invented late in the 18th century, was strongly condemned on the ground that it was an insult to God, therefore poisoned the ground and caused the weeds to grow; and until recently the old farmer laughed at the soil-analysis of the city chemist. The man who first built a water-driven saw-mill in England was mobbed; the English war department informed the inventor of the first practical telegraphic device that it had no use for that contrivance; in the last generation there was a persistent opposition to the introduction of stoves and organs into churches, and if we omit recent years, and in recent years only the scientific and practical fields, it would be difficult to find a single innovation that has not encountered opposition and ridicule. . . .

. . . The main purpose of what I have said up to this point was to show that "human behavior norms" are not only very arbitrary, but, precisely because behavior norms, so highly emotionalized that they claim to be absolutely right and final and subject to no change and no investigation. . . . [But] the norms do change, in spite of the emotional prepossessions; traditions and customs, morality, religion, and education undergo an increasingly rapid evolution, and it is evident that a system proceeding on the assumption that a certain norm is valid finds itself absolutely helpless when it suddenly realizes that the norm has lost all social significance and some other norm has appeared in its place.[5]

But why, we may ask, if a society is orderly and doing very well, is it desirable to disturb the existing norms at all. "Little man, why so hot!" And this question reduces itself ultimately to a basis of idealism. It becomes a question of happiness, of the degree of fulfillment of wishes within the society, and on the other hand of levels of efficiency as between societies in the ultimate struggle against death—as in the present war. . . .

Professor Watson [6] emphasized the meaning of higher levels of efficiency, and higher levels of social efficiency are reached through the individualization of function represented best by the scientific specialization of our time. Individualization is a relative term—the individual always remains incorporated in some world of ideas—but practically the creative man secures sufficient individualization to do his work, retains enough recognition to keep him sane, by escaping from the census of one group into the appreciation of another

[5] Cf. "The natural and naive expectation of a social group is that the definitions which have been traditionally accepted and applied to innumerable situations by many individuals will last indefinitely and bear any amount of change. It is not usual for social groups to prepare against possible disorganization except by trying to provide for the repetition of such breaks of rules as have already been experienced in the past; every break of a new and unknown kind always provokes astonishment." (*The Polish Peasant,* 1927, Vol. II, p. 1248.)

[6] J. B. Watson, "Practical and Theoretical Problems in Instinct and Habit," in Jennings and others, *Suggestions of Modern Science Concerning Education,* pp. 51–100.

group. And this escape seems to go on at a rate corresponding with the increased facility of communication. The world has become greatly diversified, containing not only races and nationalities with differing norms and cultural systems, but various worlds of ideas represented by various scientific, religious, artistic circles; and by the fact of reading alone the individual can associate himself with those persons or circles pre-adapted to his ideas, and form with them a solidary group.

Now, the superior level of culture reached by the western world is due to a tendency to disturb norms—introduced first into the material world by the physicists and gradually extending itself in connection with the theory of evolution to the biological world, and just now beginning to touch the human world. And this tendency to disturb norms becomes an end in itself in the form of scientific pursuits whose aim is the redefinition of all possible situations and the establishment eventually of the most general and universal norms, namely scientific laws. And the success of this method from the standpoint of efficiency is shown in the wonderful advance in material technique resulting from research for law in the fields of physics and chemistry, exemplified, for example, in mechanical inventions and modern medicine.[7]

[7] The last four paragraphs have been rearranged.

14 SOCIAL DISORGANIZATION AND RECONSTRUCTION

In the preceding selection Thomas suggested that group solidarity and social organization depend upon common definitions of situations, and that the modern world is witnessing a decline and disappearance of such common definitions. The present selection from *The Polish Peasant,* 1918–20, develops the same theme around the concept of "social disorganization."

In *The Polish Peasant* Thomas and Znaniecki were confronted with the necessity of describing the rapid and fundamental changes which had taken place in Polish peasant society in a relatively short time. Moreover, they were interested in achieving a level of conceptualization that would have wider applicability than to a single group. The result was a challenging general theory of social change which, in its emphasis upon "social disorganization," has had a marked influence on American sociological thought.

Essentially, any violation of a social norm is a case of "social disorganization" from the standpoint of the traditional code of a society, and adaptation to it may take place in two ways. If the violations are few and scattered, the process of "social reorganization," or the reinforcement of existing rules, is sufficient. But when social disorganization is exceptionally severe or widespread (as "revolt" or "revolution") the primary adaptation is not sufficient, and processes of "social reconstruction" are called for. This involves the creation of new institutions, codes, and schemes of behavior—a task in which the creative individual plays an important role.

Thus in the general theory social disorganization is but a phase of all change, although Thomas regarded modern national societies as being highly disorganized. The next selection, "The Individualization of Behavior," will make this clear.

It should be noted, however, that in Thomas' conception "social disorganization" is not regarded as a "cause" of various social problems. Many American sociologists have assumed that "social disorganization" accounts for such things as high divorce rates, delinquency, and the like, whereas from Thomas' standpoint these phenomena are simply a part of a whole process of change involving both norms and behavior. Social disorganization, in his view, is simply the context in which behavior problems emerge in a relatively normless society. Finally, it should be remarked that whether or not any particular activity is disorganizing depends upon the point of view taken. New norms may result from behavior which in terms of the traditional code is disorganizing.

The Concept of Social Disorganization [1]

The concept of social disorganization as we shall use it . . . refers primarily to institutions [2] and only secondarily to men. Just as group-organization embodied in socially systematized schemes of behavior imposed as rules upon individuals never exactly coincides with individual life-organization consisting in personally systematized schemes of behavior, so social disorganization never exactly corresponds to individual disorganization. Even if we imagined a group lacking all internal differentiation, *i.e.*, a group in which every member would accept all the socially sanctioned and none but the socially sanctioned rules of behavior as schemes of his own conduct, still every member would systematize these schemes differently in his personal evolution, would make a different life-organization out of them, because neither his temperament nor his life-history [3] would be exactly the same as those of other members. As a matter of fact, such a uniform group is a pure fiction; even in the least differentiated groups we find socially sanctioned rules of behavior which explicitly apply only to certain classes of individuals and are not supposed to be used by others in organizing their conduct, and we find individuals who in organizing their conduct use some personal schemes of their own invention besides the traditionally sanctioned social rules. Moreover, the progress of social differentiation is accompanied by a growth of special institutions, consisting essentially in a systematic organization of a certain number of socially selected schemes for the permanent achievement of certain results. This institutional organization and the life-organization of any of the individuals through whose activity the institution is socially realized partly overlap, but one individual cannot fully realize in his life the whole systematic organization of the institution since the latter always implies the collaboration of many, and on the other hand each individual has many interests which have to be organized outside of this particular institution.

[1] *The Polish Peasant,* 1927, Vol. II, pp. 1127–1131.

[2] See p. 52 supra for the definition of "institution" used in *The Polish Peasant.*

[3] These concepts were developed in the Introduction to the "Life-Record of an Immigrant," also in *The Polish Peasant.* For selections from this Introduction, see "A Theory of Social Personality," pp. 145–186 supra.

There is, of course, a certain reciprocal dependence between social organization and individual life-organization. . . . But the nature of this reciprocal influence in each particular case is a problem to be studied, not a dogma to be accepted in advance.

These points must be kept in mind if we are to understand the question of social disorganization. We can define the latter briefly as a *decrease of the influence of existing social rules of behavior upon individual members of the group.* This decrease may present innumerable degrees, ranging from a single break of some particular rule by one individual up to a general decay of all the institutions of the group.[4] Now, social disorganization in this sense has no unequivocal connection whatever with individual disorganization, which consists in a decrease of the individual's ability to organize his whole life for the efficient, progressive and continuous realization of his fundamental interests. An individual who breaks some or even most of the social rules prevailing in his group may indeed do this because he is losing the minimum capacity of life-organization required by social conformism; but he may also reject the schemes of behavior imposed by his milieu because they hinder him in reaching a more efficient and more comprehensive life-organization. On the other hand also, the social organization of a group may be very permanent and strong in the sense that no opposition is manifested to the existing rules and institutions; and yet, this lack of opposition may be simply the result of the narrowness of the interests of the group-members and may be accompanied by a very rudimentary, mechanical and inefficient life-organization of each member individually. Of course, a strong group organization may be also the product of a conscious moral effort of its members and thus correspond to a very high degree of life-organization of each of them individually. It is therefore impossible to conclude from social as to individual organization or disorganization, or vice versa. In other words, social organization is not coextensive with individual

[4] In this same volume, pp. 1206–1210, Thomas and Znaniecki identify two different types of social disorganization. The first is marked by the acceptance of new values by the younger generation; the second, by the decay of solidarity among older members of the community. The latter is regarded as more serious because it weakens "the very foundation of social cohesion."

morality, nor does social disorganization correspond to individual demoralization.

Social disorganization is not an exceptional phenomenon limited to certain periods or certain societies; some of it is found always and everywhere, since always and everywhere there are individual cases of breaking social rules, cases which exercise some disorganizing influence on group institutions and, if not counteracted, are apt to multiply and to lead to a complete decay of the latter. But during periods of social stability this continuous incipient disorganization is . . . neutralized by such activities of the group as reinforce with the help of social sanctions the power of existing rules.[5] The stability of group institutions is thus simply a dynamic equilibrium of processes of disorganization and *reorganization*. This equilibrium is disturbed when processes of disorganization can no longer be checked by any attempts to reinforce the existing rules. A period of prevalent disorganization follows, which may lead to a complete dissolution of the group. More usually, however, it is counteracted and stopped before it reaches this limit by a new process of reorganization which in this case does not consist in a mere reinforcement of the decaying organization, but in a production of new schemes of behavior and new institutions better adapted to the changed demands of the group; we call this production of new schemes and institutions *social reconstruction*.[6] Social reconstruction is possible only because, and in so far as, during the period of social disorganization a part at least of the members of the group have not become individually disorganized, but, on the contrary, have been working toward a new and more efficient personal life-organization and have expressed a

[5] That Thomas was responsible for this theory of disorganization and reorganization is not to be questioned. It may be found in embryo in the selection from the *Source Book for Social Origins*, 1909, p. 222 supra.

[6] The concept of "social reconstruction" is clarified in another part of *The Polish Peasant:* "The problem of social reconstruction is to create new schemes of behavior—new rules of personal conduct and new institutions—which will supplant or modify the old schemes and correspond better to the changed attitudes, that is, which will permit the latter to express themselves in action and at the same time will regulate their active manifestations so as not only to prevent the social group from becoming disorganized but to increase its cohesion by opening new fields for social cooperation." (Vol. II, 1927, p. 1303.)

part at least of the constructive tendencies implied in their individual activities in an effort to produce new social institutions.

Revolutionary Attitudes [7]

All the cases of social disorganization include an active opposition to the traditional social schemes of behavior; in this respect the rejection of a fashion, a theft or murder, an attempt to overthrow the existing class organization or political order, a religious heresy, are fundamentally similar, being equally the manifestations of tendencies which can find no adequate expression under the prevailing social system and, if allowed to develop sufficiently, lead to a decay of this system. But notwithstanding this general similarity there are . . . important differences . . . [and] the terms "revolt" and "revolution" can be utilized to mark this difference.

That kind of active opposition to existing rules which we term revolt is individualistic in its bearing, even if many members of a group happen to participate in it; it implies only, on the part of each individual, personal demands for some values which he could not have under the traditional system. A revolutionary tendency may also involve such personal demands and in so far be an act of revolt; but its essential feature is that it includes a demand for new values for a whole group—community, class, nation, etc.; each individual acting not only in his own name but also in the name of others.

Secondly, revolt does not intentionally and consciously aim at the destruction of the old system in general; its purpose is in each particular case the satisfaction of some particular wish. The break of rules is only, in a sense, incidental to this satisfaction and the decay of the traditional system comes spontaneously, as a result of an increasing number and variety of cases of revolt. Whereas the immediate aim of revolution is to abolish the traditional system or at least some of the schemes of behavior which are its part, to destroy permanently their influence within the given group, and thus to open the way to a general and permanent satisfaction of those needs which cannot be freely satisfied while the system lasts.

In view of these differences between revolt and revolution, the

[7] *Ibid.*, pp. 1265–1266.

methods which prove more or less efficient in suppressing the former often fail when applied to the latter.

The Concept of Social Reconstruction [8]

In . . . [the] process of creating new social forms the role of the individual, the inventor or leader, is much more important than in the preservation and defense of the old forms or in revolutionary movements which tend merely to overthrow the traditional system, leaving the problem of reconstruction to be solved later. For even when the defense of the traditional organization is assumed by particular individuals the latter act merely as official or unofficial representatives of the group; they may be more or less original and efficient in realizing their aim, but their aim has been defined for them entirely by social tradition.[9] In revolution, as we have seen, the individual can generalize and make more conscious only tendencies which already exist in the group. Whereas, in social reconstruction his task is to discover and understand the new attitudes which demand an outlet, to invent the schemes of behavior which would best correspond to these attitudes, and to make the group accept these schemes as social rules or institutions. More than this, he must usually develop the new attitudes in certain parts of society which have been evolving more slowly and are not yet ready for the reform; and often he has to struggle against obstinate defenders of the traditional system.

[8] *Ibid.*, pp. 1303–1304.

[9] Cf. "The task of preventing or counteracting disorganization, whether faced by the community which wants the individual to behave in accordance with traditional rules, or by the individual who wants to influence the community so as to maintain the traditional system in belief and action, can always be reduced to the following simple formula: 'How to make the individual or the community define and solve certain situations in the same way as before, in spite of changed conditions or changed attitudes or both.'" (*Ibid.*, p. 1247.)

15 THE INDIVIDUALIZATION OF BEHAVIOR

While Thomas regarded "social disorganization" as a regular feature of all social change, he was also convinced that the rapidity of change in modern society presented more problems in disorganization than had ever before been witnessed in human society. Today, the old primary-group norms have broken down and as yet the forces of social reconstruction have not appeared in sufficient strength to provide new norms. These ideas form the background for Thomas' treatment of a particular social problem in the present selection.

This selection is from Chapter III of *The Unadjusted Girl,* 1923, a study of the increased prostitution which appeared during and after World War I. In the first chapter the "four wishes" are introduced, and in the second Thomas shows how the wishes are regulated in primary-group life to the satisfaction of both the individual and the group. In the third chapter widespread culture change is introduced as a new factor.

Various forces have converged upon the modern world to weaken social organization and disturb the solidarity of the individual with his group. Commonly accepted definitions of the situation are few, and under these conditions there is a tendency for individual definitions to supplant group definitions. Wish-satisfaction is often obtained by forms of behavior which are regarded as deviant from the standpoint of traditional norms. The increased number of prostitutes is therefore a part of this general process of "individualization," and a result of both cultural and psychological forces. To support his thesis Thomas relies upon personal documents and records which are presented in sharp focus upon the backdrop of widespread social disorganization. The result is a convincing picture of how rapid and widespread change contributes to personal demoralization.

The present selection, then, is important as an illustration of how Thomas applied his general theories and methods to a concrete problem and thereby illumined it.

THE UNADJUSTED GIRL—CHAPTER III [1]

From the foregoing it appears that the face-to-face group [2] (family-community) is a powerful habit-forming mechanism. The group has

[1] *The Unadjusted Girl,* pp. 70–97.

[2] Cf. Charles H. Cooley, *Social Organization,* especially chap. III, for discussion of the primary group.

to provide a system of behavior for many persons at once, a code which applies to everybody and lasts longer than any individual or generation. Consequently the group has two interests in the individual,—to suppress wishes and activities which are in conflict with the existing organization, or which seem the starting point of social disharmony, and to encourage wishes and actions which are required by the existing social system.[3] And if the group performs this task successfully, as it does among savages, among Mohammedans, and as it did until recently among European peasants, no appreciable change in the moral code or in the state of culture is observable from generation to generation. In small and isolated communities there is little tendency to change or progress because the new experience of the individual is sacrificed for the sake of the security of the group.

But by a process, an evolution, connected with mechanical inventions, facilitated communication, the diffusion of print, the growth of cities, business organization, the capitalistic system, specialized occupations, scientific research, doctrines of freedom, the evolutionary view of life, etc., the family and community influences have been weakened and the world in general has been profoundly changed in content, ideals, and organization.[4]

[3] In 1921 Thomas had phrased this differently: "The organization of society has always a double character: it makes possible the gratification of the individual's wishes, and even the multiplication of them, but at the same time it requires that his wishes shall be gratified only in *usual* ways, that their expression shall be so regulated as not to interfere unfairly with the expression of the wishes of others." (*Old World Traits Transplanted,* p. 26.)

[4] Cf. "Under these conditions, the first result of the growing connection between the community and the outside world is . . . a more or less far-going process of disorganization; new attitudes develop in the members of the group which cannot be adequately controlled by the old social organization because they cannot find an adequate expression in the old primary-group institutions. The group tries to defend itself . . . by methods consciously tending to strengthen the influence of the traditional rules of behavior; but this endeavor, often efficient as long as the outside contacts remain limited to some particular field of interests, loses more and more of its effectiveness when these contacts continue to develop and extend gradually to all fields of social activity. The problem is then no longer how to suppress the new attitudes, but how to find for them institutional expression, . . . instead of permitting them to remain in a status where they express themselves merely in individual revolt and social revolution.

"This problem is evidently common to all societies in periods of rapid change. We

Young people leave home for larger opportunities, to seek new experience, and from necessity. Detachment from family and community, wandering, travel, "vagabondage" have assumed the character of normality. Relationships are casualized and specialized. Men meet professionally, as promoters of enterprises, not as members of families, communities, churches. Girls leave home to work in factories, stores, offices, and studios. Even when families are not separated they leave home for their work.

Every new invention, every chance acquaintanceship, every new environment, has the possibility of redefining the situation and of introducing change, disorganization or different type of organization into the life of the individual or even of the whole world. Thus, the invention of the check led to forgery; the sulphur match to arson; at present the automobile is perhaps connected with more seductions than happen otherwise in cities altogether; an assassination precipitated the World War; motion pictures and the *Saturday Evening Post* have stabilized and unstabilized many existences, considered merely as opportunity for new types of career. The costly and luxurious articles of women's wear organize the lives of many girls (as designers, artists, and buyers) and disorganize the lives of many who crave these pretty things.

In the small and spatially isolated communities of the past, where the influences were strong and steady, the members became more or less habituated to and reconciled with a life of repressed wishes. The repression was demanded of all, the arrangement was equitable, and while certain new experiences were prohibited, and pleasure not countenanced as an end in itself, there remained satisfactions, not the least of which was the suppression of the wishes of others. On the other hand the modern world presents itself as a spectacle in which the observer is never sufficiently participating. The modern revolt and unrest are due to the contrast between the paucity of fulfillment of the wishes of the individual and the fullness, or apparent fullness, of life around him. All age levels have been affected

---

find it in a savage group brought in contact with western civilization, and in the most extensive and highly complicated modern national group where the rapid growth of new attitudes is no longer the effect of external influences but of the internal complexity of social activities." (*The Polish Peasant,* 1927, Vol. II, pp. 1120–1121.)

by the feeling that much, too much, is being missed in life. This unrest is felt most by those who have heretofore been most excluded from general participation in life,—the mature woman and the young girl.[5] Sometimes it expresses itself in despair and depression, sometimes in breaking all bounds. Immigrants form a particular class in this respect. They sometimes repudiate the old system completely in their haste to get into the new. There are cases where the behavior of immigrants, expressing natural but random and unregulated impulses, has been called insane by our courts.

Case No. 37 represents despair, case No. 38 revolt, . . . [No.] 39 . . . extraordinarily wild behavior.

37. There is a saying about the peacock, "When she looks at her feathers she laughs, and when she looks at her feet she cries." I am in the same situation.

My husband's career, upon which I spent the best years of my life, is established favorably; our children are a joy to me as a mother; nor can I complain about our material circumstances. But I am dissatisfied with myself. My love for my children, be it ever so great, cannot destroy myself. A human being is not created like a bee which dies after accomplishing its only task.

Desires, long latent, have been aroused in me and become more aggressive the more obstacles they encounter. . . . I now have the desire to go about and see and hear everything. I wish to take part in everything—to dance, skate, play the piano, sing, go to the theatre, opera, lectures and generally mingle in society. As you see, I am no idler whose purpose is to chase all sorts of foolish things, as a result of loose ways. This is not the case.

My present unrest is a natural result following a long period of hunger and thirst for non-satisfied desires in every field of human experience. It is the dread of losing that which never can be recovered—youth and time which do not stand still—an impulse to catch up with the things I have missed. . . . If it were not for my maternal feeling I would go away into the wide world.*

38. I had been looking for Margaret, for I knew she was a striking instance of the "unadjusted" who had within a year come with a kind of aesthetic logic to Greenwich Village. She needed something very badly. What I heard about her which excited me was that she was twenty years

* *Forward,* March 11, 1921.

[5] Many years earlier Thomas had suggested this view. See "The Mind of Woman and the Lower Races," 1907, reprinted in *Sex and Society,* pp. 301–302, 311.

old, unmarried, had never lived with a man or had any of that experience, had worked for a year on a socialist newspaper, and a socialist magazine, was a heavy drinker and a frequenter of Hell Hole, that she came from a middle class family but preferred the society of the outcasts to any other. Greenwich Village is not composed of outcasts, but it does not reject them, and it enables a man or woman who desires to know the outcast to satisfy the desire without feeling cut off from humanity. Hell Hole is a saloon in the back room of which pickpockets, grafters, philosophers, poets, revolutionists, stool-pigeons, and the riff-raff of humanity meet. Margaret loves this place and the people in it—so they told me—and there she did and said extreme things in which there was a bitter fling at decent society.

So that night, when she came with Christine, I invited her to go with me to Hell Hole to have a drink. She drank whiskey after whiskey and showed no effect. As soon as we were seated in the back room alone she started to tell me about herself. I forget what unessential thing I said to get her started. She knew by instinct what I desired and she told me her story with utter frankness, and with a simple, unaggressive self-respect.

"I belong to what is called a respectable, middle-class family. My father is a prominent newspaper man. Whenever I was ill, as a child, he gave me whiskey instead of medicine. This began at the age of four. One of my childish amusements was to mix cordials and water to entertain my little friends with. We lived in the city, and I had from four years of age the run of the streets. At six or eight I knew everything—about sex, about hard street life. I knew it wrong, of course, for I saw it but did not feel it. I felt wrong about it all, and feared it, wasn't a part of it, except as an observer. I saw no beauty or friendliness in sex feeling. I think it was this that kept me away later from physical intimacy with men; it couldn't appeal to me after my early life in the street. I know it doesn't always happen so, but it did with me.

"When I got to be thirteen years old my father reversed his attitude towards me; before then, all freedom; after that, all restraint. I was completely shut in. Soon after that I became religious and joined the church. I had a long pious correspondence with another girl and used to brood all the time about God and about my transcendental duties. This lasted till I was sixteen, and then life, ordinary external life, came back with a rush and I couldn't stand my exclusive inner world and the outward restraint any longer, and I wanted to go away from home. So I worked hard in the High School and got a $300 scholarship in Latin and Greek. With this I went to a Western College and staid there two years, working my own way and paying my expenses. I read a lot at this time, and liked revolutionary literature; read socialism, and poetry that was full of revolt. I took to anything which expressed a reaction against the conditions of my life at home.

"I stood well in my studies, and suppose I might have completed the college course, except that I got into trouble with the authorities, for very slight reasons, as it seems to me. I smoked cigarettes, a habit I had formed as a child, and that of course was forbidden. It was also forbidden to enter the neighboring cemetery, I don't know why. One day I smoked a cigarette in the graveyard—a double offense—and then, in the playfulness of my spirit, I wrote a poem about it and published it in the college paper. In this paper I had already satirized the Y.W.C.A. A few other acts of that nature made me an undesirable member of the college and my connection with it ceased.

"After an unhappy time at home—my father and I could not get on together; ever since my early childhood he had been trying to 'reform' me—I got a job on the socialist *Call,* a New York daily newspaper, at $—— a week. It was hard work all day, but I liked it and I didn't drink—I didn't want to—and lived on the money without borrowing. Later I went on the *Masses,* and there I was well off. [Then I went to Washington to picket for the suffragists and got a jail sentence, and when I returned the *Masses* had been suspended.] It was at that time that I began to go with the Hudson Dusters [a gang of criminals] and to drink heavily. Greenwich Village seemed to think it was too good for me, or I too bad for it. Most of the women were afraid to associate with me. Only the Hudson Dusters, or people like them, seemed really human to me. I went, in a kind of despair, to the water-front, and staid three days and nights in the back room of a low saloon, where there were several old prostitutes. And I liked them. They seemed human, more so than other people. And in this place were working men. One man, with a wife and children, noticed I was going there and didn't seem to belong to them, and he asked me to go home with him and live with his family; and he meant it, and meant it decently.

"I want to know the down and outs," said Margaret with quiet, almost fanatical intenseness. "I find kindness in the lowest places, and more than kindness sometimes—something, I don't know what it is, that I want." *

39. There came a day when my wife heard that there was an Atlantic City not far from Philadelphia. So I granted her wish and rented a nice room for her in a hotel there and sent her with the two children to that seashore. . . .

The next summer I did not make out so well and could not afford to send my wife to the country, but she absolutely demanded to be sent even if I had to "hang and bring." . . . My protestations and explanations

* Hutchins Hapgood: "At Christine's" (Manuscript).

were of no avail. She went to Atlantic City and hired a room in the same hotel. . . .

I took my wife's behavior to heart and became ill. Some of my friends advised me to teach her a lesson and desert her, so that she would mend her ways in the future. They assured me that they would take care of my family, to keep them from starving. I was persuaded by them and left Philadelphia for a distant town.

My wife in Atlantic City, seeing that I sent her no money, returned home. Upon learning what had happened, she promptly sold the furniture, which had cost $800, for almost nothing and went to New York. My friends notified me of all that had occurred in my absence, whereupon I came back.

I advertised in the papers and found my wife. My first question was about the children and she replied she did not know where they were. Upon further questioning she answered that she had brought the children with her from Philadelphia but as she could do nothing with them in her way she simply left them in the street.

After great efforts made through my lawyer, I succeeded in obtaining the release of my children from the Gerry Society, after paying for their two months' keep there. . . .

Since this unhappy occurrence, my wife has many times wrecked our home, selling the household goods while I was at work and leaving me alone with the children. Whenever she feels like satisfying her cravings, or whenever she cannot afford to buy herself enough pretty clothes and hats, she deserts me. One time she was gone 9 months and never saw the children during this period. . . .

I tried to make up with her every time and give her another chance. But her cordiality lasted only until she again took a craving for some rag, when she would again leave home. She was even mean enough once to leave me with a five months' old baby who needed nursing and the only way out seemed to be the river for me and the baby. . . .

I assure you that everything I have written is the truth. If you do not believe me, you may convince yourself at the Desertion Bureau where my case has been recorded several times.*

. . . . .

The world has become large, alluring, and confusing. Social evolution has been so rapid that no agency has been developed in the larger community of the state for regulating behavior which would replace the failing influence of the community and correspond completely with present activities. There is no universally accepted body of doctrines or practices. The churchman, for example, and the

* *Forward,* December 8, 1920.

scientist, educator, or radical leader are so far apart that they cannot talk together. They are, as the Greeks expressed it, in different "universes of discourse."

41. Dr. Austin O'Malley writes rather passionately about the control of births, in the Catholic weekly, "America." Says Dr. O'Malley: "The most helpless idiot is as far above a non-existent child as St. Bridget is above a committe on birth control." Let us pause over the idiot and the non-existent child. Must we say that all potential children should be born? Are we to take a firm stand against celibacy, which denies to so many possible children the right to be baptized? And will Dr. O'Malley tell us which is the greater virtue, to bear children that they may be baptized, or to have no children for the glory of one's own soul? This solicitude over the non-existent child has certain drawbacks. How large a family, in fact, does Dr. O'Malley desire a woman to bear? May she stop after the fourteenth infant, or must she say to herself: "There are still non-existent children, some of them helpless idiots; perhaps I will bear them that they may be baptized." *

Or, if we should submit any series of behavior problems to a set of men selected as most competent to give an opinion we should find no such unanimity as prevailed in a village community. One set of opinions would be rigoristic and hold that conformity with the existing code is advisable under all circumstances; another pragmatic, holding that the code may sometimes be violated. For example, in 1919, the United States Interdepartmental Social Hygiene Board authorized the Psychological Laboratory of the Johns Hopkins University to make an investigation of the "informational and educative effect upon the public of certain motion-picture films," and in this connection a questionnaire was sent to "medical men and women who have had most to do with problems in sex education and the actual treatment of venereal infections." From the manuscript of this investigation I give below some of the replies received to question 13.

42. Question 13. Do you consider that absolute continence is always to be insisted upon? Or may it be taught that under certain conditions intercourse in the unmarried is harmless or beneficial?

Dr. A. I know of no harm from absolute continence. Intercourse in the unmarried cannot be justified on any grounds of health or morals.

* Editorial in *The New Republic,* June 19, 1915.

Dr. B. No. For some absolute continence would be easy, for others, impossible. It is an individual problem to be decided by the individual, with or without advice.

Under certain conditions in the unmarried, male or female, intercourse is harmless or beneficial; under other conditions it is harmful and injurious (irrespective of venereal disease).

Dr. C. I think it is harmless and beneficial. But our standards are against it. And who could possibly conscientiously teach such a thing, no matter what he thought?

Dr. D. Certainly not. It is probably well to teach young people that continence before marriage is in general very desirable, as contrasted with the results of incontinence.

Dr. E. It is best to teach conformity to custom.

Dr. F. Absolute continence should always be insisted upon.

Dr. G. I know of no condition where one is justified in advising the unmarried that intercourse is harmless or beneficial.

Dr. H. Absolute continence.

Dr. I. No. [Continence is not always to be insisted upon.]

Dr. J. The first should not be insisted on any more than the latter should be recommended. . . .

Dr. K. The latter may be taught.

Dr. L. Not convinced either way.

Dr. M. Absolute continence should be preached as a doctrine to the unmarried, and let the individual adjust himself to this stern law according to his lights.*

Fifty-one replies were received to this question. Twenty-four were, in substance, "not permissible"; fifteen, "permissible"; four, "in doubt"; eight were indefinite, as, for example: "Adults will probably decide this for themselves."

As another example of a general defining agency, the legal system of the state does not pretend to be more than a partial set of negative definitions. An English jurist [6] has thus described the scope of the law: "If A is drowning and if B is present, and if B by reaching out his hand can save A, and if B does not do this, and if A drowns, then B has committed no offense." All that the law requires of B is

* These materials, edited by John B. Watson and K. S. Lashley, have been printed in part in *Mental Hygiene,* Vol. 4, pp. 769–847.

6 In his article "Eugenics," *American Magazine,* June 1909, p. 191, Thomas attributes this example to Sir James F. Stephen, but adds no further reference. A very similar statement may be found in Stephen's *A Digest of the Criminal Law* (St. Louis: Soule, Thomas & Wentworth, 1877), p. 151.

that he shall not push A into the water. The law is not only far from being a system capable of regulating the total life of men, but it does not even regulate the activities it is designed to regulate. . . .

The definition of the situation is equivalent to the determination of the vague. In the Russian *mir* and the American rural community of fifty years ago nothing was left vague, all was defined. But in the general world movement to which I have referred, connected with free communication in space and free communication of thought, not only particular situations but the most general situations have become vague. Some situations were once defined and have become vague again; some have arisen and have never been defined. Whether this country shall participate in world politics, whether America is a refuge for the oppressed of other nationalities, whether the English should occupy India or the Belgians Africa, whether there shall be Sunday amusements, whether the history of the world is the unfolding of the will of God, whether men may drink wine, whether evolution may be taught in schools, whether marriage is indissoluble, whether sex life outside of marriage is permissible, whether children should be taught the facts of sex, whether the number of children born may be voluntarily limited,—these questions have become vague. There are rival definitions of the situation, and none of them is binding.

In addition to the vagueness about these general questions there is an indeterminateness about particular acts and individual life-policies. It appears that the behavior of the young girl is influenced partly by the traditional code, partly by undesigned definitions of the situation derived from those incidents in the passing show of the greater world which suggest to her pleasure and recognition. If any standard prevails or characterizes a distinguished social set this is in itself a definition of the situation. Thus in a city the shop windows, the costumes worn on the streets, the newspaper advertisements of ladies' wear, the news items concerning objects of luxury define a proper girl as one neatly, fashionably, beautifully, and expensively gowned, and the behavior of the girl is an adaptation to this standard. . . .

45. . . . My sweetheart remarked that she would like to have a great deal of money. When I asked her what she would do with it, she replied

that she would buy herself a lot of beautiful dresses. When I said that it was all right to have them but it ought to be all right without them too, she protested that she loved fine clothes and this to such exent, that——

Here she made a remark which I am ashamed to let pass my lips. I would sooner have welcomed an open grave than to have heard those words. She said that she would sell her body for a time in order to procure nice clothes for herself.

And since that day I go around like a mad person. I neither eat nor sleep. In short, I am no more a man.

She afterward excused herself, claiming that it was said in a joke, and that as long as one talks without actually doing it there is no harm in it. But this is not reassuring to me. I have a premonition that she would go further than mere talk after marriage, for if she carries such notions in her head now, what might happen after we are married.*

Intermediate between the home and work (or the school) there are certain organized influences for giving pleasure and information—the motion picture, the newspaper, the light periodical—which define the situation in equivocal terms. They enter the home and are dependent upon its approval, and are therefore obliged to present life in episodes which depict the triumph of virtue. But if they limited themselves to this they would be dull. The spectacle therefore contains a large and alluring element of sin over which virtue eventually triumphs. The moral element is preserved nominally but the real interest and substance is something else.

46. A young girl may be taught at home and church that chastity is a virtue, but the newspapers and the movies feature women in trouble along this line, now painting them as heroines, now sobbing over their mystery and pathos. Apparently *they* get all the attention and attention is the life blood of youth. The funny papers ridicule marriage, old maids and bashful men. The movies, magazines, street conversation and contemporary life are filled with the description of lapses that somehow turn out safely and even luxuriously. If the modern young girl practices virtue she may not believe in it. The preliminaries to wrong-doing are apparently the accepted manners of the time. When the girl herself lapses it is frequently because of lack of a uniform, authoritative definition of the social code.**

* *Forward,* May 4, 1920.

** Miriam Van Waters: "The True Value of Correctional Education." Paper read at the 51st American Prison Conference, November 1, 1921.

Among well-to-do girls a new type has been differentiated, characterized by youth, seeming innocence, sexual sophistication and a relatively complete depudorization.

47. The modern age of girls and young men is intensely immoral, and immoral seemingly without the pressure of circumstances. At whose door we may lay the fault, we cannot tell. Is it the result of what we call "the emancipation of woman," with its concomitant freedom from chaperonage, increased intimacy between the sexes in adolescence, and a more tolerant viewpoint toward all things unclean in life? This seems the only logical forbear of the present state. And are the girls causing it now, or the men? Each sex will lay the blame on the heads, or passions, of the other, and perhaps both sexes are equally at fault.

Whosesoever the fault may be (and that is not such an important question, since both sexes are equally immoral), the whole character of social relations among younger people is lamentable. The modern dances are disgusting—the "toddle" and its variations and vibrations, the "shimmy" and its brazen pandering to the animal senses, and the worst offspring of jazz, the "camel-walk." There is but one idea predominant in these dances—one that we will leave unnamed.

It is not only in dancing that this immorality appears. The modern social bud drinks, not too much often, but enough; smokes considerably, swears unguardedly, and tells "dirty" stories. All in all, she is a most frivolous, passionate, sensation-seeking little thing.*

48. "Flappers" usually are girls who believe personality is physical, who consider all advice as abstract, who love continual change, who converse in generalities and who are in many higher institutions of learning.

To present a picture of the normal girl as she exists today is a daring venture. She has no average, she has no group tie. She is a stranger to herself—sometimes especially to members of her own family—and cannot be compared with her kind of a previous age.

We are tempted to think of her as living in a spirit of masquerade, so rapidly and completely can she assume different and difficult roles of accomplishment.

She tantalizes us by the simpleness of her artfulness and yet unrealness. We find her light-hearted, which is the privilege of youth. She believes with Stevenson that to have missed the joy is to have missed it all. We find her harboring secrets and imbedded emotions which are her hidden treasure in the mysterious discovery of herself as a private individual.

* Editorial in the Brown University *Daily Herald* quoted in the *New York World,* February 3, 1921.

If we do not understand these symptoms we call it temperament and try to dispose of the girl as difficult or as needing discipline.*

Formerly the fortunes of the individual were bound up with those of his family and to some degree with those of the community. He had his security, recognition, response, and new experience in the main as group member. He could not rise or fall greatly above or below the group level. Even the drunkard and the "black sheep" had respect in proportion to the standing of his family. And correspondingly, if a family member lost his "honor," the standing of the whole family was lowered.

Individualism, on the other hand, means the personal schematization of life,—making one's own definitions of the situation and determining one's own behavior norms. Actually there never has been and never will be anything like complete individualization, because no one lives or can live without regard to a public. Anything else would be insanity. But in their occupational pursuits men have already a degree of individualization, decide things alone and in their own way. They take risks, schematize their enterprises, succeed or fail, rise higher and fall lower. A large element of individualism has entered into the marriage relation also. Married women are now entering the occupations freely and from choice, and carrying on amateur interests which formerly were not thought of as going with marriage.[7] And this is evidently a good thing, and stabilizes marriage. Marriage alone is not a life, particularly since the decline of the community type of organization. The cry of despair in document No. 37 is from a woman who limited her life to marriage, probably by her own choice, and is now apparently too old to have other interests. But on the other hand document No. 49 is a definition of marriage as exclusively a device for the realization of personal wishes and the avoidance of responsibility. . . .

* Mary Ide Bentley, Address at Berkeley, California. *New York Sun,* February 7, 1922.

[7] Some years before this was written Thomas had recommended jobs for married women as at least a partial solution to the strains encountered in modern marriage. See "The Adventitious Character of Woman," 1906, reprinted in *Sex and Society,* pp. 245–247; also, "The Older and Newer Ideals of Marriage," *American Magazine,* April 1909, pp. 548–552.

49. Girls, get married! Even if your marriage turns out badly, you are better off than if you had stayed single. I know half a dozen women whose first marriages were failures. They got rid of their first husbands easily and have made much better marriages than they could have made if they had stayed single. Their new husbands idolize them. One of my women acquaintances who has been married four times is the most petted wife I know.

My own marriage has turned out well. Everything seemed against it. I was well known in my profession, and when I married I was making as much money as my husband. We were of different religions. He drank.

But he had one big quality. He was generous. Since our marriage he has refused to let me work. Girls, be sure the man you pick is generous. Look out for a tightwad. If a man is liberal with his money he is sure to be easy to get along with. Liberal men in money matters do not annoy their wives in the other concerns of life. . . .

But even if my marriage had turned out badly, I would have been better off than if I had neglected the opportunity to become married. I met new friends through my husband. If I had divorced him at any time, I know many of his men friends would have courted me. There is something about the magic letters "Mrs." that gives a woman an added attraction in the eyes of men. There is a middle-aged widow in our apartment house that has more men taking her to theatres and dances than all the flappers and unmarried young women. . . .

I often wonder what men get married for. They take heavy financial responsibilities. They mortgage their free time to one woman. What a wife's clothes cost them would enable them to enjoy expensive amusements, extensive travel and better surroundings generally. Then, too, a bachelor, no matter what his age or social position, gets more attention socially than a married man. Children, too, give less pleasure and service to a father than a mother.

But for women, marriage is undoubtedly a success. It raises their position in the community. In most cases, it releases them from the danger of daily necessary work and responsibility. It brings them more attention from other men. Even when incompatibility intervenes, alimony provides separate support without work. In such cases, it also provides a more strategic position for a new and better marriage.*

In the same connection, the following cases show the growing tendency toward individualized definitions of sexual relations outside of marriage. In case No. 50 an immigrant girl explicitly organizes her life on the basis of prostitution instead of work. In No. 51

* *New York American,* September 27, 1920.

the girls commercialize a series of betrothals. In No. 52 the girl has worked out her own philosophy of love and calls herself a missionary prostitute.

50. [When I left Europe] my little sister's last words were, "Here, in hell, I will dream through the nights that far, far, across the ocean, my loving brother lives happily." And my last words were, "I shall forget my right hand if I ever forget you."

I suffered not a little in the golden land. . . . Five years passed. I loyally served the God of gold, saved some money and sent for my sister. For three years I believed myself the happiest of men. . . . My sister bloomed like a rose in May and she was kind and motherly to me. We were tied by a bond of the highest love and on my part that love had until now remained the same. But listen what a terrible thing occurred.

About a year ago I noticed a marked change in my sister—both physically and spiritually. She grew pale, her eyes lost their fire and her attitude toward me changed also. She began to neglect her work (I taught her a good trade), until half a year ago she entirely gave up the work. This angered me very much and I began to shadow her in order to discover the mystery in her life, for she had recently avoided talking to me, particularly of her life. I concluded that she kept company with a boy and that caused her trouble.

But I soon noticed that she was wearing such expensive things that a boy could not afford to buy them. She had a couple of diamond rings and plenty of other jewelry. I investigated until I discovered, oh, horrible! that my sister was a prostitute. . . .

You can understand that I want to drag her out of the mire, but . . . she tells me that I do not understand life. She cannot conceive why it should be considered indecent to sell one's body in this manner. When I point out to her the end that awaits her she says in the first place it is not more harmful than working by steam for twelve to fourteen hours; in the second place, even if it were so, she enjoys life more. One must take as much as possible out of life. When I call her attention to the horrible degradation she replies that in the shop, too, we are humiliated by the foreman, and so on. . . .

I know that if I could convince her that I am right, she would be willing to emerge from the swamp, but I am unfortunately too inadequate in words, she being a good speaker, and I am usually defeated.*

51. I read in the "Bintel" the letter of a young man who complained that his fiancée extorted presents from him and that when, as a result of unemployment, he was unable to buy her everything she demanded, she

* *Forward,* January 1, 1920.

began to make trouble for him—that she was evidently playing to have him desert her and leave her the property she had extorted.

Well, I am a woman myself, and can bear testimony that there are unfortunately such corrupted characters among my sex, who rob young men in this disgraceful manner. With these girls it is a business to "trim" innocent and sincere young men and then leave them. To them it is both business and pleasure. It gives them great joy to catch a victim in their outspread net and press as much of his hard-earned money out of him as possible.

I know a girl who . . . extracted from her naïve victim everything she laid her eyes on. When he stopped buying her so many things she began to treat him so shamefully that the poor boy was compelled to run away to another town, leaving all his gifts with the girl. The poor fellow was not aware that his so-called fiancée merely tricked him into buying her all kinds of jewelry and finery. He was afraid she would sue him for breach of promise and this fear caused him to leave town.

And don't think for a moment that that girl is ashamed of her deed. Not at all. She even boasts of her cleverness in turning the heads of young men and their pockets inside out. She expects to be admired for that. . . .

I attempted to explain to her that she is a common swindler and thief, but she replied that not only is it not wrong but a philanthropical act. Her argument was that there are many men who betray innocent girls and it is therefore no more than right that girls should betray men also.*

52. [After the marriage of a brilliant man who had flirted with her but never mentioned marriage] she went on the stage, and was immoral in an unhappy sort of way. She met a young artist whose struggles for success aroused her pity and motherly instinct. With the memory of her faithless lover uppermost she plunged into a passionate realization of sex, more to drown her feelings than anything else. She roused the best in this boy, made a man of him, and steadied him. With her sexual tempests there came an after-calm when she forbade any familiarity. This was not studied but an instinct. She hated men, yet they fascinated her, and she them.

She studied stenography and worked as private secretary in a theatrical company. She tried to face life with work as her only outlet, but the restlessness of her grief made her crave excitement. She made friends easily, but her sexual appeal made it difficult for her to fit into a commonplace social atmosphere. She married the artist to the girl he loved, after a terrible struggle to make him realize it was not herself he loved. Later he came and thanked her. "The quiet women make the best wives," he said, "but my wife would not have loved me if you had not made me into

* *Forward,* December 15, 1920.

a man. She cannot, however, give me what I get from you. I wish I could come to you once in a while?"

She said yes, and he came. That was five years ago and that is why she calls herself a prostitute. Her women friends have no idea she is not the quiet, dignified woman she appears to be, and men, many of them married men, want her for their own. She has no use for the man about town; only the man with brains or talent fascinates her at all. She says, "I suppose every one would think me a sinner; I am. I deliberately let a married man stay with me for a time. It is an art. I have learned to know their troubles. They tell me they are unhappy with their wives, wish to go away, are desperate with the monotony of existence. It is generally that they are not sexually mated, or the wife has no sex attraction. Of course she loves him, and he her. I give them what they need. It is weary for the brain to understand men, it is harder on me mentally than physically. I control them only because I have self-restraint. I send them away soon. They are furious; they storm and rage and threaten they will go to some other woman. What do I care? They know it and I send them back to their wives. They will go to her; they would not go to any other woman. That is where I do good. This sex business is a strange thing. I am a missionary prostitute. I only do this once in a while, when I think a man needs me and he is one who will come under my influence. I know I have managed to avert the downfall of several households. If the wives knew? Never mind; they don't. I am not coarse; I can be a comrade to a man and doubt if I harm him. I make him sin in the general acceptance of the term, the common interpretation of God's commandments. How do we know God didn't mean us to use all the powers he gave us? *

In the two cases following, adjustment to life is highly individualized but moral and social. The one is a response adjustment, recognizing freedom for new experience, particularly for creative work, and in the other marriage is based on the inherent values of the relationship, and on nothing else.

53. Being firmly of the opinion that nine out of ten of the alliances I saw about me were merely sordid endurance tests, overgrown with a fungus of familiarity and contempt, convinced that too often the most sacred relationship wears off like a piece of high sheen satin damask, and in a few months becomes a breakfast cloth, stale with soft-boiled egg stains, I made certain resolutions concerning what my marriage should not be.

First of all, I am anxious to emphasize that my marriage was neither

* Edith L. Smith, in Collaboration with Hugh Cabot: "A Study in Sexual Morality," *Social Hygiene,* Vol. 2, p. 537.

the result of a fad or an ism, but simply the working out of a problem according to the highly specialized needs of two professional people.

We decided to live separately, maintaining our individual studio-apartments and meeting as per inclination and not duty. We decided that seven breakfasts a week opposite one another might prove irksome. Our average is two. We decided that the antediluvian custom of a woman casting aside the name that had become as much a part of her personality as the color of her eyes had neither rhyme nor reason. I was born Fannie Hurst and expect to die Fannie Hurst. We decided that in the event of offspring the child should take the paternal name until reaching the age of discretion, when the final decision would lie with him.

My husband telephones me for a dinner appointment exactly the same as scores of other friends. I have the same regard for his plans. We decided that, since nature so often springs a trap as her means to inveigle two people into matrimony, we would try our marriage for a year and at the end of that period go quietly apart, should the venture prove itself a liability instead of an asset. . . .

On these premises, in our case at least, after a five-year acid test, the dust is still on the butterfly wings of our adventure. The dew is on the rose.*

54. I am a college graduate, 27, married five years and the mother of a three-year-old boy. I have been married happily, and have been faithful to my husband.

At six I had decided upon my husband. Jack was his name; he was a beautiful boy, fair, blue eyes, delicate and poetic looking. He was mentally my superior, he loved poetry and wrote good verses. He read a great deal and talked well. He loved me and I loved him, yet there was no demonstration of it in embraces. We played together constantly, and we spoke of the time when we might marry. His great desire was to have a colored child with light hair and blue eyes for a daughter, and we agreed upon it. All of our plans were spoken about before our parents, there was no effort made to hide our attachment. I was by nature rough and a great fighter, Jack was calm and serious, and at times I fought his battles for him. I was maternal towards him. His mother died during our friendship, and I tried to take her place. It was a pure love, nothing cheap or silly. He was killed in the Iroquois Fire and my life was dreary for a long time. I remember the hopeless feeling I experienced when I heard the news. I did not weep, I turned to my mother and said, "I don't want to live any longer."

We had always been allowed to sit across from each other at school, and after Jack's death, I was granted permission to keep his seat vacant

* *New York World,* May 4, 1920.

for the rest of the year, and I kept a plant on the desk which I tended daily as a memorial to my friend.

. . . In college, a coeducational school, I was not allowed to remain ignorant long. I was young and healthy and a real *Bachfisch* in my enthusiastic belief in goodness. I was fortunate in having a level-headed senior for my best friend. She saw an upperclassman [girl] falling in love with me, and she came to me with the news. Then she saw how innocent I was and how ignorant, and my sex education was begun. She told me of marriage, of mistresses, of homosexuality. I was sick with so much body thrown at me at once, and to add to the unpleasantness some one introduced me to Whitman's poetry. I got the idea that sex meant pain for women, and I determined never to marry.

But the next year I felt very differently about sex. I was used to the knowledge and I went with a crowd of girls who were wise, and I had a crush. I had never been stirred before, but I was by her. She told me her ambitions, and I told her mine; it was the first time I had ever been a person to any one, and I was her loyal and loving friend. I kissed her intimately once and thought that I had discovered something new and original. We read Maupassant together and she told me the way a boy had made love to her. Everything was changed, love was fun, I was wild to taste it. I cultivated beaux, I let them kiss me and embrace me, and when they asked me to live with them, I was not offended but pleased. I learned my capacity, how far I could go without losing my head, how much I could drink, smoke, and I talked as freely as a person could. I discussed these adventures with the other girls, and we compared notes on kisses and phrases, and technique. We were healthy animals and we were demanding our rights to spring's awakening. I never felt cheapened, nor repentant, and I played square with the men. I always told them I was not out to pin them down to marriage, but that this intimacy was pleasant and I wanted it as much as they did. We indulged in sex talk, birth control, luetic infection, mistresses; we were told of the sins of our beaux, and I met one boy's mistress, an old university girl. This was life. I could have had complete relations with two of these boys if there had been no social stigma attached, and enjoyed it for a time. But instead I consoled myself with thinking that I still had time to give up my virginity, and that when I did I wanted as much as I could get for it in the way of passionate love. Perhaps the thing that saved me from falling in love was a sense of humor. That part of me always watched the rest of me pretend to be swooning, and I never really closed my eyes. But there was a lot of unhealthy sex going around because of the artificial cut off. We thought too much about it; we all tasted homosexuality in some degree. We never found anything that could be a full stop because there was no gratification.

During this period of stress and heat I met a man, fine, clean, mature and not seemingly bothered with sex at all. I kissed him intimately too, but it was different. He had great respect for me, and he believed in me. I respected him, admired his artistic soul and his keen mind. There was no sex talk with him, it was music and world-views and philosophy. He never made any rash statements, nor false steps. He could sense a situation without touching it, and I felt drawn to him. I knew he had never been with a woman and he told me once that he could never express more than he felt for a person, and could sustain. After five years of friendship we married. There was no great flair to it; it was an inner necessity that drove us to it; we could no longer escape each other. We tried to figure it out, but the riddle always said marry. Sexually I had more experience than he, I was his first mistress, his wife, his best friend, and his mother, and no matter what our moods were, in one of these capacities I was needed by him. Our adjustment was difficult; he had lived alone for thirty years. I was used to having my own way, and he was a very sensitive man, nervous, sure of his opinion, and we quarreled for a while, but never very bitterly. Sexually we were both afraid of offending the other and so that was slow. But in four months we had found our heads again and were well adjusted. He was, and is, the best friend I ever had. I love him more as I know him longer. We can share everything, we are utterly honest and frank with each other, we enjoy our sex life tremendously as well as our friendship. But it was difficult for us to abandon ourselves. To allow any one to know you better than you know yourself is a huge and serious thing and calls for time and love and humor.

I have never known any one as fine as my husband. He is generous, honest, keen, artistic, big, liberal, everything that I most want in a person. I have never been tired of him. I feel confident that he loves me more now than ever before and that he thinks me very fine, a good sport. We have been thrown together a great deal through poverty, and I feel that we are alone in the world and facing it together, a not too friendly world at that. Yet with all this love and closeness, I don't feel that I possess my husband, nor that he does me. I am still the same old girl, the same personality, and my first duty is to develop my own gifts. I have no feeling of permanency with him because we are legally married, but at present a separation is unthinkable. I am worth more to myself with him, and life is infinitely sweeter and richer within the home than any other place.

But if I had married the average American husband who plays the business game as a religion, then I should long ago have been unfaithful to him. I could never disclose myself and be happy with a man who had any interest more important to him than our relationship.

As long as our relationship continues as it is I think we will both be faithful to each other. But I need to have freedom to move about now with all this. And perhaps part of my happiness consists in the fact that I do have freedom. I have had intimate friendships with other men since I am married, kissed them, been kissed, been told that they would like to have me with them. But none of this seems to touch my relation with my husband. I want, and I need to be, intimate on my own hook in my own way with other people. I don't honestly know whether I would take a lover or not. If my husband gave me the assurance that he would take me back, on the old basis, I think I would try it to see if it's as great as it's said to be. But if I had to give up my husband, I would not. I need him as I need my eyes and hands. He is the overtone in the harmony, and I am that for him. I like to experiment, but from past experience I believe the cost would be greater than the gain. I am free at home as I am not anywhere else. I love it, I express myself freely and completely emotionally, and the only reason I could have for being unfaithful would be experimentation. And if I were unfaithful I should have to tell my husband the whole affair; I could not enjoy it otherwise. I have no feeling against it, and no urge towards it. I can honestly say that I am a happy woman, that I have every opportunity to develop my potentialities in my present relation, that I am free as any one can be, that my husband is superior, as a mate for me, to any one I have ever seen. I regret nothing of the past; it could have been improved tremendously, but it was pleasant and human.*

* Autobiography (Manuscript).

16 RECONCILIATION OF THE HERITAGES

The final selection of Part III deals with a special phase of the social process which Thomas found of interest and importance, namely, the contact of individuals and groups possessing different cultures. His immediate concern here is with American immigration and the process of assimilation, but this is merely a particular case of a widespread process of culture contact and change.

This selection is from Chapter IX, "Reconciliation of the Heritages," in *Old World Traits Transplanted,* published in 1921 over the names of Robert E. Park and Herbert A. Miller. Sociological circles have known for some time that Thomas was primarily responsible for the book, and in this connection it is a privilege to quote from a recent letter written by Mr. Allen T. Burns to Professor Ernest W. Burgess. Mr. Burns was General Director of the larger project in Americanization Studies of which this volume was a part.

> The volume, *Old World Traits Transplanted,* of the Americanization Studies was written primarily by W. I. Thomas though at the time it was considered by all concerned best to have it appear under the authorship of Park and Miller who also worked on the volume. I am very glad that Professor Thomas is to receive credit for his invaluable contribution.

According to Thomas, in this selection, democratic ideals demand that all persons be permitted to participate in the social, economic, and political life of the nation. Hence, assimilation of millions of immigrants of diverse cultures presents a problem that must be solved. Since cultural differences do not depend upon innate biological differences, the problem is one of education and at least an initial tolerance of observable differences.

Psychologically, the process of assimilation means that the new experiences of the immigrant are related to the body of memories he already has accumulated in his own land. A wise policy of assimilation, therefore, will encourage immigrant organizations and the retention of native languages, since these facilitate contacts between the heritages and the new situations.

Factors determining the rate of assimilation are two: the amount of similarity between incoming cultures and the receiving one, and the attitude of Americans toward the various immigrant groups. In regard to the first factor, the various immigrant cultures are not so extremely different from American culture that common experiences and rewarding contacts cannot be made. In regard to the second, while there are some who demand a sudden Americanization, America's general tendency is one of tolerance of difference. The idea is not to achieve complete uniformity but to encourage participation by permitting the different groups to make their unique contributions to the total culture.

This selection, then, is concerned primarily with the problem of immigrant assimilation into American society. But it is more than that: it is also a valuable contribution to the literature on culture contact and change, particularly in its psychological aspects. Written almost thirty years ago, it remains a penetrating analysis of the problems produced by large-scale immigration, and makes both theoretical and practical contributions to their solution.

Old World Traits Transplanted—Concluding Chapter [1]

Immigration in the form it has taken in America differs from all previous movements of population. Populous countries have planted colonies, states have been conquered and occupied, slaves have been imported. But when a single country is peacefully invaded by millions of men from scores of other countries, when there are added to one American city as many Jews as there are Danes in Denmark, and to the same city more Italians than there are Italians in Rome, we have something new in history.

Naturally the mass and quality of this immigration is important to us because it cannot fail to have an influence on our whole system of life. Every country must have an organization for securing order and efficiency, not only to insure the happiness and prosperity of its citizens within its boundaries, but also to protect it from foreign attack. The various nationalities and civilizations of the world are in a state of rivalry, and a low efficiency in any country may lead to its destruction, actual or economic. Our wish to assimilate [2] the

[1] *Old World Traits Transplanted* (New York: Harper & Brothers, 1921), pp. 259–308.

[2] It should be pointed out that such terms as "assimilate" and "assimilation" have had various meanings attached to them, and that there is some question as to their scientific use. In general, Thomas and his followers used the term "assimilation" to define a general social process; it was of the same level of conceptualization as

immigrants who remain here means that we want to make them a practical part of our organization.

There is an interesting parallel between the influence which a country wishes to exercise over its members and the influence of what geographers and naturalists call an "area of characterization." In the natural world an area of characterization is a geographical region sufficiently marked in its physical features to put a characteristic imprint on its flora and fauna. In the same way, the human inhabitants of a country develop a body of characteristic values. A country is an area of cultural characterization.[3]

REQUIRED IN A DEMOCRACY

Among the distinguishing features of the American "area of characterization" is the principle that no man is to be used as a tool and thus placed in the category of purely material values, and we have consequently repudiated the ancient conception of the state, in which by a system of "ordering and forbidding" great things were achieved, indeed, but only by keeping the masses permanently in the category of things.

Our state system is based on the participation of every member and assumes in all the wish and ability to participate; for in the last analysis we mean by democracy participation by all, both practically and imaginatively, in the common life of the community. Our democracy is not working perfectly at present because not even the native born are participating completely. Our old order was a territorial one. The autonomy of the political and social groups was based on size and geographical isolation. So long as the group remained small and isolated, individuals were able to act responsibly, because the

---

"conflict," "accommodation" and the like. In other words, it could be used in both intragroup and intergroup conditions.

The relationship between assimilation and such other terms as "diffusion," "acculturation," "culture contact," and "transculturation" remains rather vague even at this date. See, for example, the discussion in Melville J. Herskovits, *Man and His Works,* especially chap. 31.

[3] Cf. the "culture area" concept used by the American anthropologists, for example in Clark Wissler, *Man and Culture* (New York: Thomas Y. Crowell Company, 1923), especially pp. 55–61.

situations they dealt with came easily within their understanding and capacity. But the free communication provided by the locomotive, the post, the telegraph, the press, has dissolved distances. As a result men find themselves in a system of relationships, political and economic, over which, in spite of their traditional liberties of speech and action, they no longer have control. The conditions of their daily living are vitally affected by events occurring without their knowledge, thousands of miles away.

It is similarly impossible for average citizens to grasp all the elements of the political issues on which they give decisions. The economic nexus holds them in an inevitable interdependence; they are politically disfranchised while retaining the ceremony of a vote. No longer able to act intelligently or responsibly, they act upon vagrant impulses. They are directed by suggestion and advertising. This is the meaning of social unrest. It is the sign of a baffled wish to participate. It represents energy, and the problem is to use it constructively. While we are forming a new definition of the situation, we are subject to emotional states and random movements.

The founders of America defined the future state as a democracy characterized by the largest possible amount of individual freedom, but this ideal has not been fully realized. At best we can say that we are in the process of giving this country the cultural characterization of such a democracy.

While we have on our hands this problem we are importing large numbers of aliens, representing various types, in the main below our cultural level. Some of them bring a greater and more violent unrest than we know here: psychoses acquired under conditions where violence was the only means of political participation. Others belong to the nationalistic, opportunistic, or in fewer numbers to the radical elements, who not only do not regard this country as their country, but do not regard it as a country at all—do not recognize that we have a characteristic body of values and the right to preserve these values.

The immigrant usually brings a value which is very important to us—labor—and it would be possible to regard him in a narrowly practical way as a merely material value, just as the Negro in slavery and Chinese labor in earlier days were regarded as material values, and as the Germans regarded the 600,000 laborers from Austria and Russia who crossed their borders annually and returned to their homes at the end of the harvest season. But we know from our experience with slavery and from the German experiences with the *Sachsengänger,* that this attitude has a bad effect both on the aliens and on the culture of the group which receives and uses them as mere things. If visitors are disorderly, unsanitary, or ignorant, the group which incorporates them, even temporarily, will not escape the bad effects of this.

Every country has a certain amount of culturally undeveloped material. We have it, for instance, in the Negroes and Indians, the Southern mountaineers, the Mexicans and Spanish-Americans, and the slums. There is a limit, however, to the amount of material of this kind that a country can incorporate without losing the character of its culture. For example, the "three R's" represent our minimum of cultural equipment, and we are able to transmit this much to practically everybody. With this equipment the individual is able to penetrate any sphere of life; without it, he cannot move upward at all. But if we should receive, say, a million Congo blacks and a million Chinese coolies annually, and if they should propagate faster that the white Americans, it is certain that our educational system would break down; we could not impart even the "three R's." We should then be in a state of chaos unless we abandoned the idea of democracy and secured efficiency by reverting to the "ordering and forbidding" type of state.

This is the general significance of immigration to our problem of democracy. We must make the immigrants a working part in our system of life, ideal and political, as well as economic, or lose the character of our culture. Self-preservation makes this necessary; the fact that they bring valuable additions to our culture makes it desirable.[4] Now we can assimilate the immigrants only if their attitudes

[4] All too seldom has it been recognized that in culture contact the process of transmission is two-way. Thus William F. Ogburn and Meyer F. Nimkoff in their *Sociology* (Boston: Houghton Mifflin Company, 1940), pp. 383–384, say: "A common but mistaken notion about assimilation is that it is a one-way process. . . . Close contact of persons of dissimilar cultures always results in mutual interpenetration and

and values, their ideas on the conduct of life, are brought into harmony with our own. They cannot be intelligent citizens unless they "get the hang" of American ways of thinking as well as of doing. How fast and how well this is accomplished depends (1) on the degree of similarity between their attitudes and values and our own, giving them a certain preadaptation to our scheme of life and an ability to aid in their own Americanization; and (2) on how we treat them—our attitude toward their heritages. These are, roughly, the elements in our problem of assimilation.

SIMILARITY OF HERITAGES

It is one of the ordinary experiences of social intercourse that words and things do not have the same meanings with different people, in different periods of time, in different parts of a country—that is, in general, in different contexts. The same "thing" has a different meaning for the naïve person and the sophisticated person, for the child and the philosopher. The new experience derives its significance from the character and interpretation of previous experiences. To the peasant a comet, a plague, an epileptic person, may mean, respectively, a divine portent, a visitation of God, a possession by the devil; to the scientist they mean something quite different. The word slavery had a connotation in the ancient world very different from the one it bears to-day. It has a different significance to-day in the Southern and Northern states. "Socialism" has a very different significance to the immigrant from the Russian pale living on the "East Side" of New York City, to the citizen on Riverside Drive, and to the native American in the hills of Georgia.

The meaning any word has for an individual depends on his past experience, not only with the thing the word means, but with many other things associated with it in his mind. For example, the concept evoked in his mind by the word "food" is determined not only by the kinds of food he has eaten, but also by the normal state of his

---

fusion of culture traits, although the borrowing may not be as pronounced in the one direction as the other." Evidently Thomas was aware of this as early as 1921.

On this point see also B. Malinowski, *The Dynamics of Culture Change* (New Haven: Yale University Press, 1945).

appetite and digestion, the ease or difficulty with which he secures his daily ration, whether he grows, hunts, or buys it, whether or not he prepares it, whether he has ever been near starvation, and so forth. No two people have exactly the same experience by which to define the same word, and sometimes the resulting difference in meaning is immeasurably great. This is the meaning of the saying of the logicians that persons who attach different meanings to the same words and the same things are in different "universes of discourse,"—that is, do not talk in the same world.

All the meanings of past experience retained in the memory of the individual form what is called by psychologists the "apperception mass." It is the body of memories with which every new item of experience comes in contact, to which it is related, and in connection with which it gets its meaning. The difference in the interpretation of words is merely an example of the fact that persons whose apperception masses are radically different give a different interpretation to all experience. The ecclesiastic, the artist; the mystic, the scientist; the Philistine, the Bohemian—are examples of classes not always mutually intelligible. Similarly, different races and nationalities, as wholes, represent different apperception masses and consequently different universes of discourse, and are not mutually intelligible. Even our forefathers are with difficulty intelligible to us, though always more intelligible than the eastern European immigrant, because of the continuity of our tradition.

The set of attitudes and values, which we call the immigrant's heritage, are the expression in ideas and action of his apperception mass. "Heritages" differ because the races and nationalities concerned have developed different apperception masses; and they have developed different apperception masses because, owing to historical circumstances, they have defined the situation in different ways. . . .

Certain prominent personalities, schools of thought, bodies of doctrine, historical events, have helped to define the situation and determine the attitudes and values of our various immigrant groups in characteristic ways in their home countries.[5] To the Sicilian, for

[5] Cf. "It is a notorious fact that the course of human history has been largely without prevision or direction. Things have drifted and forces have arisen. Under these conditions an unusual incident—the emergence of a great mind or a forcible per-

example, marital infidelity means conventionally the stiletto; to the American, the divorce court. These differences sometimes go so far that it is impossible for those concerned to talk to one another. The Western World, for example, appreciates learning, and we have signalized this in our schools. The Jews also show this appreciation . . . and even the Polish peasant . . . appreciates learning, though not for his class. . . .

If the immigrant possesses already an apperception mass corresponding in some degree to our own, his participation in our life will, of course, follow more easily. While we have given . . . examples of heritages strange to us, the body of material presented shows that he does not differ from us profoundly. We can best appreciate the immigrants' mental kinship with ourselves negatively, by comparing them with what they are not. If the immigrants practiced and defended cannibalism and incest; if they burned their widows and killed their parents and broke the necks of their wayward daughters, customarily; if (as in a North African Arab tribe) a girl were not eligible for marriage until she had given her older brother a child born out of wedlock, to be reared as a slave; if immigrant families limited their children by law to one boy and one girl, killing the others (as in the Ellice Archipelago); or (as in the Solomon Islands) if they killed all, or nearly all, their children and bought others from their neighbors, as our farmers sell young calves to butchers and buy yearlings; if immigrant army recruits declined target practice because the bullet would go straight anyway if Allah willed it—then the problem of assimilation would be immensely complicated.

In comparison with these examples immigrant heritages usually differ but slightly from ours, probably not more than ours differ from those of our more conservative grandfathers. Slavery, dueling, burning of witches, contempt of soil analysis, condemnation of the view that plants and animals have been developed slowly, not suddenly created, are comparatively recent American values and attitudes.

---

sonality, or the operation of influences as subtle as those which determine fashions in dress—may establish social habits and duties which will give a distinct character to the modes of attention and mental life of the group." ("The Mind of Woman and the Lower Races," 1907, reprinted in *Sex and Society,* pp. 287–288.)

PSYCHOLOGY OF ASSIMILATION

It it evidently necessary that the people who compose a community and participate in common enterprises shall have a body of common memories sufficient to enable them to understand one another. This is particularly true in a democracy, where it is intended that the public institution should be responsive to public opinion. There can be no public opinion unless the persons who compose the public are able to live and think in the same world. The process of assimilation involves the development in the immigrant and the native of similar apperception masses.[6] To this end it is desirable that the immigrants should not only speak the language of the country, but also know something of the history of the people among whom they have chosen to dwell. For the same reason it is important that native Americans should know the history and social life of the countries from which the immigrants come.

It is important also that every individual should share as fully as possible a fund of knowledge, experience, sentiments, and ideals common to the whole community, and himself contribute to that fund. It is for this reason that we maintain and seek to maintain freedom of speech and free schools. The function of literature, including poetry, romance, and the newspaper, is to enable all to share vicariously the inner life of each. The function of science is to gather up, classify, digest, and preserve, in a form in which they may be available to the community as a whole, the ideas, inventions, and technical experience of the individuals composing it. Not merely the possession of a common language, but the widest extension of the opportunities for education, is a condition of Americanization.

For the immigrant to achieve an apperception mass in common with the American community involves the development of new attitudes on his part, and his old experiences are the only possible foundation for the new structure. If a person becomes interested in anything whatever, it is because there is already in him something to which it can appeal. Visitors to the Dresden Gallery are all affected by the Sistine Madonna in approximately the same way because they bring to it a similar body of socially created apprecia-

[6] It appears that this view is at some variance with the position taken further on in the selection.

tions—the sanctity of motherhood, the sufferings of our Lord, the adoration of Mary, the aesthetic appreciation of female beauty, and so forth. No amount of explanation or persuasion would arouse the same feeling in an African black man. . . .

A certain identity of experiences and memories between immigrants and Americans is of main importance for assimilation, because, in the process of learning, a new fact has a meaning and makes an appeal only if it is identified with some previous experience, something that is already known and felt. Thus, when we appealed to the patriotism of our immigrants during the war, we found a ready response, because they knew what patriotism is. The Bohemians in a Cleveland parade carried a banner with the inscription: "We are Americans through and through by the spirit of our nation," and interpreted this by another banner: "Americans, do not be discouraged. We have been fighting these tyrants for three hundred years." . . .

This process of making warm and personal something that would otherwise remain cold, extraneous, irrelevant, and foreign, by identifying it with a body of sentiments that is already intimate and warm, is illustrated in more detail by the case of the Italian boy whose first disillusionment in America is referred to . . . [in a previously quoted document].

159. I go about the streets to find the great history, to feel the great emotion for all that is noble in America. I do not see how the people can think to compare the American city with the beauty of Rome, or Venice, or Naples. Even in big city like New York I do not find much monuments to the great deeds, to the great heroes, and the great artists. I was deeply surprised not to find the fountains. I do not find the great art to compare with the art of Italy. . . . But one day I see very, very big building. My mind is struck. With all I have seen in Italy, in Rome, in Venice, in Genoa, in Milano, in Florence, in Naples—I have never seen anything like that! I say, "There is the thing American. It is a giant!"

When I went to night school, I had a good impression to me. The teacher treat every one just the same. The Jew just the same the Chinaman, and the Chinaman just the same the Italian. This was a wonderful impression. When I saw the principal of the school, he look to me like Italian nobleman, the way he hold his eyeglasses. I went to this school just because I like the principal. He give it to me welcome like I was an

American. I learn little English, and about the American government, and how the people can make change and progress by legislation without the force of revolution, and I like very much this idea. The teacher told me why not to become an American? . . .

I have good impression to become an American. But I do not become American because I think always of the grandeur of the Italy civilization of the past! . . . [Then I fall in love and] . . . I do not wish at all to go back to Italy. I think to take a wife. A man must situate himself. I think about many things, but I think especially about the future. Everything begin to look different. I have not think much about the future before, I have think about the past. Maybe I have a son, it is the future that is for him. America is to be his country. What is the past? It is gone. The future is to come, and I think that when my son shall live I wish it to be some great time. For the future I cannot see so much Italy as America. The grandeur of the Italian cities, Venice, Genoa, Florence, Naples, held Italy in the world's highest place for nearly one thousand years. But the world continue. It go on. Now comes the great day for America, the great financial, the great mercantile power, and I think with that the great science, the great art, the great letters. Why to live always in the memory of past grandeur? They were only men. I am a man, and my son will be a man. Why not live to be somebody ourselves, in a nation more great than any nation before, and my son perhaps the greatest of any great man?

And I see that big work to build the future. I see the necessity to learn the English, to become the citizen, to take part in the political life, to work to create the better understanding between the races that they come to love each another, to work for better conditions in industry, for health and safety and prosperity, to work for the progress in science, for the better government, and for the higher morality—and it become more pleasure to work than to take the leisure. Suddenly it looks to me like that is the American, that is what the American is always to do, always to work for the achievement. It come to me, like I am born—I am American! *

In this case a new experience makes an appeal because it is identified with a wish. The Italian boy specifies that he wishes a wife, child, home, but more generally he wishes success, and he identifies this with the American principle of "achievement."

Most frequently the appreciation of America begins in connection

* . . . [Life history of Alessandro Daluca, a tailor on the East Side of New York. Emily F. Robbins, "If One Speak Bad of Your Mother, How You Feel?" in *Red Cross Magazine*, September 1919.]

with a wish or a general ideal which was not attainable in the old country, but is attainable here. In document 160 the writer realizes that America is a country where everybody can get an education:

160. The strongest reason for my preference of America to other countries is perhaps my appreciation of education and its opportunities. This is probably explained by my previous experience as a worker in the educational field in the old country—Russia. After graduating from a teachers' college at Petrograd I served as director of a pedagogical class in Esthonia during three years, from 1897 to 1900. As my views upon education conflicted with those of higher "Russianizing" authorities, I chose to leave the teaching field and entered a university to study law and political economy.

The children in the public schools in Esthonia had to study everything except religion in Russian. They had to study Russian (Slavic) history instead of that of their own country and people. A good deal of time was given to lessons in religion and the singing of church hymns. But the saddest thing of all was that the children going through public school learned nothing or very little of the rudiments of the sciences. For adults there were no facilities for learning. The people forming private classes were pursued and in many instances arrested and fined.

Later I went to Germany and other West European countries and found that though public schools there gave some knowledge to the children, their individuality was suppressed by a system of discipline and punishment, and by being forced to learn rather by memorizing than by understanding, and rather by compulsion than by their own love for learning.

America is not only a "melting pot" for races but also a testing ground or laboratory for ideas, original American as well as imported European. Here they are compared in practical application, through which the degrees of their vitality can be determined. This makes America an interesting country in which to learn—to learn through observation and experience and through amply provided educational institutions and facilities, from the evening schools to the great universities, from various expositions to libraries. I know no other country where opportunities for learning by everybody are so rich as here.

The immigrants arriving on American shores soon find out that they need to learn, and first of all to learn the American methods of their prospective trades if they are going to make good in the New World. Formerly many of them were discouraged by not knowing or not finding opportunities for learning here. But nowadays they are, as it were, discovering these opportunities. For this reason I believe that the immigrants in the future will come here not only for higher earnings, but also for the sake of learning, desiring industrial training as well as general education.

The appreciation of America as a wonderful country in which to learn dawned upon me after years of wanderings, study, and observation here and in Europe, and as a result of comparing this country with the European countries, within the limitations of my personal experience.

My field study and observations led me to the conclusion that in the public school programs and methods in America and in European countries there is a still more pronounced difference than in the field of higher education. In Europe the main emphasis is laid upon form, authority, obedience, discipline, while in the American public schools freedom of action, imagination, initiative, and self-reliance are pursued as the main goal in the training of youth. The European public school suppresses individuality, while the American builds it up, or at least leaves it untrammeled.*

The identification of immigrant groups with America takes place on the psychological basis shown in the preceding documents. Points of contact are found in the respective apperception masses, where interests merge, and as a result of the increased community of interests other contacts are made progressively. Assimilation may be compared with skin grafting, where the new tissue is not applied to the whole surface, but spots are grafted, and from these the connecting tissues ramify.

TOLERANCE VS. SUPPRESSION

The apperception mass of the immigrant, expressed in the attitudes and values he brings with him from his old life, is the material from which he must build his Americanism. It is also the material we must work with, if we would aid this process. Our tools may be in part American customs and institutions, but the substance we seek to mold into new forms is the product of other centuries in other lands. In education it is valuable to let the child, as far as possible, make his own discoveries and follow his own interests. He should have the opportunity of seeking new experiences which have a meaning for him when connected with his old experiences. A wise policy of assimilation, like a wise educational policy, does not seek to destroy the attitudes and memories that are there, but to build on them.

There is a current opinion in America, of the "ordering and forbidding" type, demanding from the immigrant a quick and complete Americanization through the suppression and repudiation of all

* *Autobiography of an Intellectual Esthonian* (manuscript).

the signs that distinguish him from us.* Those who have this view wish the repudiation to be what the church fathers demanded of a confession of sin—"sudden, complete, and bitter."

It is notable that this destruction of memories is the plan of both those who demand a quick and complete Americanization and those who demand a quick and complete social revolution—the extreme Americanists and the extreme radicals. . . . Both positions imply that there is nothing of value for the future in the whole of past experience; whereas we have shown, in speaking of the psychology of assimilation (particularly in the case of the Italian boy) that "reminders" are precisely what the individual uses in making constructive changes in his life; and in the chapter on demoralization we pointed out that the absence of reminders, forgetfulness of the standards of the community, failure to live in the light of the past, reduce a man to the basis of the instincts, with which humanity first began. . . .

There is an element of pure prejudice in this theory of Americanization. It appears as intolerance of the more obvious signs of unlikeness. Where color exists, it is the mark specially singled out by prejudice, but since our immigrants are mainly not colored, language becomes the most concrete sign of unlikeness and the foremost object of animosity. It is certainly true that a man cannot participate fully in our life without our language, and that its acquisition is rightly considered a sign and rough index of Americanization. But the American who does not know the details of the immigrant's life and problems cannot imagine how useful his language is here in the first stages. Take an actual case. The Danes are distinguished farmers, but here the soil, the demand, are unfamiliar and they have trouble. The American government could help them, but they do not know this. Even if they did they could not inquire in English; they would not know whether to address the President or the Senate; and they would not address either because they would not know with what honorific form to begin the letter. A certain Danish editor invites

* "Broadly speaking, we mean [by Americanization] an appreciation of the institutions of this country, absolute forgetfulness of all obligations or connections with other countries because of descent or birth."—Superintendent of the New York Public Schools, *N. Y. Evening Post,* August 9, 1918. Quoted by I. B. Berkson . . . [*Theories of Americanization: A Critical Study,* New York: Teachers College, Columbia University, 1920, p. 59].

communications on specific plans and troubles of this kind. In each case (and the number is relatively large) he sends with his reply a letter in English, addressed to the Department of Agriculture, asking for the proper bulletin. The Dane is to copy the letter and send it. This much he will do, and the bulletin somehow gets read. Here again is the typical process of assimilation—the identification of the immigrant's success with America; here, too, is an example of what we mean when we say that the immigrants must assist in their own Americanization. Prejudice against language thus means bringing into disrepute one of the tools most useful in assimilation.

Again, the Yiddish language is a very useful heritage to the Jew, and this is a clear case of utility, without any obstinacy or sentimentality. The Jews associate their nationalism with Hebrew, the language of the Jews and the one that their national idealists are seeking to restore. Yiddish is a German dialect, with a mixture of Hebrew, Polish, and so forth, developed originally by the Jews as a business expedient. It is an uncouth speech, with very limited power of literary expression, and nothing with which a man would seek to identify himself. The Jews in America drop it as soon as possible, and it is really difficult to induce a Jew to speak a few words of it in order to show you what it is like. And yet the Jewish community in New York City pays annually more than $2,000,000 for Yiddish newspapers. These newspapers and other Jewish institutions do thousands of particular and very personal services for Jews which American institutions could not do and which no one could undertake without the use of Yiddish.[7] Language is a tool which its possessor cannot afford to throw away until he has another.

Quite aside from the question of utility, immigrants, especially the older ones, cherish the memories of their former home, and wish to preserve some signs identifying them with their past. This is a natural sentiment. It is frankly expressed in the following documents from groups which have no nationalistic psychoses and represent the settler type:

[7] Over a period of years Thomas collected a considerable amount of data on the Jews in America, with particular reference to their adjustment. Study of this material is now being completed by Marvin Bressler, of the University of Pennsylvania, and should soon be available.

161. In a news item in *Skandinaven,* the editor of the *Lutheran Herald* . . . is quoted as saying . . . with reference to the Norwegian flag, that in this country it did not belong anywhere outside of the dictionary and the Norwegian legation headquarters in Washington. . . .

No flag except the American has a place as a national emblem in the heart of any good citizen. But how is it that we have here the flags of all the nations of the earth? During the war, when the country surely required the loyalty of every citizen as never before, there were foreign flags around us wherever we went. The English flag, the French, the Belgian, the Italian—they were to be seen everywhere. They were used at patriotic and other meetings; people displayed buttons with these flags on them, and it was very common to see automobiles decorated in this way. . . . No one feared enemy purposes from the nations these flags represent. The same can with even greater truth be said about Norway. In the first place, Norway's relatively small military strength makes this thought untenable. Also that country's pronounced peace policy puts the idea out of the question; also its later historical traditions. Norway is one of the few nations which have managed a decisive national crisis without resorting to war. . . .

When the Norwegian flag is seen here the object of its display is to celebrate the intellectual and spiritual values which Norway has achieved. In the same way we honor the important intellectual and spiritual revivals and achievements in all nations. If this had not been permitted, the Rev. Mr. Lee or any other American would not have a bible to teach from.

But when people of Norwegian extraction in this country hold fast to their Norwegian cultural heritages, then it is because a people who have lived together in the same country through centuries must have given birth to spiritual and intellectual values which are peculiar to such a people. . . .*

162. . . . The small Danish society of which I am the secretary has a membership of only twenty-eight, and while in regard to American ideas these men are as loyal as if they were born Americans—and this is the case with the immigrated Danes as a general rule—yet I cannot say that our society does much to Americanize its members. At their meetings they speak their mother tongue and sing their old country songs, looking upon one another almost as members of the same family, and their object is to help each other in case of necessity, especially, of course, in case of sickness. . . .

When the different Liberty loans were floated I found all of us personally deeply interested and buying to our capacity, and at my initiative our little society bought $500 worth of bonds, practically using all the

* Simon Johnson, *Skandinaven* (Chicago) December 1, 1919.

cash money we had in the treasury; I, personally, managed out of my $35 per week job to buy bonds to the value of $600.*

Any fine fund of personal feeling is valuable in identifying the present with the past in the life of the immigrant, but aside from this these sentimental memories should command respect, and we should let them remain unmolested in the region of personal life. We should know by this time that under tolerance, peculiar group values—such as language and religion—are only means to a fuller life; under oppression, they become objects of life.

IMMIGRANT ORGANIZATIONS VALUABLE

Following the instinctive prejudice against strangeness,[8] many Americans distrust immigrant organizations, as such, and consider them obstacles to assimilation. On the contrary, we have emphasized throughout this study the importance of these organizations. Indeed, the amount of immigration which we can continue to tolerate or encourage depends on their character.

Organizations, beginning in the family and community, are the means by which men regulate their lives. The healthy life of a society always depends more on the spontaneous organization of its members than on formal legal and political regulations. It is only in an organized group—in the home, the neighborhood, the trade union, the cooperative society—where he is a power and an influence, in some region where he has status and represents something, that man can maintain a stable personality. There is only one kind of neighborhood having no representative citizen—the slum; a world where men cease to be persons because they represent nothing. In

* Communication from Mr. Fred Thomsen.

[8] For what Thomas meant by "instinctive prejudice" see "The Psychology of Race-Prejudice," *American Journal of Sociology,* March 1904, pp. 593–611. His position is that the analogue to human prejudice may be found in the tendency of organisms to reject harmful stimuli; on this biological basis, men become hostile toward those parts of the environment with which they are unfamiliar and hence regard as dangerous. Then he concludes: "Race-prejudice is an instinct originating in the tribal stage of society, when solidarity in feeling and action were essential to the preservation of the group. It, or some analogue of it, will probably never disappear completely" (p. 610). See also "The Significance of the Orient for the Occident," *ibid.,* May 1908, p. 729, for another statement of this position. Cf. Sumner's concept of "ethnocentrism," *Folkways,* pp. 13 ff.

the slum men live in an enforced intimacy, but they do not communicate. They suspect one another and keep away from one another. They cannot maintain a personality because there are no standards; if standards of decency, morality, and sanitation exist they are imposed from without. A slum is a place, composed at first of the poor, which has become inevitably a refuge for criminals and disorderly persons—a place of missions and lost souls.[9]

If the face-to-face organization which made the immigrant moral at home is suddenly dissolved in this country, we have . . . [this] general situation . . . that men, removed from the restraining influence of an organized community, tend to follow their immediate impulses and behave in monstrous ways. Ethnologists have shown that when the uncivilized races come into contact with the products of our civilization they appropriate the vices and ornaments, the whiskey and beads, and leave the more substantial values.[10] The same tendency appears among immigrants, especially the children. The term "Americanization" is not used popularly among the immigrants as we use it. They call a badly demoralized boy "completely Americanized." . . .

The organization of the immigrant community is necessary as a regulative measure. Any type of organization which succeeds in regulating the lives of its members is beneficial. If you can induce a man to belong to something, to cooperate with any group whatever, where something is expected of him, where he has responsibility, dignity, recognition, economic security, you have at least regulated his life.[11] From this standpoint even the nationalistic societies do more to promote assimilation than to retard it. There is no doubt, for example, that the nationalistic newspapers do not want

[9] Cf. Harvey Zorbaugh, *Gold Coast and Slum* (Chicago: University of Chicago Press, 1929), and R. E. Park, E. W. Burgess, and R. D. McKenzie, *The City* (Chicago: University of Chicago Press, 1925).

[10] In one of his earlier writings, while discussing modesty, Thomas remarked: "A wholesale unsettling of habit is seen when a lower culture is impinged upon a higher." See "The Psychology of Modesty and Clothing," 1899, reprinted in *Sex and Society,* p. 213.

[11] Although the well-known "four wishes" were used in the book from which this selection is taken, the above usage is curious. Here, only two of the wishes are stated (recognition and security), while the other two (response and new experience) are here supplanted by "dignity" and "responsibility."

their readers to become Americanized, but they make them more intelligent, more prepared to be Americans, simply by printing the news of what is going on in America, and this they have to do in order to circulate at all.[12] The nationalistic organizations are the means by which certain men make their living and get their distinction; they assist the home countries materially in their struggle for freedom, they stimulate some older people to return to Europe, but they have almost no effect in keeping the immigrant, especially the young generation, estranged from American life. . . .

The propaganda of hate carried on notably by the Italian press, and described by an Italian in the note below,* is also partly nationalistic in its aim. While not among the dependent nationalities, Italy has been particularly active in preserving the allegiance of her emigrated subjects, and her leaders have acted, so to speak, as representatives of a country that is trying to control a colony. They have used hate, because enmity is the motive through which men can be aroused and controlled most easily. But here also, if we recognize the fact that editors are playing on attitudes that are already there, not creating them, the propaganda has slight importance. Italians who returned to Sicily after the war are now returning to America. They found that it was "too small" over there. They had entered their own country as immigrants, and suffered again the disillusionment of the immigrant. The fault to be found with the nationalistic organizations is not that they do the damage they imagine they are doing, but that they fail to do the constructive work of which, as organizations, they are capable; that they do not help their people

* "I have seen a large number of articles from Italian newspapers, written by Italian professional men concerning America, which if translated and published, would open the eyes even of the blind. America is described in these articles as a ruthless, rapacious, hypocritical, puritanical country. American men are superficial, weak, ridiculous; American women are vain and prefer to have a good time rather than to be good wives and mothers; churches in America are places of business; social and philanthropic work is established to furnish fat salaries to innumerable officeholders; the political life is incurably corrupt; and everything else is termed 'Americanate,' meaning the quintessence of foolishness. A sensational divorce case, a scandal at the City Hall, Dowie or Billy Sunday, anything and everything is used as a pretext for a long philippic against America. I have seen Italian newspapers with laudatory articles on America written in English, which no Italian would read, and with an article in Italian in the same issue, that the American would not understand, painting America in the blackest colors."—E. C. Sartorio, *Social and Religious Life of the Italians in America,* p. 50.

[12] Cf. R. E. Park, *The Immigrant Press and Its Control* (New York: Harper & Brothers, 1922).

to identify their success with America, in such ways as we have exemplified above in the case of the Danes and Jews.

We have not developed American institutions adapted to meeting the first needs of the immigrant and preserving in him the good qualities which he brings. Usually he reaches our institutions only after he has become a failure. The immigrant organizations are doing very positive services for their members by maintaining their sense of social responsibility, of responsibility to some type of community. . . . But more than this, our experience has shown that, while it is possible for an individual immigrant, especially if he represents a relatively cultured type, to identify himself directly with American society without an intermediate connection with a group of his own nationality, in the main the immigrants are becoming Americanized *en masse,* by whole blocks, precisely through their own organizations. The organization as a whole is influenced, modified, Americanized by its efforts to adjust itself to American conditions. This happened, for example, when the immigrant athletic organizations recently joined the American Amateur Athletic Association; for this alliance implies acceptance by the immigrant of all the American athletic standards. Similarly, the immigrant who penetrates American society as a member of an immigrant group forms a bond between this group and American society. The Letts in New York City felt pride in a young violinist who had played at their weekly entertainments. For his further development the Lettish organization sent him to the American teacher, Damrosch. The individual thus forms a link between the immigrant society and American society. He will transmit the influence of his American contacts to the immigrant organization.

We [have] illustrated . . . the important fact that the immigrant is not a highly individualized person. He has been accustomed to live in a small, intimate, face-to-face group, and his conduct has been determined by this group. Naturally he needs the assistance of such a group for a time in America, and naturally this group is composed of his own people.[13] This general condition explains the perfect success of our government in its appeal to the immigrant population

[13] Cf. "In order to reorganize his life on a new basis . . . [the immigrant] needs a primary-group as strong and coherent as the one he left in the old country. The Polish-

for subscriptions to the Liberty loans. The appeal was not made to the immigrant individually, but through his organizations.

The type of organization which the immigrants bring with them from home . . . is one which we ought to appreciate. It represents the individual's responsibility to society which we have in a measure lost, and are consciously attempting to restore by the reorganization of the local community. It is a type of organization which can be made the basis of all kinds of cooperative enterprise—the basis, in fact, on which the local community will again function. Cooperation is an attitude already present in immigrant consciousness, and cooperative economic enterprises are arising spontaneously among immigrant groups—the Finns, the Italians, the Poles, and others. This is especially true since younger men of immigrant parentage, who have gone through our schools, who are American in feeling, are beginning to assume the leadership in the immigrant groups and to employ constructively the traditional spirit of cooperation.

If we wish to help the immigrant to get a grip on American life, to understand its conditions, and find his own role in it, we must seize on everything in his old life which will serve either to interpret the new or to hold him steady while he is getting adjusted. The language through which his compatriots can give him their garnered experience, the "societies" which make him feel "at home," the symbols of his home land, reminding him of the moral standards under which he grew up. Common courtesy and kindness exact tolerance for these things, and common sense indicates that they are the foundation of the readjustment we seek.

PERPETUATION OF GROUPS IMPOSSIBLE

The evident value of these immigrant organizations during the period of adjustment raises another question. Is he to remain permanently in one of these . . . organizations, and are they to continue as centers of cultures diverse from and competing with that of America? This question touches a larger aspect of the heritages, relating to the ideal character of our national life—whether we shall

---

American society gives him a few new schemes of life, but not enough to cover all of his activities." (*The Polish Peasant,* 1927, Vol. II, p. 1650.)

strive for a uniform or a diversified type of culture and whether the perpetuation of immigrant traits and organizations will accomplish this diversity.

We have recognized the importance of a resemblance between the members of a community which will enable them to understand and influence one another. In a peasant community, as in a herd or flock, great unanimity in following tested habits is sufficient, without any great intelligence, to enable all to live. But as communities progress the members behave more and more independently, use more freedom. Communities progress, indeed, because certain of their members insist on using more freedom.

The civilization we have is the product of an association of individuals who are widely unlike, and with the progress of civilization the divergence in individual human types has been and must continue to be constantly multiplied. Our progress in the arts and sciences and in the creation of values in general has been dependent on specialists whose distinctive worth was precisely their divergence from other individuals. It is even evident that we have been able to use productively persons who in a savage or peasant society would have been classed as insane—who were, perhaps, insane. Until recently our conception of insanity has been to some extent determined by the standards of the "primary group," which demands uniformity in its members. . . . We have already pointed out that the Mohammedan could regard a modern scientist as insane. However, we have had so many profitable returns from the queer behavior of such men as Mayer, Darwin, and Langley (whose experiments with the flying machine were regarded by many as insane), that we have changed our definition of insanity and regard any man as sane the sum of whose activities is valuable to the community.*

The value of the principle of diversity has already been fully recognized in the scientific world and in the specialized occupations. Efficiency in these fields is based on far-going individualization of function. The astronomer or the physiological chemist awaits the result of the physicist or the chemist as condition of further steps in his own investigation. The more diversified the personalities, the

* "When we begin to acknowledge *many standards of normality* we take away the sting of a stigma."—Adolf Meyer, *Suggestions of Modern Science Concerning Education,* p. 143.

more particularized the products of these personalities, the greater the likelihood that we shall find among them the elements for the realization of our own plans, the construction of our own values.

In the civilization having the highest efficiency all are not in the same "universe of discourse," but there tend to be smaller groups or circles who understand one another and cooperate. Although they are not understood by everybody, their products become useful to everybody. The physicists, for example, represent such a circle. The physicist demonstrates a law which the public cannot understand; but the engineer understands it and applies it in the invention of machines which become of general use.

Now representatives of the different immigrant groups claim a similar social value—that, on account of their racial peculiarities and the fact that they have developed by their past experiences different apperception masses, they are predisposed to individualized functions as groups, and that by permanently organizing along the lines of their aptitudes they will not only express their peculiar genius, but contribute unique values to America:

165. Democracy rejected the proposal of the superman who should rise through sacrifice of the many. It insists that the full development of each individual is not only a right, but a duty to society; and that our best hope for civilization lies not in uniformity, but in wide differentiation.

The movements of the last century have proved that whole peoples have individuality no less marked than that of the single person; that the individuality of a people is irrepressible and that the misnamed internationalism which seeks the obliteration of nationalities or peoples is unattainable. The new nationalism proclaims that each race or people, like each individual, has a right and duty to develop, and that only through such differentiated development will high civilization be attained. Not until these principles of nationalism, like those of democracy, are generally accepted, will liberty be fully attained, and minorities be secure in their rights.*

166. In contradistinction to fusion is the attitude which deals with the entire problem of Jewish life as the problem of a community, which wishes to preserve the integrity of its group life. Those who hold this attitude believe that the continued conservation of those values which are worth while in Jewish life can but work for the enrichment of the

* Louis D. Brandeis, *Jewish Rights and the* [Jewish] *Congress,* Address, Carnegie Hall, January 24, 1916.

character of the American Jew, and must therefore redound to the benefit of America. They contend that America will accomplish its destiny to the fullest only if it will permit complete social expression on the part of all the people which come to its shores, provided, of course, such expression is cooperative and does not militate against the common good. . . . In his political and civic life, therefore, the individual must necessarily have a single affiliation. But it is possible for one individual to know many languages, to be acquainted with many literatures, and to be imbued with the ideals of many groups. Democracy not only permits such multiple spiritual affiliations, but encourages them to the utmost.*

167. The ethnic groups are justified in organizing among themselves for the perpetuation of what they consider to be of significance for their heritage, providing that by so doing they do not preclude the influence of what the state considers to be of significance to its own heritage. The adjustment of the individual born within an ethnic group to the total life must rightly be made through the cooperative work of the public and the ethnic schools.**

This position would seem very secure only if the groups represented in immigration were specialized by heredity, so that some of them could do certain things that others could not do, or do them better—if some of them were poetical, some philosophical, some born physicists. But it is not apparent that even the most distinct races, the black, white, and yellow, are characterized in this way. The anthropologists think that if such differences exist they are not very great. Certainly the Japanese have shown that in general they can do anything that we can do, and have not shown that they can do anything that we cannot do. It is easier to explain why the Jew is in the needle trades, is not a farmer, and is intelligent, on the ground of circumstances—that he has had a given racial history—than on the ground of inborn aptitudes.

In any case, so far as European immigration is concerned, we do not have to do with races at all in the proper sense. The "races" of Europe are all mongrel, and are classified on the basis of language and custom. The Magyars, for example, came in from Asia only a thousand years ago, but they are so interbred with Germans, Ruthenians, Slovaks, Rumanians, Serbians, Croatians, that it is difficult to find an example of the original Magyar type. The Prussians were not

* Alexander M. Dushkin, *Jewish Education in New York City,* pp. 4 and 386.
** I. B. Berkson, [*Theories of*] *Americanization: A Critical Study . . .*

originally Germans at all, but a Baltic tribe, akin to the Lithuanians. Even the Jews are greatly intermixed with both Asiatics and Europeans. Twenty per cent of the Jews are blond.* . . .

We see no objection to an immigrant group remaining perpetually in America as immigrant group or as racial element on the basis claimed by the Jews in documents 165–167, if it is able to do so. Certainly our opposition would fan the wish to a flame, as, on the contrary, laws compelling immigrants to remain in such groups would arouse their fanatical resistance. But since we must ascribe the peculiarities of these groups to a long train of common experiences, not to inborn and ineradicable traits, there are apparently only three grounds on the basis of one or more of which an immigrant group could remain culturally separate for an indefinite time: (1) the ability to perpetuate in the new generations the traditional memories of the group without loss; (2) the ability to create values superior to those of America, and the maintenance of separation in order not to sink to the cultural level of America; or (3) an ineradicable prejudice on one or both sides.

(1) Actually, individuals and groups cling to their memories only so long as they are practically or sentimentally useful. The efficiency of the newer immigrants depends on their not forgetting, and on contact with their own past, as is illustrated in the following document, which was sent from America to Norway, and advises against certain radical changes in the Norwegian language.

168. The Norwegians in America are and intend to remain Americans. They do not consider themselves colonists in a foreign land. They regard this country as their own. They have helped to build large sections of it. Here their children are born and here they will remain. But a supply of cultural values from the old country will strengthen them individually and collectively and make them even better citizens than they already are. . . .

Norwegian-Americans will continue for many years to need cultural supply from the mother country. The need will continue until our people have become so far assimilated that they can supply their own cultural requirements from American sources. But that will take a long time, because, while the pioneers, or those who are left of them, and their descendants are thoroughly Americanized, there are still hundreds of thousands of people of the first generation who are not yet in touch with American

* Details are in Franz Boas' *The Mind of Primitive Man.*

cultural sources and therefore depend upon Norway for their supply through the medium of their own language. . . . The continued cultural connection between Norway and the Norwegian-Americans ought, in my judgment, to be built up on a solid language foundation. If the language be lost we may be absolutely sure that cultural supply from Norway will cease.*

We know, however, that the grandchildren of Norwegian immigrants have become practically indistinguishable from other Americans and that Norway has for them, at most, only a poetic value. All immigrant groups are losing, even too completely and rapidly, their languages, which would be the chief sign and instrument of their separate identity.

(2) There are frequent cases where a people of superior culture remains indefinitely separate in a culturally inferior group. The English in India and the Saxons in Transylvania have remained separate for centuries. But no immigrant group here can claim so great a diversity of values as is produced by America as a whole, and to the degree that an immigrant group is separated from American life, voluntarily or by geographical isolation, it will be pauperized in even the culture which it brings. . . . No existing state or nation, and certainly no nation within a nation, can create alone the values necessary to a high degree of efficiency. In a world characterized by individualization of function, values must be secured from wherever they exist in the whole world.

(3) The question of prejudice and discrimination may be put aside as not serious enough in America to affect the persistence of immigrant groups. The Jews have felt it, but in general the Jew is losing the marks of his identity as fast as possible, and to the degree that he does this the prejudice disappears. "To the degree that racial minorities are not secure in their rights" (as Justice Brandeis puts it), the separateness will continue.

The present immigrant organizations represent a separateness of the immigrant groups from America, but these organizations exist precisely because they enable the immigrants to overcome this separateness. They are signs, not of the perpetuation of immigrant groups here, but of their assimilation. We know no type of immigrant

* H. Sundby-Hansen, in a communication from America to the Norwegian newspaper *Stavangeren,* October 4, 1919.

organization which is able to live without some feature related to the needs of the immigrant in America. The success of the nationalistic societies is based on such features as insurance. In addition they provide entertainment and recognition, which represent universal needs. On the other hand, American organizations for the immigrant interest him only to the degree that they understand and supply his needs as immigrant.

We have recorded the wish of the Italian editor . . . that the Italians would organize as do the Jews. From his standpoint this meant a gain to be made at the expense of the Americans, for the sake of "what constitutes a gain for our race over the Anglo-Saxon race." From our standpoint, the Jewish community is serving the Jew by enabling him to identify his interests with America. Because Jewish organizations make the Jew efficient they prepare him to use all the American institutions. If you open a school for immigrants it is filled with Jews; if you open a school for immigrant women it is filled with Jewish women. Some Americans are disquieted by the persistence of immigrant organizations even in groups of longstanding in this country. But they disregard the continual intake of recruits from the old country who need the support and schooling of their fellow countrymen, and the fact that these organizations are constantly graduating their members into general American life.

Assimilation is thus as inevitable as it is desirable; it is impossible for the immigrants we receive to remain permanently in separate groups. Through point after point of contact, as they find situations in America intelligible to them in the light of old knowledge and experience, they identify themselves with us. We can delay or hasten this development. We cannot stop it. If we give the immigrants a favorable milieu, if we tolerate their strangeness during their period of adjustment, if we give them freedom to make their own connections between old and new experiences, if we help them to find points of contact, then we hasten their assimilation. This is a process of growth as against the "ordering and forbidding" policy and the demand that the assimilation of the immigrant shall be "sudden, complete, and bitter." And this is the completely democratic process, for we cannot have a political democracy unless we have a social democracy also.

Part IV

PERSONALITY AND CULTURE

17 OUTLINE OF A PROGRAM FOR THE STUDY OF PERSONALITY AND CULTURE

In 1933 Thomas submitted a report to the Social Science Research Council on the organization of a program in the field of personality and culture. This report, minus the ninety-seven appendices which accompanied it, comprises Part IV. It has not been published before. In it, however, many of the ideas scattered through the preceding selections will be found to converge upon a single major problem of social research.

The problem is taken to be that of "adjustive striving" of individuals and groups as it is revealed in behavior. Two approaches are possible. One is the biological, wherein behavior is viewed as organically determined. The other is the cultural, which claims in general that adjustment is a product of experience and cultural situations. Each approach has its own characteristic solution to behavior problems, eugenics and sterilization for the one, and altered cultural situations for the other.

Recognizing that these approaches complement each other, Thomas formulates the basic question in this way: "Individuals differentiated in what ways and placed in what situations react in what patterns of behavior, and what behavioral changes follow what changes in situations?" This is a complex question, involving the divergent capacities of men to be adjusted, the manner in which they are helped or retarded by existing codes and institutions, and the way in which culture changes precipitate the necessity of new adjustments. Thus biological, physiological, psychological, social, and cultural factors in human life must be considered, as well as methods for determining their various relationships.

Basically, two different kinds of studies are called for: the comparative study of individuals in given cultures from various points of view (biological, psychological, etc.), using life histories, case records, and genetic-maturational material; and comparative statistical studies of whole populations, including regions, nations, and races, together with descriptions of their cultures, and the contact, conflict, and acculturation which occurs among them. In the first kind of study, emphasis is upon the effect of specific cultural factors (family, law, occupation) upon variable individuals, and how these relationships are conditioned by the larger context of which they are a part. In the second kind of study, this larger context itself is explored, the problem being the relative incidence of personality traits and behavior patterns in whole populations. Throughout both kinds of studies, the factors of change and development in situations and reactions must be taken into account.

Clearly this maps out a vast research terrain in which it is necessary to do "first things first." Thomas did not think it desirable to make a formal distinction between "normal" and "abnormal" behavior, but for reasons of urgency recommended that behavior problems, or maladjustments, be given priority when studied as part of a total biological, social, and cultural context.

This selection, then, while somewhat sketchy and incomplete as to details, is a rather systematic presentation of Thomas' basic ideas and methods. When seen in light of Thomas' total work, it brings these questions to the attention of social science:

1. How the adjustive efforts of fundamentally similar men have led to so many different cultures;
2. How men with different heredities and constitutions can, within a single group, reveal so many similarities of behavior;
3. How, despite social learning and rewards and punishments, some members of every population deviate from behavior norms;
4. How individuals in any culture can be so similar to each other, and so different, at the same time?

The importance of this selection[1] ultimately lies in the fact that here Thomas asks fundamental questions about the variables involved in human behavior and the way in which behavior must be studied to be understood.[2]

I. The Problem of Personality and Culture

The social sciences are fundamentally concerned with relationships between either individuals and individuals, individuals and groups, or groups and other groups. Language, gossip, customs, codes, institutions, organizations, governments, professions, etc., are concerned with the mediation of these relationships.

[1] "Report to the Social Science Research Council on the Organization of a Program in the Field of Personality and Culture" (1933, typescript), pp. 1–35.

[2] The verdict of two eminent scholars on this selection is relevant: "This document . . . forms a major landmark in the growth of organized research on the relationship between individual development and the biological, social, and cultural matrix in which it occurs. Thomas' insistence upon the necessity for a multi-dimensional attack is worth recalling at a time when so many publications are set in a framework that in fact is purely biological, or social, or cultural—however much verbal hat-tipping there may be to the other dimensions." (Kluckhohn and Murray, *Personality in Nature, Society, and Culture,* p. xiii.)

The central problem in the general life-process is one of adjustment, and the forms of adjustive effort are "behavior." In a human as distinguished from an animal society the problem of the adjustments of individuals and groups is related to a cultural situation, that is, one in which a body of values has been accumulated and preserved (mainly through the instrumentality of language) in the form of institutions, mores and codes, together with a reinforcing set of "attitudes" or tendencies to act in conformity with prescribed behavior patterns or "norms." The attitudes and values, or more properly the attitudes toward values, which may be said to reflect the personality of the individual are the result of a process of conditioning by the influences of the cultural milieu, eventuating in a body of habits.

The reaction of different individuals in the same culture to identical cultural influences will depend partly on their different trains of experience and partly on their biochemical constitutions and unlearned psychological endowments. Local, regional, nationalistic and racial groups are in turn conditioned in the formation of their behavior patterns and habits, by their several trains of experience and conceivably by their particular biochemical and psychological constitutions.[3]

"Personality" has been defined in various ways.[4] The psychologists are inclined to use the term as representing a constellation of innate "traits" (extravert or introvert; dominant or submissive, etc.) but in the present report the term refers to the efforts of the individual to adjust himself to other individuals and to institutions and social codes.[5] . . .

Defining the general problem as one of adjustive striving, the question arises whether concentration in the programs of study should be

[3] Thomas used these same paragraphs at the beginning of *Primitive Behavior,* 1937 (see pp. 98–99 supra).

[4] Appendix 1, pp. 36–42 in the unpublished report, is a compendium of definitions of personality. Most of them may also be found in the American Psychiatric Association and Social Science Research Council, *Proceedings: Second Colloquium on Personality Investigation* (Baltimore: Johns Hopkins Press, 1930), pp. 146–155.

[5] The wording of this sentence varies slightly in Thomas' original report and in the mimeographed version distributed to the members of the Council in April 1933. Where such differences exist, the more detailed version is quoted in this selection.

on the successful or the unsuccessful efforts of adjustment. It is, however, desirable that no formal separation should be made of the so-called "normal" and "abnormal" aspects of personality and behavior. The two phases should be taken as aspects of a process and as representing different degrees of adjustment. On the other hand, the unadjustments are the critical and practical aspects of the problem and it will be methodologically important and necessary to give particular attention to the maladjustments represented by delinquency, crime, insanity, divorce, alcoholism, drug addiction, unemployment, vagabondage, etc.[6] . . . And while investigations of these maladjustive aspects of behavior should be made with reference to the cultural context in which they occur, and can, in fact, be adequately made in no other way, it will be desirable in some cases to take the maladjustment as the point of departure of the investigation.

The disciplines involved in the study of personality and culture may be taken as: biochemistry, physiology, neurology, endocrinology, genetics, psychology, geography, human ecology, anthropology, sociology, psychiatry, criminology, political science, law, economics, history.

Related to these disciplines there are two fundamentally different conceptions of the problems of personality and adjustment, which may be called the biological and the cultural. The one assumes that behavior reactions are for the most part a constitutional matter, organismically predetermined, and that the problem of controlling unsocial behavior lies along the lines of eugenics, sterilization and segregation. The other recognizes the presence of a considerable number of organic "spoils" in the general population in the way of idiots, imbeciles, morons, predestined psychotics, etc., but claims that an at-present-incalculable number of cases of maladjustment are the result of life-experiences and are remediable or evitable through a readjustment of cultural situations. From this standpoint the process is one of learning, or education in the broadest sense. Nevertheless, a fundamental body of interest runs through and unites all the disciplines and a program of personality and culture would be limited to this common body of interest.

[6] Cf. the problems cited in *The Polish Peasant,* 1927, Vol. I, pp. 78–86, and those listed in *The Unadjusted Girl,* pp. 255–257.

With reference, however, to the question whether Personality and Culture is a suitable field for concentration it may be desirable to point out what are the attitudes, claims and programs of these two approaches.

II. The Biological Standpoint

The European programs relating to personality, culture and human relations have more generally a biological basis than the American. As examples:

The Belgian prison system together with its "psychiatric annexes" is based on the theory that the criminal and the psychotic are "degenerates," that degeneracy is revealed by physical measurements and can be correlated with the height of the subject compared with his "grand stretch," or distance between his finger tips, with arms extended.[7]

The superior program of the *Deutsche Forschungsanstalt für Psychiatrie* studies the heredity of the psychoses in different populations, but neglects the cultural factors.[8]

The prison system of Bavaria is an attempt to apply the studies of the *Forschungsanstalt* to the prison population, and is one exemplification of the procedure of the prevalent European school of biocriminology.[9]

The Kretschmerian type of research claims a relation between body-build and the psychoses, and attempts have been made to correlate body-build with crime and types of criminals.[10]

The researches of W. Jaensch and his associates on the capillaries at the base of the finger-nail have resulted in the claim that physical

[7] W. I. and D. S. Thomas, "The Criminological and Psychopathological Service in Belgium under the 'Law of Social Defense,'" Appendix 3, pp. 46–55.

[8] E. Rüdin, "The Significance of Eugenics and Genetics for Mental Hygiene," *Proceedings of the First International Congress on Mental Hygiene, Washington, D. C., 1930*, Vol. I, pp. 473–475; cited in Appendix 4.

[9] W. I. and D. S. Thomas, "Organization and Objectives of the Criminal-Biological Service in Bavaria," Appendix 5, pp. 58–67.

[10] E. Kretschmer, *Physique and Character* (tr. W. J. H. Sprott; New York: Harcourt, Brace and Company, 1925); George J. Mohr and Ralph H. Gundlach, "The Relation between Physique and Performance," *Journal of Experimental Psychology*, 10:155–157 (1927); and F. I. Wertheimer and F. E. Hesketh, *The Significance of the Physical Constitution in Mental Disease* (Medicine Monographs, Vol. 10, 1926); cited in Appendix 6.

and social maladjustments are correlated with capillary structure and are corrigible by certain forms of therapy.[11]

In the ten volumes on *Races, Stocks, Nationalities and Families among the German People* (edited by Professor Eugen Fischer) which have appeared since 1929 the emphasis is almost exclusively on physical characters and hereditary factors.[12] . . .

III. The Cultural Standpoint

On the other hand, students of cultural influences claim that profound changes in the behavior patterns of individuals and populations occur rapidly in changed situations. In studies of delinquency areas the Chicago sociologists have shown that in one local area 37% of all boys of juvenile court age have been in the juvenile court (or before the police) and in another area not 1% of the boys; that the boys of any nationality whose families move into the area of high delinquency show the high delinquency rate, and that the boys of any nationality whose families move out of the area of high delinquency show a diminishing delinquency rate.[13]

An example of extent to which habits may change for the worse, where the possibility of bad heredity is excluded, is found in the Russian Molokan colony of Los Angeles. About a thousand families of this pious sect settled in that city twenty years ago. Children born in the first years had no juvenile court records, but at present the

[11] W. I. and D. S. Thomas, "Report of the Researches of W. Jaensch and His Associates on the Relation of Psychophysical Constitution to Capillary Structure," Appendix 7, pp. 73–84, cites W. Jaensch, "Kapillaren und Konstitution," *Bericht über den Fünften Kongress für Heilpadagogik in Köln,* 301–302; Gertrud Gehri, "Giebt es bei Schilddrüsenkranken ein pathognomisch characteristiches Kapillarbild," *Schweizerische Medizinische Wochenschrift,* 60:1084–1092 (1930); and J. Kirow, "Kapillaroskopie bei Geisteskranken," *Wratschepole Dels.* Nos. 5 and 6 (1930).

[12] Appendix 8, pp. 85–94, refers to the series edited by Fischer under the general title: *Deutsche Rassenkunde: Forschungen über Rassen und Stämme, Volkstum und Familien im Deutschen Volk.*

[13] Ernest W. Burgess, "The Determination of Gradients in the Growth of the City," *Proceedings of the American Sociological Society,* Vol. 21, pp. 178–184; Clifford R. Shaw, "Correlation of Rate of Juvenile Delinquency with Certain Indices of Community Organization and Disorganization," *ibid.,* Vol. 22, pp. 174–179; Frederic M. Thrasher, *The Gang* (Chicago: University of Chicago Press, 1927); and Clifford R. Shaw, *U. S. National Commission on Law Observance and Enforcement: Report on the Causes of Crime,* Vol. II, No. 13 (1931), p. 98; cited in Appendix 9.

delinquency rate of the boy population of this group is approaching 90%.[14] . . .

The crime rates in different countries, states and cities vary so enormously that no one would claim that the differences are due to constitutional rather than cultural factors. In a given year there were in London 3 murders per million inhabitants and in Chicago 73. In the whole of France in a given year there were 29 highway robberies, in St. Louis 1,087, in Chicago 1,862. It has been pointed out that in order to keep pace with Chicago it would have been necessary for France to have 830 times as many robberies as occurred.

Among the immigrant populations in America strikingly different degrees and kinds of demoralization are evident, and it is possible to relate this fact to the different bodies of social heritages or conditionings brought to this country by these groups. To a bright Italian boy in America admission to the society of big gangsters with an opportunity to work up may appear the most brilliant career possible, and the criminal world the normal world.[15] . . .

The caution which must be used in attributing behavior deviations to constitutional traits is indicated by the fact that children frequently employ totally different behavior patterns in different cultural situations—the home and the nursery school.[16]

IV. The Relation of the Biological and the Social Sciences in a Program of Personality and Culture

At this point the question arises as to the place of biological-psychological-genetic studies in a program of personality and culture. The physiologist Claude Bernard has emphasized the point that the individual is related to two environments, the inner in which he lives and the outer in which he acts:

14 Pauline V. Young, "The Russian Molokan Colony in Los Angeles," *American Journal of Sociology*, 35:393–402 (1930) is cited in Appendix 10. In this connection, see also her *The Pilgrims of Russian-Town* (Chicago: University of Chicago Press, 1932).

15 W. I. Thomas, "Methodological Experience in the Study of an Immigrant Group" in *Conference on Racial Differences* (Washington: National Research Council, 1928, mimeographed), pp. 24–29; and Illinois Association for Criminal Justice, *Illinois Crime Survey* (1929), pp. 1043–1057 and *passim;* cited in Appendices 13–14.

16 Grace M. Caldwell, Records of the Boston North End Habit Clinic (manuscript); cited in Appendix 16.

Life goes on, not in the external environment, air, fresh water, or salt water, as the case may be, but in the liquid internal environment composed of the organic circulating liquid which surrounds and bathes every cell.[17]

This internal medium contains an incredibly complicated integration of cells, blood chemicals, hormones, enzymes, various nervous systems, chromosomes, endogenous electrical stimuli, catalytic transformations, tensional relationships, etc. The limits to prediction based on the inner environment are indicated[18] . . . Moreover, the situation is further complicated by the fact that the human organism is itself developing and changing under influences which cannot be measured. Its responses change with periods of physical, mental and emotional maturation and as result of experiences in an endless variety of preceding situations.

In the projected program it is therefore desirable to set some limits to the scope of the inquiries. In order to understand an individual completely it would, indeed, be necessary to understand completely the "inner environment" but this is not undertaken even by the natural scientist. The natural scientist is able by experimentation to establish certain laws or regularities, but he does not attempt the determination of ultimate causation; he fixes some limits to his material universe. It is, in fact, desirable to abandon everywhere the idea of "causation" and approach problems in terms of "what antecedents have what consequences?" In the field of personality and culture the formulation of an adequate approach is: "Individuals differentiated in what ways and placed in what situations react in what patterns of behavior, and what behavioral changes follow what changes in situations?" The question is not *why* but *how* actions follow and relationships obtain.[19]

Definitions of what the human material is, in terms of its quality,

[17] Leçons sur les Phenomenes de la Vie, 112, quoted by L. J. Henderson, "The Physico-Chemical Changes in Blood during the Respiratory Cycle," in H. H. Dale and others, *Lectures on Certain Aspects of Biochemistry* (London: University of London Press, 1926), pp. 176–178.

[18] R. G. Hoskins, "The Endocrine Glands in the Second Decade," *Proceedings of the Conference on Adolescence, Cleveland, Ohio, October 17 and 18, 1930*, pp. 54–85; and H. S. Jennings, "American Society of Naturalists: Heredity and Personality," *Science*, 34:902–910 (December 29, 1911); cited in Appendices 17–18.

[19] Cf. p. 79 supra for a similar statement made in 1928.

its deviations from given norms, its capacity and disposition to be influenced by social stimuli (with reference particularly to the quantification of data) will involve the biochemical, physiological, psychological and psychiatric disciplines in different degrees in the different programs to be elaborated in the field of personality and culture.

In view of the inseparable nature of structure and function,[20] . . . it will be important to organize some studies in which both the biologists and social scientists participate. Certain approaches and set-ups, for example, psychiatric and genetic studies (as indicated below), will require this rather than others. . . .

V. The Cultural Approaches

Three general patterns of approach are indicated:

1. The documentation of personality.
2. Studies of personality in relation to specific cultural factors.
3. Studies of personality in culture areas.

These approaches are presented in more detail below.

1. *The documentation of personality.* Personality documents may be prepared by (1) the life-history method, (2) the case record method, (3) the observational method, (4) the psychological testing method, (5) the genetic method, or by a combination of these methods.

(1) *The life history:* The life history is an autobiographic narrative which should be as detailed as possible, and unguided except for inventories of items to assist the subject in a relatively complete anamnesis. The psychoanalytic technique is also available and has a unique value when its employment does not indoctrinate the subject.

> The unitary life of the person is known only in movement, not in organic structure. This life is . . . a movement observed through a period of time and recorded in a narrative. This narrative tells of acts of attention, in which through recognition and expectancy memory organizes and purpose forms.*

Documents of this kind should be prepared representing the general, the criminal and the psychotic populations and different cul-

* Hughes, P., "The Normative in Psychology and Natural Science," *Journal of Philosophy,* 24:150.

[20] Appendices 20 and 21, pp. 119–122, cite two memoranda prepared especially for the report: C. Macfie Campbell, "The Relation of Biological and Social Factors as Exemplified in Psychiatric Studies" (manuscript), and Stanley Cobb, "The Artificial Distinction between Organic and Functional, Physical and Mental" (manuscript).

tural areas and social strata, showing cultural relationships and experiential and behavioral crises and sequences.[21]

(2) *The case record:* The life history represents the train of experience or life movement as observed by the subject. It has the disadvantage of being never completely quantifiable, and is always to some extent a "rationalization of attitudes to protect the real personality." The case record is constructed by others, has the advantage of employing more techniques (psychometric, psychiatric, etc.), and of the arrangement of data in a form suitable for comparison and statistical treatment. Furthermore, the case method may involve the observations of many persons—members of the family, social workers, teachers, employers, etc.—and the family interview where the reaction of all the family members to the same situation (e.g., delinquency of one of the members) is recorded. Or the continuous interview of a family member (assisted by a questionnaire) may secure an extensive record which is superior in reliability to the autobiography.[22] . . .

Life histories and case records have hypothesis-forming importance, and provide data of the following character:

(a) The systems of ideas and purposes of individuals as related to the general culture patterns of society, and the relative compulsiveness of the various specific cultural stimuli.[23]

(b) The trains of experience through which the individual's conception of his role in society is developed.[24] . . .

(c) How organizations and institutions as they are (family,

[21] See the statements by Ernest W. Burgess, Truman L. Kelley, and Harold D. Lasswell, in *Proceedings: Second Colloquium on Personality Investigation,* pp. 11–12, 150, 142–143 (among others); also R. L. Whitley, "The Case Study as a Method of Research," *Social Forces,* 10:573 (1932); cited in Appendix 22. For Thomas' views on the subject, see pp. 79–81 supra.

[22] Appendix 23, pp. 132–175, quotes a communication from Jean Walker Macfarlane, with special reference to the "continuous interview."

[23] Edward Sapir, "Cultural Anthropology and Psychiatry," *Journal of Abnormal and Social Psychology,* 27:235–242 (1932); cited in Appendix 24.

[24] On this point Thomas includes three life histories in Appendices 25–27, pp. 182–314. Two of them, "Autobiography of a Chinese Student" and "Record of Carl Panzran," are unpublished manuscripts. The third, "The Autobiography of a Fox Indian Woman," was published by Truman Michelson, *U. S. Bureau of American Ethnology, 40th Annual Report, 1918–1919,* pp. 295–349.

school, occupation, etc.) promote and interfere with individual adjustment.

(d) Whether the personality is essentially structuralized in infancy, and later maladjustments in the adolescent period (schizophrenia, crime) date back to that period, or whether childhood maladjustments are to a degree self limiting.

(e) What are the determining crises at adolescence and other periods of maturation and experience.[25]

(f) The incentives involved in personality development and what necessities of human nature (organic and social urges) must always and everywhere be satisfied as condition of an adjusted personality.[26]

(g) The desire for intimacy, forms of intimacy, and the size of groups within which intimacies are possible, with special reference to the psychoses.[27]

(h) The different reactions of different individuals to the same critical experience. For example, one may become insane, another commit suicide, another commit a crime, another continue unchanged, another adjust on a higher level of efficiency.

(i) To how many and what codes does the individual respond and what conflicts arise from this source. "There seem to be different codes for the different situations, such as a home code, a school code, a Sunday school code, a club code." [28]

(j) Differences between verbal and actual behavior.[29]

[25] E. B. Hurlock and S. Sender, "The 'Negative Phase' in Relation to the Behavior of Pubescent Girls," *Child Development,* 1:325–329, 338–339 (1930); cited in Appendix 44.

[26] Clarence J. Leuba, "A Preliminary Analysis of the Nature and Effects of Incentives," *Psychological Review,* 37:432–434 (1930); cited in Appendix 28. Also Thomas wrote a report on "Physiological Tensions and Psychological Incentives in Behavior Reactions," Appendix 29, pp. 316–320.

[27] See the discussion of intimacy by H. S. Sullivan, E. Sapir, and W. I. Thomas, in *Proceedings: Second Colloquium on Personality Investigation,* pp. 52–54; cited in Appendix 30.

[28] Hugh Hartshorne, Mark A. May, and others, *Testing the Knowledge of Right and Wrong* (Religious Education Association Monograph No. 1, 1927), pp. 50–51.

[29] Since the report was written some suggestive studies of this problem have been published. See, for example, Stephen M. Corey, "Preferred Attitudes and Actual Behavior," *Journal of Educational Psychology,* 28:271–280 (1937), and Richard T.

(3) *Observational studies:* Observational methods have been employed, mainly with young children as subjects, to determine the order of appearance of responses and conditionings, the spontaneous forms of social interaction and the differences in the personality traits exhibited, such as extraversion or introversion, ascendance or submission, etc.[30]

(4) *Psychological testing:* The psychologists have developed a multitude of tests for the measurement of mental and personality traits. Mental testing has had a longer history, intelligence is not so difficult to define, and standard tests have been developed which have a useful and widespread application in relation to the learning process (education). But with regard to personality traits it has been difficult to establish the validity of the trait itself or to provide test situations which will be valid indications of the assumed trait. There have been proposed no less than two hundred and fifty personality tests or testing techniques, the usual assumption being that traits are entities and capable of measurement as such. It is, however, recognized that psychological traits as entities are fictions. But if the tester undertakes to record responses instead of measuring entities indices of personality differentia become possible.[31]

(5) *Genetic studies:* In contrast with the life history and case record, which attempt to reconstruct personality development by inquiries into the past, the genetic method proposes to begin with infancy and work forward through the life span, making records of physical and mental maturation and behavior patterning at various age levels, and at the same time correlating the behavior with the physical and mental maturation on the one hand and the cultural situation in its various aspects on the other. These two methods are thus equally longitudinal, with different points of departure.

The present emphasis on the genetic method represents a reaction

---

LaPiere, "The Sociological Significance of Measurable Attitudes," *American Sociological Review,* 3:175–182 (1938).

[30] Appendix 31, pp. 324–331, quotes, among others, D. S. Thomas' remarks in *Proceedings: Second Colloquium on Personality Investigation,* pp. 20–23.

[31] Mark A. May, "Problems of Measuring Character and Personality," *Journal of Social Psychology,* 3:131–145 (1932), and Knight Dunlap, "Response Psychology," in *Psychologies of 1930* (Worcester: Clark University Press, 1930), pp. 318–319; cited in Appendix 32.

against the practice of observing behavior at a given moment by a given technique (e.g., psychological, observational) and drawing inferences as to causation. It is realized that the conception can no longer be entertained that it is adequate to correlate any two variables —a given behavior manifestation with nutrition, or skeletal development, or mentality, or birth trauma, or family, or bad company, taken separately. The genetic method proposes, therefore, to study human growth as a maturational and experiential process from early infancy through adolescence and beyond, in individuals, groups and control groups, with reference to both physical maturation and the complex of cultural factors (family, school, moral code, etc.) by the simultaneous and continuous employment of all available techniques—anatomical, physiological, psychological, etc.[32] . . .

A number of programs of child study have taken the genetic direction with varying emphases. In Minneapolis and Iowa City physical development and the order of growth of structures have been emphasized.[33]

In Cleveland a "biological assay" of children from birth to late adolescence is under way, with periodic clinical examinations over a period of years and the employment of quantitative scales of change. The emphasis is on skeletal growth and the direction of the study is toward the determination of developmental discrepancies (retarded or precocious) which may be correlated with personality deviations.[34]

In the Yale Psycho-Clinic the study of the child is concentrated on the development of patterns of mental growth and concerned mainly with normal infants in the first year of life. Monthly clinical examinations are made and quantitative indices are constructed for each characteristic.[35]

At the Merrill-Palmer School the physical and behavioral character-

[32] Lawrence K. Frank, "Childhood and Youth," in President's Research Committee on Social Trends, *Recent Social Trends in the United States* (New York: McGraw-Hill Book Company, 1933), Vol. 2, pp. 795–797; cited in Appendix 33.

[33] W. I. and D. S. Thomas, *The Child in America,* pp. 491–497; cited in Appendix 35.

[34] "Report on the Maturation Program of the Brush Foundation," Appendix 36, pp. 349–352, cites a communication from T. Wingate Todd.

[35] See Dr. Arnold Gesell's discussion in *Proceedings: Second Colloquium on Personality Investigation,* pp. 18–20; cited in Appendix 37.

istics of nursery-school children are systematically studied, together with family relationships, and a "biogram" is constructed showing the relative asymmetries of growth and development.[36]

At the University of Toronto groups of infants, pre-school children, school children, adolescents and delinquents are studied simultaneously and observed and examined over a period of time with reference to sequences of physical, mental and social development. An important feature of this program is the cooperation secured from families, schools and courts.

The study at Berkeley has numerous ramifications, and constitutes, in fact, a group of studies covering the first two decades of life. In one of these studies a group of new-born infants is divided into an experimental and a control group. The experimental group is examined at frequent intervals by all available techniques, and the control group twice a year. In 1931 a six-year study was undertaken of the physical and mental development and family and school relationships of 250 adolescents, beginning at the ages of 10 to 12 years. As in the Toronto study, the cooperation of families was secured, and of schools in the case of the adolescents. A notable feature of this study is a detailed schedule for the family interview referred to above which makes possible a documentation of behavior having the general significance of a life-history.[37]

In the School of Education, University of Chicago, the concentration is on the learning process, and the same individuals are studied from the pre-school period through college, with reference to the physical, mental and cultural factors.[38]

The general significance of these specific genetic programs is that, in so far as the individual is striving for adjustment to institutional patterns, the whole course of personality development is genetic.

2. *Personality in relation to specific cultural factors.* The social, moral and legal codes which regulate the patterning of behavior by the individual are determined by definitions of situations made by

[36] See Lawrence K. Frank's discussion, *ibid.*, pp. 14–17; cited in Appendix 38.

[37] See p. 298, n. 22, supra for the citation in Appendix 23.

[38] Appendix 40, pp. 368–369, contains a statement from Charles H. Judd concerning this program.

parents to children, by gossip and discussion, by ecclesiastical and legal formulations and decisions, etc., and eventually by personal interpretations. The definition of the situation is a conditioning influence, and studies may take the direction of examining and measuring the sources of influence. Among the major defining agencies and influences are family, gang, school, adult education, church, government, law, boys' and girls' clubs, art, sport and recreation, occupation, forms of commercialized pleasure (movies, dance-halls), the press, forms of propaganda (e.g., advertising), other personalities, etc.

(1) *The family as defining agency:* The family may be taken as an example of these agencies and studied in order to determine:

(a) What is or may be the function of the family in forming the personality of its members in the present stage of evolution of society. It is desirable that studies including the following items should be undertaken:

(b) What the family is able to do and unable to do to promote the interests of its members. An extensive and long-time investigation of this character is under way in Germany.[39]

(c) The effect of social status on the behavior development of children by the study of large numbers of families classified on this basis and showing variations in the cultural content of the home and in the treatment of children. An important study of this character has shown that wide variations in cultural situation do exist, but has not undertaken to measure the effects upon the child of the cultural environment to which he is exposed.[40]

(d) The significance of the "broken home" in personality formation. The more recent studies from this standpoint claim that broken homes as customarily defined in terms of separation, divorce, desertion, death, do not contribute a larger rate of delin-

[39] Alice Salomon and Marie Baum, *Das Familienleben in der Gegenwart* (Berlin: F. A. Herbig, 1930), and eight other volumes in a series of studies under the auspices of the Deutsche Akademie für soziale und pädagogische Frauenarbeit; cited in Appendix 41.

[40] Appendix 42, pp. 402–405, cites a Report of the Committee IIIb, White House Conference, John E. Anderson, Chairman (manuscript).

quency than unbroken homes in the same social strata of the population.[41]

(e) The relation of family characteristics to delinquency areas. The data on this point are meagre, limited almost entirely to divorce and desertion, and inadequate as covering these items.

(f) The characteristics of the families of non-delinquent children in delinquency areas.

(g) Family relations with reference to the various psychoanalytic concepts (mother fixation, father fixation, birth trauma, anal eroticism, the castration complex, inferiority feeling, etc.), in order to secure more objective and quantifiable data.[42] The significance of other particular characteristics as they appear in infancy. The psychiatrists, for example, have elaborated such items as "overprotected child," "unwanted child," "neglected child," but it is not known how significant these conditions are nor the ways in which they work.

(h) The failure of the family to adapt its functions to the evolution of the greater society of which it is a part (cultural lag). In some cases problem behavior represents a tendency of the individual to organize his life on lines deviating from those laid down in the familial patterns, and the childhood maladjustment or revolt represents not personal disorganization but a preliminary stage of reorganization, and the assumption of a role in the great society which involves the repudiation of familial norms and is felt by the family as demoralization.

(i) The degree to which delinquency and crime are a continuation and culmination of the maladjustments reported in childhood, and in what fields of crime (homicide and suicide, robbery, fraud, etc.) the criminal behavior is such a continuation and culmination. A working hypothesis in this field would be that crime is not a continuation of childhood attitudes and behavior nor a youth movement to the degree assumed at present, especially by psychoanalysts and mental hygienists.[43] . . .

[41] Clifford R. Shaw, *U. S. National Commission on Law Observance and Enforcement: Report on the Causes of Crime,* Vol. II, No. 13, pp. 283–284; cited in Appendix 43.

[42] Cf. Robert R. Sears, *Survey of Objective Studies of Psychoanalytic Concepts* (Social Science Research Council Bulletin 51, 1943) for a review of some evidence on this point.

[43] See p. 299, n. 25, supra for a study relating to this point; cited in Appendix 44.

(j) Attitudes and changes of attitudes in families toward the child as a value in different social strata and in different cultures. For example, in Sweden and Germany the birth rate is now reported as lower in the laboring class than in the middle and upper classes.[44]

(k) Family situations where the inner relationships are harmonious, the economic conditions good, etc., and where family members nevertheless become delinquent and criminal. For example, in imitation of the adult criminal gangs Italian children in a certain Chicago area begin to use the vocabulary of crime at the age of three and at the age of twelve may participate in burglaries, perhaps without a previous appearance in juvenile court or other indications of maladjustment.

(l) The adjustive behavior of families and family members in critical situations, e.g., periods of economic depression.[45]

(m) The interrelationships of the members of a number of successfully adjusted families. . . .

There are available a vast number of valuable records of the behavior of delinquent and non-delinquent family members, usually prepared from the standpoint of treatment or advice, which could be examined comparatively from the general standpoint of personality and culture. . . .

(2) *Commercialized defining agencies:* The newspaper, the motion picture and radio are examples of defining agencies whose influence reaches great masses of the population continuously. There is no question as to the quantitative importance of this influence and there are claims that the newspaper and motion picture presentations of crime and adventure are the models on which delinquents and criminals pattern their behavior to a large degree. Certain investigations, however, claim that while spectators and readers enjoy crime films and crime news they nevertheless bring to bear on the situation the

[44] Karl A. Edin, *Ekonomisk Tidskrift,* 1929, pp. 123–152; cited in Appendix 45.

[45] Cf. Samuel A. Stouffer and Paul F. Lazarsfeld, *Research Memorandum on the Family in the Depression* (Social Science Research Council Bulletin 29, 1937); Robert C. Angell, *The Family Encounters the Depression* (New York: Charles Scribner's Sons, 1936); and Mirra Komarovsky, *The Unemployed Man and his Family* (New York: Dryden Press, 1940).

moral judgments prevalent in society, and wish and expect the punishment of the "bad man."[46] . . .

(3) *Personality as related to the occupations:* The present distribution of occupations among populations represents the selection of stimulating types of performance, or, negatively, the rejection of unstimulating types of performance ("work") by those individuals and classes able to do so.[47] . . .

In this connection the situation of the industrial worker has become perhaps the most critical point in our social system. The performance is inherently irksome because it is an adaptation to one aspect of a total performance. In addition there may be no correspondence between this aspect of the work and the attitudes of the worker, and on this account, and because of the instability of industry and changes in industrial trends threatening unemployment, there is a state of strain and feeling of insecurity.

With reference both to increased production and the welfare of the worker, technologists and psychologists have concentrated on tests of occupational aptitudes and personality traits with a view to the assignment of suitable work and on the study of industrial trends in order to regulate the policy of the industry and assure a degree of stability to the worker.[48]

Stimulated by the present situation of unemployment a number of important studies have been organized and proposed involving the preparation of life histories and case records of industrial workers,

[46] Appendices 48 and 49, pp. 424–442, cite, among others, Joseph L. Holmes, "Crime and the Press," *Journal of Criminal Law and Criminology,* 20:39 (1929); M. K. Wisehart, "Newspapers and Criminal Justice," in Cleveland Foundation Survey Committee, *Criminal Justice in Cleveland,* Part VII, pp. 544–546; William Healy, *The Individual Delinquent* (Boston: Little, Brown, and Company, 1915), pp. 301–304; William Healy and Augusta F. Bronner, *Delinquents and Criminals* (New York: The Macmillan Company, 1926), p. 181; and the Report of the British Cinema Commission. In this same connection see such other studies as Herbert Blumer, *Movies and Conduct* and Herbert Blumer and Philip M. Hauser, *Movies, Delinquency, and Crime* (New York: The Macmillan Company, 1933), and other Payne Fund studies in this series. For a critique of these studies, see Mortimer J. Adler, *Art and Prudence* (New York: Longmans, Green and Co., 1937).

[47] See p. 125, n. 6, supra for the gist of this statement.

[48] M. R. Trabue, "Occupational Ability Patterns," *Personnel Journal,* 11:344–351 (1933); Clark L. Hull, "The Differentiation of Vocational Aptitudes," *Psychological Clinic,* 19:201–209 (1930); cited in Appendices 51–52.

the measurement of attitudes, the study of the effects of employment changes on efficiency and health, the influence of lay-off on individuals of different temperaments, comparison of the attitudes of the unemployed worker with those of the employed with respect to certain aspects of governmental function (for example, their reaction to communism), investigation of the employment of leisure time, the impairment of the morale of the unemployed with consequent tendencies to vagrancy, alcoholism and crime, the relation of the psychoses to industrial occupations, etc.[49] . . .

The three conditioning situations just mentioned were selected as examples of the influence of cultural factors on personality, but the school, religion, art, government and law should be emphasized in a program of this character, especially in view of their function in providing and stabilizing the symbols and values whose common possession is the basis of an orderly society, and of developing a leadership capable of adjusting populations in an orderly way to the rapid cultural transformations.

3. *Personality as related to the total cultural situation.* It seemed desirable to indicate above in some detail the approaches to the study of specific cultural situations, but studies in human ecology or "the position in a spatial grouping of interacting human beings and interrelated human institutions" (McKenzie) [50] have shown that no single conditioning factor or situation can be separated from its whole cultural context, and that studies of the relation of personality and culture should be formulated with reference to the convergence on the individual of all the conditioning factors of his environment. This "spatial concentration of interacting human beings" has the same methodological importance as the longitudinal studies of individuals mentioned above.

Thus the family is found to be a very different situation in different localities. In a localized population of 4,000 in Chicago there

[49] Report of a conference, March 21–22, 1931, under the joint auspices of the Personnel Research Federation and the Social Science Research Council, on the "Effects of Part Time and Layoff: The Need for Research During Industrial Depression," *passim;* and Rex B. Hersey, "Is Industrial Psychology Making the Most of the Depression?" *Personnel Journal,* 10:157–166 (1931); cited in Appendices 54–55.

[50] R. D. McKenzie, "The Scope of Human Ecology," *Publications of the American Sociological Society,* Vol. 20, p. 141.

are only 154 females, or 96% males to 4% females, and less than 2% of the population is under 20 years of age, while the percentage for Chicago as a whole in 1930 was 32.8%.[51] . . .

While it is therefore possible to make studies of personality and culture at any given point in the cultural system (family, delinquency, gang, boys' club, school, motion picture, economic situation, etc.) the studies should be related to the conditioning influences of the locality.

Regional studies are also the approach which will disclose the relation of personality and culture in the general population. From this standpoint the problem becomes, "What personality traits and behavior patterns are present in what proportions in given populations?" This is therefore the necessary approach for the quantitative evaluation of culture in relation to personality.

It should be noted that the application of studies of the personality of individuals is related in a practical way to their adjustment in their own cultures while studies of the personality traits of populations have their practical applications in the restructuralization of given cultures and the readjustment of relations between cultures. The implications of studies of individuals are with the fields of psychology, education, medicine and penology, while the implications of studies of personality in populations are with the fields of political science, economics, sociology and law.

The regional concept has been developed by the geographers, with emphasis on the physical features of regions, and by the anthropologists, sociologists and political scientists, with emphasis on the social determinants.[52] . . .

These regional studies may take several directions:

(1) *Studies of local areas:* In the studies of urban neighborhoods referred to above . . . the concentration is on delinquency, but it will be important to develop comparable studies in Chicago and other urban centers, such as Cleveland, Philadelphia, Boston, New

[51] Appendix 57, pp. 479–482, cites a manuscript prepared by E. W. Burgess.

[52] Minutes of a "Conference on Regional Phenomena, Washington, D. C., April 11 and 12, 1930" (National Research Council, mimeographed); R. D. McKenzie, *op. cit.;* and Howard W. Green, "Cultural Areas in the City of Cleveland," *American Journal of Sociology,* 38:356–367 (1932); cited in Appendices 58–62.

Orleans, Minneapolis, San Francisco, etc., and in towns and in rural communities, in which the convergence of all the cultural influences on delinquent and non-delinquent individuals and groups are measured. The survey of social work for boys in Brooklyn is an attempt of this kind, though directed primarily toward the improvement of the work of social agencies and confessedly inadequate as a research program.[53]

In addition, programs may be developed for larger territories which exhibit characteristic populations and cultures. For example, the Central Northwest Regional Survey of the University of Minnesota is developing a continuous program which up to the present has emphasized geographic and economic conditions, markets, trade areas, crop zones, distribution, etc.[54] Studies of personality as related to culture could very appropriately be placed within the frame of this program, and since the population of this region is predominantly of Scandinavian origin it would be advantageous to develop a working relation with the Scandinavian program mentioned below. A similar study could be organized in Canada in connection with the study of pioneer belts.

(2) *Studies of national and racial culture areas:* It will have methodological importance and hypothesis forming value if monographic studies are prepared on the social structures and behavior patterns of selected present civilized nationalities and races. The study projected by the Social Science Institute of the University of Stockholm is a program of this kind.[55] . . . Rumania, Turkey, Russia, Poland, Finland, Hungary, Italy, Germany, France, Mexico, China, Japan, India, Hawaii, are among the modern cultures which should be considered for comparable studies. Sociologists, criminologists, psychologists, psychiatrists, statisticians and cultural anthropologists could be associated in these studies.

The cultural anthropologists have described the structuralization

[53] *Annual Report of the Welfare Council of New York City,* 1931, pp. 2, 7–13, 16–35; cited in Appendix 64.

[54] Remarks of William Anderson in minutes of a "Conference on Regional Phenomena," *op. cit.,* pp. 68–74; cited in Appendix 65.

[55] Appendix 66, pp. 542–549, cites an unpublished statement from a Committee of the Socialvetenskapliga Institutet of the University of Stockholm. Other data pertaining to a social study of Scandinavia are given in Appendices 67–71, pp. 550–579.

of primitive groups in great detail and have pointed out the astonishing differences in the patterning of culture in different groups and even in contiguous tribal groups of the same ethnic stock,[56] but have given relatively little attention to the individual in his interaction with the cultural situation. A study of personal adaptation to a primitive culture would be of major importance, and in the following section further desirable contributions from anthropology are mentioned.

VI. Comparative Studies of Personality and Culture

It will be desirable to study certain aspects of culture in a comparative way, employing the data assembled in the studies of separate culture areas supplemented by specific cross-cultural investigations.

1. *Studies of race relations.* Studies of this character would investigate the effects of the impact of cultures on cultures when divergent racial stocks come together in a common territory through migration, invasion, conquest or incorporation, and the development of the personality traits of populations in these situations. Among the problems involved are miscegenation, bilingualism, exterritoriality, nationalistic aspirations of minorities, race prejudice, caste hierarchization, importation of foreign labor (e.g., Chinese) in connection with a capitalistic organization replacing a familial and communal organization, etc.[57] Rumania, for example, with a predominantly peasant population, as many as ten language-groups, as many as four languages spoken in the same area, and Hawaii, with a complex mixture of racial stocks, are favorable points for the development of programs.

A study in Rumania could be conveniently associated with the Yiddish Scientific Institute which is developing a program for the study of the Jew in eastern Europe,[58] and with the Universities of Bucharest and Cluj which are studying the Rumanian populations.

[56] Ruth Benedict, "Configurations of Culture in North America," *American Anthropologist,* 34:4–23 (1932); cited in Appendix 72.

[57] Robert E. Park, "Memorandum on the Proposed 1934 Conference on Relations in Honolulu" (manuscript); cited in Appendix 73.

[58] Statement of Max Weinreich, Director of the Yiddish Scientific Institute; cited in Appendix 74.

The Hawaiian study could be associated with the University of Hawaii which is also preparing the program . . . [cited in n. 57].

In addition to the study of immigrant populations in America, which should be associated with studies of the cultures of these groups in Europe, the Negro in America (as a forcibly transplanted and extremely disadvantaged ethnic stock, strongly migratory toward urban centers, marginal to white society but crossing with the white stock to the point of color disappearance, and struggling among its own members for status on the basis of color distinctions) presents the problems of personality, culture and race relations on a magnified scale and affords an exceptional opportunity for methodological contributions.

2. *Studies of acculturation.* In the foregoing statement the emphasis is on the conflict of cultures, but another important aspect of race relations is the process of acculturation, or the diffusion and appropriation of cultural patterns and values. For example, the culture traits borrowed from one group by another never have the same meaning in their new context and the study of diffusion throws light on the general process of social change. Cultural anthropologists have made notable but by no means adequate contributions to the study of acculturation.[59] . . .

3. *Studies of communal living.* Studies of "essential communism" or collective living, as distinguished from doctrinal communism, may be undertaken in order to determine the degrees and kinds of intimacy which human nature requires in its adjustive efforts or to which it is capable of habituation. Such studies would be important to problems of family life, sexual relations and government and

[59] Proposed studies of acculturation by Edward Sapir (American Indians), G. Gordon Brown (East African tribe), and Clark Wissler (Polynesia) are cited in Appendices 75–77, pp. 599–605. Also cited in this connection (pp. 606–632) are: R. Thurnwald, "The Psychology of Acculturation," *American Anthropologist,* 34:557–563 (1932); and Paul Radin, "A Sketch of the Peyote Cult of the Winnebago: A Study in Borrowing," *Journal of Religious Psychology,* 7:1–22 (1914). For later works on acculturation, see Robert Redfield, Ralph Linton, and Melville J. Herskovits, "A Memorandum for the Study of Acculturation," *Man,* 35:145–148 (1935); Melville J. Herskovits, *Acculturation,* (New York: J. J. Augustin, 1938); the Symposium on Acculturation (M. J. Herskovits, F. Eggan, D. G. Mandelbaum, S. Tax, W. R. Bascom, and J. H. Greenberg) in *American Anthropologist,* 43:1–61 (1941); Ralph Linton, ed. *Acculturation in Seven American Indian Tribes* (New York: D. Appleton-Century Company, 1940).

would have psychiatric bearing. Two points of concentration might well be the primitive societies and Russia at the present time. The Soviet government is promoting its program for a "communal man" by a number of methods, e.g., communally motivated textbooks, communal farms, and legislation unfavorable to the intimacy of marriage, for the sake of consecrating all individuals to the state.[60]

4. *Comparative psychiatric studies.* It is unnecessary to point out the importance and magnitude of the problem of insanity among modern populations. In 1930, 736,000 persons were reported in hospitals in the United States and of these 419,000, or 57%, were suffering from nervous and mental disorders. . . .

Recognizing that constitutional factors may well be the main determinants, it is evident that constitutional conditions and predispositions in the case of the psychoses, as in tuberculosis and perhaps in cancer, represent "a susceptibility and not a sure fate" [61] . . .

Reference was made above to definitions of situations as determining conduct and codes. The definition may be innate, determined in the structure of the organism . . . or, more especially in humans, the definitions may be given by experience and by the past and present generations of society. Certain of these definitions of situations originate in certain social structures—the family, the community, the church, the state, etc.—certain features of the codes may in certain areas and historical times be measurably observed "always and everywhere by everybody," certain features possess a peculiar inviolability (e.g., avoidance of incest), certain rival definitions of situations arise encouraging the violation of the sanctity of codes,[62] etc., and in this

60 Avrahm Yarmolinsky, "Research in Collective Living" (manuscript), and Fedor Stepun, "Das Problem der Liebe und die Kulturpolitik Sowjet-Russlands," in Frank Thiess, ed. *Wiedergeburt der Liebe: Die unsichtbare Revolution* (Berlin: P. Zsolnay, 1931), pp. 191–210; cited in Appendices 81–82.

61 This quotation is attributed by Thomas to E. B. Wilson without a specific reference.

Appendices 83–87, pp. 650–707, contain various statements relating mental disease to organic processes; most of these are from the report of a "Conference on Mental Health October 21–26, 1931, Held at the Norwich Inn, Norwich, Connecticut" (2 vols., typescript), a conference initiated by the Rockefeller Foundation. See also p. 293, n. 9, supra.

62 Lawrence K. Frank, "The Concept of Inviolability in Culture," *American Journal of Sociology,* 36:607–615 (1931); and (for "rival definitions of the situation") *The Unadjusted Girl,* pp. 78–80; cited in Appendices 88–89.

whole connection it is desirable to study racial, national and local cultures in order to determine the relative frequency of the psychoses among the populations of different cultural areas and, if possible, relate the problem to the various social codes.

The primitive groups are of singular importance in this connection because they offer a great variety of social structures with divergent emphasis on social values, but the anthropological reports mention insanity infrequently and anthropologists are just beginning to approach the problem of the relation of the insanities to the codes.[63]

There is, however, an accumulation of evidence and opinion of the following character: The precipitation of mental disorders is related in some degree to cultural crises and conflicts. It is claimed that the incidence of schizophrenia, like the incidence of juvenile delinquency, varies by neighborhoods in the same populations, that the rates tend to correspond by neighborhoods and that the frequency of insanity in the same race or language-group (e.g., Jews, Negroes) varies in different neighborhoods in relation to density of population, economic status and numerical proportion of this element of the population. The migration of a racial group, e.g., the Negro from the West Indies to the United States, or from the southern to the northern states, increases the rate of insanity in the migrating group, and the distribution of insanity among the sexes varies in relation to the conception of roles of the two sexes.[64]

Schizophrenia, or the praecox diseases, is a favorable point for concentration in view of the facts that it is a characteristic adolescent manifestation, that it seems most clearly related to cultural situations, and that about 40% of all mental cases in the hospitals of the United States are schizophrenic.

As to the possibility of organizing adequate studies, the present

[63] Ruth Benedict, "Configurations of Culture in North America," *op cit.;* cited in Appendix 72.

[64] Karl Birnbaum, "The Social Significance of the Psychopathic," *Proceedings of the First International Congress on Mental Hygiene, Washington, D. C., 1930,* Vol. I, pp. 567–572; A. J. Rosanoff, "Exciting Causes in Psychiatry," *American Journal of Insanity,* 69:351–353 (1912); H. Warren Dunham, Jr., "Urban Distribution of Schizophrenics" (manuscript); and Mandel and Irene Sherman, "Social Factors Influencing Mental Abnormalities" (manuscript); cited in Appendices 90–94.

For a later study of this subject, see Robert E. L. Faris and H. Warren Dunham, *Mental Disorders in Urban Areas* (Chicago: University of Chicago Press, 1939).

program of Rüdin and his associates in Munich [65] has unexampled excellence in its organization for securing intimate population data. It is at present confined almost exclusively to the heredity of the insanities but there is reason to believe that cultural studies would willingly be incorporated in the present procedure, perhaps in cooperation with American social scientists. And a number of other European psychiatrists visited during the preparation of this report are prepared to cooperate. The study of behavior and social structure in Scandinavia emphasizes the cultural situation as related to the insanities, and this emphasis would be appropriate in other projected studies of national cultures.[66] The majority of American psychiatrists recognize the importance of cultural factors, and certain hospitals, for example the Worcester State Hospital, have incorporated social scientists for the purpose of cooperative study, giving them the same status as members of the hospital staff.

Anthropologists have emphasized the difficulty of making psychiatric studies among primitive groups, but there are hospitals for the insane, or congregations of the insane, among these peoples, notably in Madagascar and in what was German East Africa (Lutindi, Tanganyika Territory) favorable to such research.[67] . . .

5. *Comparative criminological studies.* A number of criminological programs and proposals have been mentioned above, and it would, in fact, be possible to apply this whole report from either the psychiatric or the criminological standpoint. . . . But it will be important to study the forms and prevalence of crime in different cultures comparatively, through life histories, case records and statistical analysis, prepare indices of crime, and examine the effectiveness of the various legislative and penal policies in connection with the various crime trends.

6. *The transformation of cultures.* At several points above reference was made to the definition of situations by and for the individual. At several points also (e.g., under the topics of "race relations" and "acculturation") there were indications of processes by

[65] See p. 293, n. 8, supra.
[66] See p. 309, n. 55, supra.
[67] Appendix 95, pp. 757–760, cites an unpublished manuscript by Ralph Linton.

which situations are themselves changed. In this direction it will be desirable to study cultural changes in a longitudinal way with concentration on the role of institutions, families, social classes, occupations, individuals and ideologies as instrumental in the transformation of cultures, with corresponding transformations of individual attitudes and personality traits.

Unavailability of objective data has been one of the obstacles to the development of studies of cultural and behavioral trends over periods of historical time. There exist, however, certain materials which lend themselves to this approach. The description of the Swedish *Community Books* [68] . . . shows the possibility of studying changes in the *same family and neighborhood groups* backwards over several centuries. Social mobility (occupational and geographic) and to some extent the behavior (crime, psychoses, illegitimacy, etc.) of the population can be studied for the same groups over long periods. The history of individuals from the standpoint of their rise and fall from one social and economic class to another can be at least briefly indicated.

These demographic longitudinal studies are important not only in showing status at any given point, and developments leading to that point, but they become a frame of reference for studies in this field starting with the present and going forward.

In studies of social change a distinction may be made between "reaction" and "response" [69] . . . The "reaction" is taken as something spontaneous and immediate, and the "response" as something involving effort or deliberation. From this standpoint "reaction" would be represented by organic conditions and traditionally transmitted attitudes, and "response" would be represented in part by propaganda or "the advocacy of attitudes" [70] . . . as expressed in reform programs, race and class conflicts, preaching, political agitation, advertising, etc. It can therefore be anticipated that the "re-

[68] Dorothy S. Thomas, "The Continuous Register System of Population Accounting," in U. S. National Resources Committee, *The Problems of a Changing Population* (Washington: Government Printing Office, 1938), pp. 276–297.

[69] Thomas indicates that he was following E. A. Bott's use of these concepts but no specific reference is given.

[70] Again, this term is attributed to Peter Odegard without a citation.

sponse" aspect of social change as seen in studies of cultures comparatively will be a contribution to the program of the Council on Pressure Groups and Propaganda.[71]

VII. The Selection and Sequences of Programs

Evidently not all the studies mentioned above can be undertaken at once or simultaneously, and in the studies which are undertaken it will usually be necessary to employ sampling. If a program of considerable proportions is undertaken . . . it will be important to determine what phases of the work shall be selected for the first approaches and what additional phases shall be introduced progressively, and in what order. It will be important also to determine that separate studies, in so far as they are comparable, shall employ procedures making comparisons possible.

It is suggested also that one of the main objectives of a program in the field of personality and culture should be the improvement of methods of research, and the promotion of specific programs should be undertaken partly with a view to the probability of securing methodological contributions. . . .

VIII. The Unifying Concept in a Program of Personality and Culture

The important question remaining is whether a unitary character can be given to the whole field whereby the several studies in the general frame will be continuously interrelated in a plan which will give the program an aspect of totality.

It will probably appear that any formulation of studies which attempts to predetermine rigidly the relation of all the parts of a general program to each other and to the whole will remain largely verbal and metaphysical. This is not the plan followed in the natural and biological sciences.

Theoretically it will be possible to structuralize the whole program around the "learning process" . . . as follows: [72]

[71] Unpublished report of the Committee on Pressure Groups and Propaganda (H. D. Lasswell, chairman) to the Social Science Research Council, 1931; cited in Appendix 97.

[72] Cf. p. 99 supra where this program appears in "The Comparative Study of Cultures," *Primitive Behavior*, p. 3.

1. The culture situations to which the individual is to make adjustments (studies of cultures).
2. The devices and instrumentalities for adjusting the individual to the cultural situations (education in the broadest sense).
3. The capacity of the individual to be adjusted (constitutional factors, studies of incentives, genetic studies).
4. The failures of adaptation (crime, the psychoneuroses, etc.).
5. Changes in cultural situations (e.g., movements of population, technological advance, unemployment, family disorganization, etc.) requiring continuous readjustment of individuals and reorganization of culture and learning.

But it will probably appear that this schematization is not sufficiently concrete to lend itself to a practical working program.

It will, however, be possible to structuralize the general program in such a way that certain groups of studies shall be more particularly directed toward certain objectives and the particular studies related to these objectives. . . .

The program would thus fall into two parts, the one with emphasis on the growth and development of individuals in given cultures, and the other with emphasis on the behavior reactions of populations in given cultures (mass phenomena). The first of these approaches would extend backwards, from the point of view of origins, and involve questions more properly relating to biology and psychology, and the second would be more directly connected with government, economics and law.

Another grouping of studies would be in the direction of developing techniques (statistical, observational, interview, testing, etc.) suitable for application in the whole field.

An overlapping of studies in this field, as in the natural and biological sciences, may be regarded as inevitable, in the sense that the same phenomena are viewed from different standpoints.[73] While

[73] Cf. "It is not claimed that the materials used are entirely new, nor that the problems arising here may not arise in connection with other sciences . . . But, after all, there is but one reality, and a new science never represented anything more than a new direction of the attention. The legitimacy of viewing the same materials from different standpoints can hardly be questioned." (W. I. Thomas, "The Province of Social Psychology," *American Journal of Sociology,* January 1905, p. 455.)

. . . I have emphasized . . . the arbitrary character of a separation of the "normal" from the "abnormal," the organization of studies around crime and the psychoneuroses seems desirable on account of the urgency of these problems, and these studies could be coordinated with and would benefit from the relevant aspects of other studies. . . .

But this policy would by no means exclude the support of projects presented by individuals who have "hunches," provided the project shows a probability of extending the limits of knowledge in the general field, although there may be no means of estimating what may be the importance of the contribution or the nature of its practical applications. Science has advanced by pursuing random inquiries (Faraday, the Curies, etc.) and society has profited by taking every one of the results and examining if and how it will apply to practical problems.

In my opinion, the critical point as related to projects in this field is not the preservation of unity, or the semblance of unity, but a more adequate provision for the critical examination of projects as they are submitted . . . with reference to relevance, proposed techniques, underlying theory or bias, capacity of the investigator, etc. And in this connection I suggest that every seemingly important project should not only be discussed but investigated. . . .

BIBLIOGRAPHY OF W. I. THOMAS[1]

BOOKS

Sex and Society: Studies in the Social Psychology of Sex. Chicago: University of Chicago Press, 1907. (The articles reprinted in this volume are indicated by asterisks in the following list.)

Source Book for Social Origins: Ethnological Materials, Psychological Standpoint, Classified and Annotated Bibliographies for the Interpretation of Savage Society. Chicago: University of Chicago Press, 1909; Boston: Richard G. Badger, 1909.

The Polish Peasant in Europe and America. With Florian Znaniecki. 5 vols. Boston: Richard G. Badger, 1918–20 (Vols. I and II originally published by the University of Chicago Press, 1918). Second edition, 2 vols. New York: Alfred A. Knopf, 1927 (content unchanged, but with alterations in organization and pagination).

Old World Traits Transplanted. [With] Robert E. Park and Herbert A. Miller. New York: Harper & Brothers, 1921. A volume in the Americanization Studies, Allen T. Burns, Director.

The Unadjusted Girl: With Cases and Standpoint for Behavior Analysis. Boston: Little, Brown, and Company, 1923, 1925, 1928. Criminal Science Monograph No. 4. Supplement to the Journal of the American Institute of Criminal Law and Criminology.

The Child in America: Behavior Problems and Programs. With Dorothy Swaine Thomas. New York: Alfred A. Knopf, 1928, 1929, 1932.

Primitive Behavior: An Introduction to the Social Sciences. New York: McGraw-Hill Book Company, 1937.

ARTICLES AND OTHER CONTRIBUTIONS

"The Scope and Method of Folk-Psychology," *American Journal of Sociology,* 1:434–445 (January 1896).

*"On a Difference in the Metabolism of the Sexes," *American Journal of Sociology,* 3:31–63 (July 1897). Ph.D. dissertation, University of Chicago; reprinted by the University of Chicago Press, 1897.

*"The Relation of Sex to Primitive Social Control," *American Journal of Sociology,* 3:754–776 (May 1898).

*"Sex in Primitive Industry," *American Journal of Sociology,* 4:474–488 (January 1899).

[1] Compiled by A. Paul Hare.

* Reprinted in *Sex and Society,* 1907.

*"Sex in Primitive Morality," *American Journal of Sociology,* 4:774–787 (May 1899).

*"The Psychology of Modesty and Clothing," *American Journal of Sociology,* 5:246–262 (September 1899).

"The Gaming Instinct," *American Journal of Sociology,* 6:750–763 (May 1901).

*"Der Ursprung der Exogamie," *Zeitschrift für Socialwissenschaft,* 5:1–18 (1902). Translated as "The Psychology of Exogamy."

"The Relation of the Medicine-Man to the Origin of the Professional Occupations," in *Decennial Publications of the University of Chicago,* First Series, Vol. 4 (1903), pp. 241–256. Reprinted in *Source Book for Social Origins,* 1909, pp. 281–303.

*"The Sexual Element in Sensibility," *Psychological Review,* 11:61–67 (January 1904).

"The Psychology of Race-Prejudice," *American Journal of Sociology,* 9:593–611 (March 1904).

"The Province of Social Psychology," *Psychological Bulletin,* 1:392–393 (October 15, 1904). Abstract of a paper read before the Congress of Arts and Science, St. Louis, September 23, 1904.

Printed in full, with the same title, in *American Journal of Sociology,* 10:445–455 (January 1905); reprinted in *Congress of Arts and Science Universal Exposition, St. Louis, 1904* [Proceedings], edited by Howard J. Rogers, Vol. 5, pp. 860–868. Boston: Houghton, Mifflin and Company, 1906.

"Is the Human Brain Stationary?" *Forum,* 36:305–320 (October 1904).

"Der Mangel an Generalisationsvermögen bei den Negern," *Zeitschrift für Socialwissenschaft,* 7:215–221 (1904).

*"The Adventitious Character of Woman," *American Journal of Sociology,* 12:32–44 (July 1906).

*"The Mind of Woman and the Lower Races," *American Journal of Sociology,* 12:435–469 (January 1907).

"The Significance of the Orient for the Occident," *Publications of the American Sociological Society: Papers and Proceedings, Second Annual Meeting . . . 1907,* Vol. 2, pp. 111–124 (discussion, pp. 124–137, pp. 136–137 by W. I. Thomas). Also in *American Journal of Sociology,* 13:729–742, 754–755 (May 1908).

"The Psychology of the Yellow Journal," *American Magazine,* 65:491–496 (March 1908).

* Reprinted in *Sex and Society,* 1907.

"The Psychology of Woman's Dress," *American Magazine,* 67:66–72 (November 1908).

"The Mind of Woman," *American Magazine,* 67:146–152 (December 1908).

"The Older and Newer Ideals of Marriage," *American Magazine,* 67:548–552 (April 1909).

"Eugenics: The Science of Breeding Men," *American Magazine,* 68:190–197 (June 1909).

"Votes for Women," *American Magazine,* 68:292–301 (July 1909).

"Woman and the Occupations," *American Magazine,* 68:463–470 (September 1909).

"Standpoint for the Interpretation of Savage Society," *American Journal of Sociology,* 15:145–163 (September 1909). Introductory chapter in *Source Book for Social Origins,* 1909.

"Race Psychology: Standpoint and Questionnaire, with Particular Reference to the Immigrant and the Negro," *American Journal of Sociology,* 17:725–775 (May 1912). Reprinted by the Helen Culver Fund for Race Psychology.

"Education and Racial Traits," *Southern Workman,* 41:378–386 (June 1912).

"The Prussian-Polish Situation: An Experiment in Assimilation," *Publications of the American Sociological Society: Papers and Proceedings, Eighth Annual Meeting . . . 1913,* Vol. 8, pp. 84–99. Also in *American Journal of Sociology,* 19:624–639 (March 1914).

"The Origin of Society and of the State," *Studies in Social Science,* Vol. 1, No. 1. Chicago: Zalas Corporation [c. 1915].

"The Persistence of Primary-group Norms in Present-day Society and Their Influence in Our Educational System," in *Suggestions of Modern Science Concerning Education,* by Herbert S. Jennings, John B. Watson, Adolf Meyer, W. I. Thomas, pp. 159–197. New York: The Macmillan Company, 1917. Reissued by the National Committee for Mental Hygiene (with The Macmillan Company's imprint), February 1946.

"The Problem of Personality in the Urban Environment," *Publications of the American Sociological Society: Papers and Proceedings of the Twentieth Annual Meeting . . . 1925,* Vol. 20, pp. 30–39.

"The Configurations of Personality," in *The Unconscious: A Symposium,* by C. M. Child, Kurt Koffka, John E. Anderson, John B. Watson, Edward Sapir, W. I. Thomas, Marion E. Kenworthy, F. L. Wells, William A. White (with an Introduction by Ethel S. Dummer), pp. 143–177. New York: Alfred A. Knopf, 1927.

"The Behavior Pattern and the Situation," *Publications of the American Sociological Society: Papers and Proceedings, Twenty-second Annual Meeting . . . 1927,* Vol. 22, pp. 1–13. Reprinted in *Personality and the Social Group,* edited by Ernest W. Burgess, pp. 1–15. Chicago: University of Chicago Press, 1929.

"Methodological Experience in the Study of an Immigrant Group," in *Conference on Racial Differences* [Proceedings of a conference held under the auspices of the National Research Council and Social Science Research Council, February 25–26, 1928], pp. 24–29. Washington: National Research Council, Division of Anthropology and Psychology, 1928. Mimeographed.

Statements in *Proceedings: Second Colloquium on Personality Investigation Held under the Joint Auspices of the American Psychiatric Association Committee on Relations of Psychiatry and the Social Sciences, and of the Social Science Research Council, November 29–30, 1929,* pp. 41–43 and passim. Baltimore: Johns Hopkins Press, 1930.

"The Relation of Research to the Social Process," in *Essays on Research in the Social Sciences: Papers presented in a general seminar conducted by the Committee on Training of The Brookings Institution, 1930–31,* by W. F. G. Swann, Walter W. Cook, Charles A. Beard, John M. Clark, Karl N. Llewellyn, Madison Bentley, Arthur M. Schlesinger, William F. Ogburn, and W. I. Thomas, pp. 175–194. Washington: The Brookings Institution, 1931.

"Comment by W. I. Thomas" in *An Appraisal of Thomas and Znaniecki's The Polish Peasant in Europe and America,* Social Science Research Council Bulletin 44, by Herbert Blumer, pp. 82–87; other comments, Part II, passim. New York, 1939.

"The Comparative Study of Cultures," *American Journal of Sociology,* 42:177–185 (September 1936). Reprinted in *Primitive Behavior,* 1937, pp. 1–9.

BIOGRAPHICAL NOTE

W. I. Thomas was born on a farm in Russell County, Virginia on August 13, 1863. His youth was spent in Virginia and Tennessee. After graduation from the University of Tennessee in 1884 he spent four years there as an instructor in classical and modern languages. During 1888–89 he studied at Berlin University and Göttingen University. From 1889 to 1895 he taught at Oberlin College, first English and later sociology. In 1893 while on leave from Oberlin College he entered the University of Chicago for graduate study. In the summer of 1894 he gave his first course at the University of Chicago in the Department of Sociology. He received his doctorate in sociology at Chicago in 1896 after serving for a year as an instructor; he became professor in the Department in 1910. From 1908 to 1918 he was in charge of the Helen Culver Fund for Race Psychology, in connection with which he travelled extensively in Europe, collected much of the material on which *The Polish Peasant* was based, and prepared the manuscript for the five-volume edition of this work.

The association of W. I. Thomas with the Department of Sociology at the University of Chicago continued unbroken until 1918, shortly after he was arrested on a charge involving allegations of violation of the Mann Act and of an act forbidding false registration at hotels. Although the charge was thrown out of court, the extensive publicizing of the arrest, particularly in the Chicago press, resulted in the termination of his appointment at the University. He moved to New York, where in 1918–19 he worked on the manuscript of *Old World Traits Transplanted*—a volume in the series of Americanization Studies sponsored by the Carnegie Corporation of New York—in association with R. E. Park and H. A. Miller. In 1923 he published *The Unadjusted Girl,* for which research funds had been provided by Mrs. W. F. Dummer of Chicago. He lectured at the New School for Social Research from 1923 to 1928. In 1927—again with Mrs. Dummer's support—he organized a conference on "The Unconscious," under the auspices of the Illinois Society for Mental Hygiene. In the same year he became president of the

American Sociological Society. In 1928 research begun two years earlier for the Laura Spelman Rockefeller Memorial culminated in the publication of *The Child in America.* For the next few years he carried out a number of assignments for Lawrence B. Dunham at the Bureau of Social Hygiene, and prepared an extensive series of unpublished reports on the behavioral sciences, with particular emphasis on criminological and personality research in Germany, Belgium, and Sweden. He spent part of each year from 1930 through 1936 in Sweden, where he had an informal connection with the Social Science Institute of the University of Stockholm. In 1932–33 he served as a staff member of the Social Science Research Council, in charge of the work in the field of personality and culture. His last academic appointment was as lecturer in sociology at Harvard University in 1936–37. The remainder of his career was spent in independent research and writing, in New Haven until 1939, and in Berkeley, California from 1940 until his death at the age of 84 on December 5, 1947.

Thomas married Harriet Park on June 6, 1888. They had five children, two of whom survived to adulthood. This marriage was terminated by divorce in 1934. On February 7, 1935 he married Dorothy Swaine Thomas.

INDEX OF NAMES

INDEX OF SUBJECTS